SURRENDER

www.grandcanyonpress.com

Publisher's Note: This memoir reflects the author's life faithfully rendered to the best of her ability. Some names and identifying details have been changed to protect the privacy of others.

Cover Design: Marylee MacDonald

Names: MacDonald, Marylee, author.

Title: Surrender : a memoir of nature, nurture, and love / Marylee MacDonald.

Description: First edition. | Tempe, AZ : Grand Canyon Press, [2020] | Includes bibliographical references.

Identifiers: ISBN: 978-1-951479-29-9 (Paperback) | 978-1-951479-30-5 (Ebook - ePIB) | 978-1-951479-31-2 (Ebook - Adobe PDF) | 978-1-951479-32-9 (Ebook - EPUB) | 978-1-951479-33-6 (Ebook - iBook) | 978-1-951479-34-3 (Ebook - Mobipocket) | 978-1-951479-35-0 (Downloadable audio file)

Subjects: LCSH: Adoptees--United States--Biography. | Unmarried mothers--United States--Biography. | Autobiography--Women authors. | Adoption--Psychological aspects. | Birth parents--United States--Identification. | Adopted children--United States--Identification. | Nature and nurture. | Dysfunctional families. | Adult children of dysfunctional families. | Mothers and daughters. | Man-woman relationships. | Interpersonal relationships. | Resilience (Personality trait) | Self-actualization (Psychology) | LCGFT: Autobiographies.

Classification: LCC: HV874.82.M33 S87 2020 | DDC: 362.734/092--dc23

A touching personal account of a journey to understanding and acceptance; informative and unsettling.

— KIRKUS REVIEWS

Surrender is a fine memoir that speaks to the very essence of our evolution as women in modern America. MacDonald adds a puzzle piece that illustrates both how far we've come and how far we still have to go.

— STORY CIRCLE BOOK REVIEWS

Surrender

a memoir of nature, nurture, and love

MARYLEE MACDONALD

Grand Canyon Press
Tempe, Arizona

ALSO BY MARYLEE MACDONALD

Bonds of Love and Blood

Body Language

The Rug Bazaar

Montpelier Tomorrow

The Big Book of Small Presses & Independent Publishers

For John and Michelle

"Whole societies have an astonishing ability to deny the past—not really forgotten, but maintaining a public culture that seems to have forgotten. . . . These forms of knowing shade into the archetypal open secret: known by all but knowingly not known."

— STANLEY COHEN, author of *States of Denial: Knowing About Atrocities and Suffering*

CONTENTS

Part **I**   1
Nature vs. Nurture

Chapter 1   5
The House of Shrouded Mirrors

Chapter 2   8
The Crying Baby

Chapter 3   15
Collage

Chapter 4   22
The Search

Chapter 5   31
Reunion

Chapter 6   38
The Request

Part **II**   47
An Adoptee's Childhood

Chapter 7   49
The Christmas Chick

Chapter 8   55
Wrongful Death

Chapter 9   58
The Chosen Child

Chapter 10   67
Peaches

Chapter 11   74
Vera Cruz

Chapter 12   83
Life Among Aliens

Chapter 13   88
Blood Money

Chapter 14   91
Fog

Part III 97
Romeo and Juliet

Chapter 15 99
Public-School Girl

Chapter 16 106
Tillie's Party

Chapter 17 112
Friar John

Chapter 18 115
Making Out

Chapter 19 125
Disaster

Chapter 20 130
A Visit to the Doctor

Chapter 21 136
Homework

Chapter 22 141
The Meeting

Chapter 23 147
Paperwork

Chapter 24 152
Going Away

Part IV 159
Phoenix

Chapter 25 161
Heat

Chapter 26 171
Lingerie

Chapter 27 175
The Crittenton Mission

Chapter 28 178
The Waiting Room

Chapter 29 184
Pam

Chapter 30 193
The Card Table

Chapter 31 196
Diane

Chapter 32 201
Roonay

Chapter 33   207
Clinic

Chapter 34   214
A Voice from Home

Chapter 35   217
Marianne

Chapter 36   220
Amber

Chapter 37   226
Thanksgiving

Chapter 38   233
Signed Out

Part V   237
Dark Night of the Soul

Chapter 39   239
Catholic Charities

Chapter 40   243
Therapy

Chapter 41   250
Changing of the Guard

Chapter 42   253
Developmental Tasks

Chapter 43   258
Banana Split

Chapter 44   261
The Rug

Chapter 45   266
Chris-Town Mall

Chapter 46   270
From Monday

Chapter 47   273
Movie Night

Chapter 48   277
The Kitchen

Chapter 49   281
The IQ Test

Chapter 50   285
Dwarves

Chapter 51   290
Festivities

Chapter 52   296
Christmas

Chapter 53   301
John's Visit

Chapter 54   308
Birth

Chapter 55   311
Surrender

Part VI   317
So Called "Normal Life"

Chapter 56   319
Driving Home

Chapter 57   322
Skyline

Chapter 58   326
The Dream of West Point

Chapter 59   330
My Senior Year

Chapter 60   336
Bruce and Me

Chapter 61   340
Thanksgiving

Chapter 62   345
Seattle

Notes   349

Acknowledgments   355

About the Author   357

Works Cited   359

Book Club Questions   363

PART I

NATURE VS. NURTURE

This studio photograph was taken in 1969. Pictured left to right are Bobby MacDonald, John and Marylee MacDonald, Teddy MacDonald, and Jackie MacDonald.

John Michael, the couple's youngest, was born seven months after his father's death.

CHAPTER 1

THE HOUSE OF SHROUDED MIRRORS

When I was sixteen and not yet wise enough to know what it meant to have a child and lose him, I surrendered my firstborn son. He was adopted. For the years of his youth, he was my ghost child. On good days I imagined him biking to the library or knocking helmets in a Pop Warner game. On bad days I pictured him dying and in need of a bone marrow transplant. I had never held him, not even as a newborn, and I had only briefly seen his face. Two years after his birth, I married his father, and we had four more children, full siblings to my absent child. When he turned twenty-one, I searched for him.

Back in 1962, when a mother surrendered a child, she signed a waiver that stripped her of her legal right to know anything more about her baby. She could not know his name or even whether he had been adopted. And yet, as an adoptee myself, I knew firsthand the difficulties of assembling an identity without the crucial, and missing, pieces that came from DNA.

From an early age, I knew I did not fit with the family that had adopted me. There was something inside me, trying to come out. I didn't know what it was, but growing up, I sensed my parents watching and waiting for the real me to emerge.

Why did I suspect that inside lurked a more authentic self? The little jokes they told. The innuendos that I did not then understand. All of these had to do with my genetic heritage. Rather than confirm my feeling of belonging to them, my adoptive family's speculative asides hinted at the opposite—that I was not *of them*.

After a difficult seven-year search, I reunited with my own birth family. For the first time in my life, I met people who looked, sounded, and acted like me. Now, I am a seventy-four-year-old former carpenter, sister, grandmother, and wife. My husband lives in Arizona, where he is a professor, and I live in Sonoma County, California, where redwood trees grow in my backyard. I often drag a blow-up mattress out to my back deck and enjoy the miracle of sleeping under the stars.

Each decade—each birth or move or life event—has caused me to revisit my own origin story and to try to make sense of two cataclysmic events that shaped my life. In the first instance, I was a baby, not much bigger than a shoebox, handed from one family to another. That transfer disconnected me from my genetic roots. In the second instance, I was the one doing the handing off. I did not literally hand my baby to his adoptive mother. I was not even allowed to touch him. However, the wheels of the transfer were set in motion the instant I signed my name to the surrender papers, thus surrendering a part of myself.

I do not blame myself for surrendering my son, nor do I seek forgiveness. Given my age at the time (sixteen), feelings of obligation to my adoptive mother, and societal norms, my signing those papers was not so much a decision as an inevitability.

As Albert Camus wrote in his novel *The Fall*, "Alas, after a certain age, every man is responsible for his own face." Throughout each person's life, during all our acts of self-discovery and self-creation, we become the face we will one day see in the mirror—our own, authentic self.

The author was six weeks old at the time of her adoption. Pictured left to right are Rex and Lorene Benham (father and mother), Orville and Celicia Pitney (maternal grandparents), and Marshall and Louise Pitney (mother's brother and his wife). The photo was taken on Thanksgiving (1945) at the adoptive parents' avocado ranch in Camarillo, California.

CHAPTER 2

THE CRYING BABY

*R*evisiting the past is never easy. It was 2008, I was living in Evanston, and I did not want to move to Phoenix, where I had once lived in a home for unwed mothers. Already in my parka, awaiting my husband's arrival, I stood looking down at a black-and-white border collie running back and forth in a neighbor's yard. Light streamed through the dining room's windows. I was nearing the age, just at the edge of it, when the world suddenly took on a sharp beauty, each pane of the steel windows framing a seasonal tableau: maples bursting into a lime-green spring; the lush, variegated greens of summer; and now, late September, with its red, yellow, and orange leaves fluttering to the ground. Soon, it would be winter. Ice would coat the bare branches. This decade would bring one final burst of health and vitality, and I did not intend to be dislodged for the sake of my husband's job.

Coming in from his office two blocks away, Bruce unlocked the front door, came up behind me, and wrapped me in his arms. His muscled chest was the wall I had leaned on during the ups and downs of my children's teenage years and the reunion with my oldest son, the one I had surrendered for adoption. Now, unless I could figure out some way to convince my husband otherwise, he was all set to move from Northwestern University to Arizona State. The therapist was squeezing us in.

Ten minutes later, Jim, a minister's husband with gray hair and the long-legged, rangy body of a distance runner, showed us into his basement office, both he and Bruce dodging the heating duct. Bruce, unwinding his muffler, took his usual seat in a leather chair near the door. Fit and muscular and with the quiet, gathered intensity of a man who never missed a day at the gym, he was at the top of his game, a leader in the world of science and a person who maintained strict control over his emotions. Jim, steepling his fingers, took the Eames chair across from us and asked what had brought us in—the therapist's standard opening gambit.

"Bruce received a formal offer from Arizona State," I said.

"They're giving me everything I could hope for," Bruce said. "A huge amount of lab space. A million dollars for remodeling. An endowed professorship. Permission to hire faculty. Oh, and moving expenses."

"Sounds great." Jim smiled benignly. "So, what's the hang-up?"

"My wife doesn't want to move."

"I want to," I said. The back of my neck prickled. My face lit up. "I just can't."

"Why don't you turn to Bruce and tell him what concerns you?" Jim said.

Take a deep breath, I told myself. Raising your voice won't do any good.

I swiveled my chair around and leaned forward. The corner of Bruce's mouth crimped. If he heard the drumbeats of anger, he would flee. Oh, sure, his body might stay seated in that chair, but he would shut down like a liquor store on Sunday, its metal grille pulled across the plate glass. How to convey my white-hot rage without scaring him? What words would open his heart?

"I need you to listen to my feelings and not be scared," I said.

"All right," he said. "What is it?"

"The research institute you're going to is an anthill of activity. All those multimillion-dollar grants. All those big egos. I'm scared that if you take this job, you'll work even more than you do now."

"That's not my intention." Grimacing as if I had stepped on his toe, Bruce looked at Jim. "For years, Marylee has been saying I work too much. With this job, I'll have a lab manager and an administrative assistant. I'm actually doing this for us."

Bullshit, I thought.

"Will you work Saturdays?" I asked.

One by one, he pulled his fingers until his knuckles cracked. Finally, he said, "I don't want to make promises I can't keep."

I hated his integrity almost as much as I hated myself for trying to extort a promise. It was like trying to shame a puppy. Chewing on shoes was in its nature. However, I was not one to give up easily. In my nights of stewing about this, I had come up with some "appeals to reason."

I reminded Bruce that he was in the middle of a visiting lectureship that would take him to one or two universities every week during the fall. Even with the best job in the world, surely he could see that the logistics of the move would fall on me. I'd have to get bids from moving companies, oversee the packing, and get our apartment ready to put on the market.

"I know that's not fair," Bruce said, "but Marylee has always been the one to handle the practical details of life. That's why we make a good team," he told Jim.

"Yes," Jim said, "we are often drawn to our opposites."

Very true. Both my husbands were engineers.

"Also," Bruce said, "when I went down there last January to give a talk, I couldn't believe how nice the weather was. I won't be walking to work in snow."

"We live only two blocks away from Northwestern," I said. "It's not like you ever freeze."

"She's not out there on the sidewalk at six thirty," Bruce said, appealing to Jim. "It's slippery as hell."

"And you've never been to Phoenix in the summer," I said. "It's *hotter* than hell."

"They tell me it's a dry heat."

"You could fry an egg on your head," I said.

Jim held up his hands. "Whoa, whoa, let's lower the temperature."

I gripped the arms of my chair. My eyes welled with angry tears. A box of Kleenex sat on the table between us. A bottled-up scream made my throat shrink to the size of a straw. I needed to lower my voice and use "I" messages.

"Phoenix is where I surrendered my son," I whispered.

"I know," Bruce said.

"You wouldn't ask a Vietnam vet to relocate to Vietnam."

"I'm not asking you to move to Vietnam." Bruce turned to Jim. "She thinks she has some kind of PTSD issue with Phoenix."

"Oh?" Jim said. "Do you?"

"I'm no psychologist, but yes, I probably do. A hand clutches my throat and cuts off the air. I wake up at night and obsess. What it comes down to is, I wish Bruce would honor my feelings."

"You didn't want to move to Urbana either," Bruce said, "but that turned out okay."

"Okay? For you, maybe, but for three years, I was fighting off major depression."

"You weren't depressed. You were just angry." Bruce turned to Jim. "When I came home from work, I could never tell what kind of mood she'd be in."

"It wasn't like that when we moved to Evanston," I said.

"No, of course not. You wanted to move."

"That's what I'm talking about, Bruce. I can't buy into this move. My whole life is here. I have friends of the heart."

"One thing I'm good at is recognizing an opportunity," Bruce said, "and something like this won't come my way again."

Twenty-five years earlier, we'd convened a high school youth group. With long hair and bangs that he cut himself with a Swiss Army knife, he had not looked like potential husband material. His hair had thinned, but inside, he was still the same sweet, introverted nerd he'd always been, with rare exceptions—like today.

"I know this is the job of a lifetime for you. Arizona State values what you can bring to the campus. Your vision. Your leadership."

"Yes?" He sat back and smiled.

"More than anything, I want you to take this job, but my life is here. I don't know a single soul in Phoenix."

"I'm starting from scratch, too."

"Yes, but you have an institutional affiliation. Departmental colleagues."

"I don't know them."

"I have a profession, too. Where am I supposed to find other writers?"

"Put up a sign in Whole Foods?"

"If you didn't have that offer, would you think that putting up a sign in a grocery store would help you find work colleagues?"

"No, but then, if it weren't for my job, you wouldn't have the luxury of calling yourself a writer."

Ouch, but fair enough.

I took a printed email from my purse and handed it to Jim. The email had come at 7:30 a.m., just after I finished my muffin and settled down to write. After reading it, I had walked down Noyes Street toward the lake, past Bruce's office on the second floor of McCormick Technological Institute. I saw that he'd turned on his office light, but rather than go up there and throw a fit, I continued down the alley and onto the running path that skirted the athletic fields, the duck pond, the student union, and the theater department, where we had season tickets. A sailing club overlooked the swimming beach where I liked to swim in summer and where Bruce, when we'd first moved to Evanston, often met me for a walk to dinner at the Fish Market or the opera café that had been our favorite, Verdi & Puccini.

I sat down at a picnic bench and, taking the email from my pocket, read it again. The writer, one of the few literary writers I'd been able to find, had moved to Tempe because of her husband's fabulous job at Arizona State. The Valley of the Sun was so spread out, she had not met any other writers. Her husband worked all the time. Her daughter needed to finish high school. Trapped, she had fallen into a clinical depression.

If I could have felt one ounce of reassurance, of gladness, one single ray of hope that I could create a life for myself in Arizona, it would have eased my mind. Instead, I was unable to put on my "good sport" beanie. Ashamed of myself, bitterly angry that I could not find it in my heart to be the wife I wanted to be, I sat there, numb with misery, staring at the flat, calm lake. I had just turned sixty, and yet I felt as lonely and as lost as I had at sixteen, standing on the walkway of the Phoenix Florence Crittenton Home for unwed mothers, the sun beating down on my head. A part of me was still the high school student with her new learner's permit and rag rug rolled beneath her arm, dreading experiences she could not yet imagine and did not want to have.

That was my Phoenix.

Bruce's Phoenix was all promise and glory.

Jim handed the email to Bruce, and he read it. Then he handed it back to me.

"This is only one person's opinion," Bruce said.

"One person's experience," I said. "An experience is different from an opinion. This is her reality. It's what she's living through, day by day."

"But you always make friends."

"I cannot and will not uproot myself again," I said. "Especially not to Phoenix."

Call me a romantic, but I have always believed that love conquers all. Bruce just needed time to think through the implications. Then he would come around.

I reached for his hand. It felt warm and firm. "If I said to you, 'Choose between me and your career,' what would you say?"

His eyes darted about. He looked up, as if the keys of an invisible typewriter were striking his forehead. He pulled his hand free and cracked his knuckles.

Finally, he said, "If you force me to give this up, I'm afraid I would hate you for the rest of my life."

I gasped. Wind whooshed through my ears. The pressure in the room shifted. The torrential rain of arguments gave way to a dead calm. An upright humidifier stood in the corner. Its whirr filled the silence. Then I heard a sniffing sound, air sucked through a nose. Then a snort, similar to a sneeze, followed by a deep, short grunt.

The sound of a cat in heat or a baby in distress. Mortified that I could not hold back the tears, I rocked forward, my face hot, palms covered in snot. A loud *Waa, waa* welled up from my throat and went on and on. It wasn't a cry of pain. Those were sudden and shrill. It wasn't hunger. It wasn't a whiny or fussy cry, either, but it would not stop. My face flashed hot and cold. I tried to rein myself in, and the crying grew in volume, until hiccups made me choke. Why couldn't I bring myself under control? I wanted to be rocked, I wanted to be held, but when I peeked out from between my fingers, I saw the therapist sitting wide-eyed and my husband standing with the doorknob in his hand. The clock above the door told me I had cried for a full half hour.

Jim looked at Bruce. "I think we're at the end of the session."

Bruce pulled a check from his pocket. "Here you go." And to me: "Pull yourself together. I've got an important conference call, and I need to get back."

Chin trembling, eyes aching, I blew my nose. Numbness washed over me. It was as if I were standing in a cold shower, my face, my chin, my shoulders, my hands, all going dead.

This was why Bruce and I were a good match. I was emotional. He was nonreactive. And now I had another important piece of information about his priorities. My fear of displacement didn't count; at least, it didn't count more than his job. Goddamn talk therapy. It never helped. I was going to have to figure out how to cope on my own, and I didn't have a clue.

CHAPTER 3

COLLAGE

*S*olving environmental problems was Bruce's calling, not his job. The move wasn't about status or salary, but about his trying to save the world. He and I had the same values. That's what had attracted me to him in the first place. Plus, he did his own laundry, was intensely loyal, and paid the bills. If Bruce went out on the dating market, he'd be snapped up instantly. I was just being unreasonable and selfish. Army wives moved all the time. Why did I think I was so special? I wished I hadn't thrown such a hissy fit.

I unbuckled my seat belt and waited in the alley for Bruce to park the car. His first academic job had been at the University of Illinois in Champaign-Urbana, and that was where we'd raised the kids. Our two-bedroom apartment in the Rookwood Gardens—a 1927 castle with a crenelated parapet—was where we had downsized. The kids were off at college, and Northwestern had made him chair of environmental engineering.

Bruce closed the garage door and then reached out and drew me to him. I rested my cheek on his chest, feeling the metal snap on his jacket against my face.

"I was thinking on the way home," he said, "that we don't have to sell the apartment."

"Can we afford two homes?" I asked, pushing back so that I could see if he was serious.

His eyes, looking down through his glasses, searched my face. "With what they're paying me? Yes," he said. "That way, you could come back for your writing workshops. You can stay as long as you like, and if you don't want to be in Tempe during the summer, you could come up here."

"Thank you," I said, my throat still raw.

As I watched him head down the alley, his step springy, his navy jacket shimmering in the sun, I realized how many times in this marriage I'd underestimated him. Occasionally, not just with Bruce, but with my first husband, too, marriage felt like a jail cell, a place I had to spring myself from. I wished I were the kind of person—a normal, "good wife" kind of person—who could just go with the flow. Instead, I was like a shopper in a shoe store, wanting the sales-person to bring me box after box, until finally, tired of myself, I settled for a pair that was an "almost good" fit, simply because I had to have something to wear. In most ways, Bruce and I were a good fit. However, his passion for his career pinched my toes. Similarly, my flying back and forth would be an almost good fit. I didn't relish the idea of living apart.

As I climbed the steel stairs to the second floor and turned the lock in the kitchen door, I heard the phone ring. Inside, I grabbed the receiver from the wall.

"It's Jim here," the voice said.

"Jim the therapist," I said, "or Jim from the condo board?"

"The therapist. I apologize for cutting off our session," he said. "What was going on today?"

I put my hand on my stomach. Like torn strips of paper, my abdominal muscles felt shredded. "Oh, nothing," I said. "I'm better now."

"I doubt that."

Jim told me to take a deep breath. Reach down inside and see if I could find that voice inside that had cried so desperately and for so long.

I wasn't sure I wanted to. I was probably the only person in the world who cared whether I was depressed or not. It was better to ignore my feelings, pretend they weren't there. But all right. If he thought it would help.

Elbows on the cool granite counter, I pressed my fingers to my eyes. It was weird trying to talk to a therapist while standing in the kitchen with a Princess phone in hand. I told him that, like it or not, I was going to have to move. I wasn't the first woman, or the only one, who was financially dependent on her husband, and I supposed that was part of the reason for the tears. It hurt my pride to acknowledge the truth: that in exchange for the freedom to write, I'd stopped paying my share of the bills.

"I don't think that's what brought on the tears," Jim said.

"Then what did?" I said.

"The tears sounded like those of a very angry baby," he said.

"I should have stuffed a sock in its mouth," I said.

"Don't be embarrassed," he said.

"It was like being possessed by a demon," I said. "I just totally let it take me over."

"You felt threatened."

"Threatened? How?"

"Like a child torn from its mother's arms."

"I'm adopted," I said.

"Yes, I know," he said. "That's what I'm talking about."

He suggested I find a small notebook, something I could carry in my purse. He wanted me to make a collage. "Find images that represent other parts of you, parts you can draw on to protect that baby."

A collage. All right. I'd always been sort of artsy-fartsy. Maybe this would, in some weird way, soothe the crying baby.

After the call, I found a stack of *National Geographic* magazines and a Moleskine notebook. In it I pasted a picture of a feisty little girl riding her first bicycle; also, a mountain gorilla, a redwood grove, and fog rolling in over the Golden Gate Bridge. California was where I had grown up and where I felt most at home. If I'd had my druthers, I would have moved back years ago. As I dabbed Elmer's glue on each image and smoothed it onto the page, I went from feeling desolate to feeling the knot in my stomach loosen. If I held tight to this notebook, I might be able to make this move with more good grace than I had imagined.

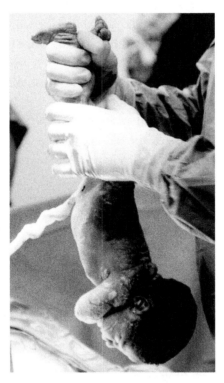

Some psychologists believe that babies who are not reunited with their birth mothers soon after delivery experience a form of infant PTSD.

THE NOTEBOOK WAS MY TALISMAN. It soon filled with names and phone numbers of moving companies, human resources managers, real estate agents and title companies, and doctors and dentists.

Even though I was going through the motions, doing the tasks expected of me and trying to do them with a spirit of generosity, the crying in Jim's office still troubled me. Had I embarked on that crying jag because of my incipient feelings of displacement, or was the problem Phoenix itself, the place I had surrendered my son?

At the very bottom of the long-buried layers of emotion I was experiencing, akin to the geologic layers in the Grand Canyon, lay the rage that had spilled out in my therapist's office and that author Nancy Newton Verrier, herself an adoptive mother, wrote about so eloquently in *The Primal Wound*, a book that examines the displacement felt by an infant transferred from its mother's arms to the arms of its adoptive parents.[1]

> The [adopted] child actually experiences being left alone by the biological mother and being handed over to strangers. That he may have been only a few days or a few minutes old makes no difference. He had a 40-week experience with a person with whom he probably bonded in *utero*, a person to whom he is biologically, genetically, historically, and perhaps even more importantly, psychologically, emotionally, and spiritually connected. . . . It is a real experience about which [adoptees] have had and are having recurring and conflicting feelings, all of which are legitimate. These feelings are their response to the most devastating experience they are ever likely to have: the loss of their mother. The fact that the experience was preverbal does not diminish the impact. It only makes it more difficult to treat. It is almost impossible to talk about, and for some even difficult to think about.

Reading Verrier's book and occasionally bringing up adoption as a potential issue with the various therapists I have seen over the years should have expunged adoption as a force that could still cause me to behave irrationally. After all, I was a smart person. I understood that this rage was a raw and primitive form of anger, a response to abandonment that is typical of many adoptees.

But I was wrong. The crying told me that my feelings, much as I might want to deny them, still blew at hurricane force.

Therapist Jack Hinman, who has worked with adopted teenage girls who are "acting out," explains it this way:[2]

An infant's world changes radically when her biochemical connection to Mom is suddenly absent. The baby is programmed, at the neurological, biochemical, and limbic levels, to attach to its biological mother. Separation can constitute an actual trauma and drive significant developmental changes. Some experts are even entertaining a diagnostic label of "developmental PTSD" for infants or children who experience attachment issues as a result of separation from the birth family.

Despite the evidence that carrying around my little notebook with its collages—my security blanket—actually helped, some part of me did not want to believe that my own adoption "trauma" was a trauma at all, or that it continued to ripple through my life. I was a grandma many times over. I wished my whole adoption history would just go away. I didn't want to feel *it* anymore (the emptiness and desolation) or have *it* jump out of nowhere and bite me in the ass.

In the book *Birthbond*,[3] the authors, Judith S. Gediman and Linda P. Brown, say that some adoptees can "thrust their adoption into the background of their sense of self. For others, it is absolutely primary, an awareness that begins the moment they learn they are adopted and is never outgrown." The book quotes one adoptee, a woman in her forties:

> Being aware that I was adopted was a cloak that I wore around me at all times. I was always aware of my adoption; it had become a part of me. Wherever I looked, whatever I did, I took the feeling of adoption with me.

Adoption creates a deep scratch on the LP of the soul. Every time the record revolves, the needle drops into that scratch. A normal person might be tempted to throw the record away. As hyperaware as many adoptees are about the various ways adoption has left us with scratches that cannot be repaired, we would also give anything for those feelings to be erased. If only the feelings would go away, we could feel "normal." Thus, we try and try again to push this adoption angst into the background, to keep it below the level of consciousness.

Here's a quote that sums up the fallacy of this thinking: "Insanity is doing the same thing over and over again but expecting different results."[4]

Every time I play the record of my life, every time I contemplate its various episodes, I think, *Ouch, there's that damned scratch again.* The scratch continues to astonish me. In other words, I want so desperately for the scratch not to exist that I would do almost anything to remain in denial. And the thing I was most in denial about was that there was a connection between my own adoption and my having surrendered a child.

CHAPTER 4

THE SEARCH

*A*lthough I had surrendered my oldest child, I had managed to put my life back together. In my early twenties, I found myself in a period of relative stability. I had finished college and was busy raising my other children and baking apple pies. However, all the years of my oldest son's growing up, I lived in a state of dread that something might happen to him before we could reconnect. He had been born in Phoenix and adopted through Catholic Social Service. Call it a premonition, but around the time he turned ten, I began to feel that something just wasn't right, that he was in danger.

In 1971, I was living in Germany. My husband, his father, John MacDonald, had a postdoctoral research fellowship near Munich, and one day when John was at work, I summoned the courage to write to the agency that had handled my son's adoption. I wanted to know if my son had indeed been adopted, and whether he was alive or dead. I did not expect any information beyond a yes or no. Yes, he was adopted. No, he was not dead.

I knew that in surrendering him, I had signed away my legal rights. Even so, I was a mother—his mother—and whatever document I had put my name to at age sixteen did not erase the feeling of longing in my heart.

My letter to the agency explained that the boy's father and I had married two years after his birth and that we had both graduated from Stanford, I with honors in English and my husband with a PhD. I wanted to present my bona fides so the director, Ramona Sherron, didn't think I was some kind of flake.

As it happened, she knew my son's adoptive grandmother and took the unusual step of calling to find out how he was doing. My son was active in Scouts and Little League, his grandmother said. He was doing well in school. The family had adopted other kids, so he was not their only child. Agency policy and Arizona adoption law did not allow Mrs. Sherron to disclose anything more.

I showed the letter to his father, my high school sweetheart, thinking he would be thrilled. After all, this was his oldest son. He read the letter and handed it back. "Why don't you let it alone?" he said. His reasoning was that I had relinquished all rights and that the adoption agency had told me to "put it out of my mind and go on with my life." We had other children, and I should concentrate on them.

All right, I thought, even if he didn't want to know about his son, I did. (Only years later did I understand that John may have been trying to protect me, and possibly himself, from the inevitable heartbreak of endlessly wondering what had happened to our child.) I wrote back, thanking Mrs. Sherron. She responded with another letter, asking me to make a tape. Catholic Social Service held classes for prospective adoptive parents. She thought a "birth mother's story" would be valuable. Without any expectation that this would get me access to my son—sealed adoption records made such contact illegal—I made the tape and talked about how my situation was typical of the birth mothers I had known. I was Catholic and had a long-term boyfriend. We'd gotten "caught." I talked about my marriage and about how John and I had worked our way through Stanford. Mrs. Sherron wrote back, thanking me.

During my son's teenage years, I made no further inquiries. Then, when he turned twenty-one, I wrote again. By that time, the director had retired, but the letter was forwarded to her. She remembered me. I told her my husband had been killed in a car accident in Germany. At the time, 1971, I had been six weeks pregnant with our fifth child. Our son had four full siblings and a mother who had never forgotten him.

The director still had contact with my son's adoptive family. She learned where his adoptive mother lived and drove two hundred miles across the desert to speak to her in person. Mrs. Sherron proposed an exchange of addresses and phone numbers.

His mother said no. No to contact. No to giving me information.

"But is he okay?" I asked Mrs. Sherron.

"I think so," she said, then added, "but she hasn't spoken to him in several years."

"He's only twenty-one," I said.

"I believe they had some sort of falling-out."

"What kind?"

"She wouldn't say."

Mrs. Sherron did get an update on his life and whereabouts. My son had grown up in the Northwest, which I took to mean Seattle. He had majored in accounting and had been an honor student. It was legal to give this sort of non-identifying information. However, without his mother's permission, the director couldn't tell me more.

I thanked Mrs. Sherron for her trouble. She said it was nothing and that many birth mothers were searching. If I was serious, I should get in touch with an organization in Phoenix called Search Triad. They were familiar with the Arizona laws regarding adoption. Maybe they could help.

I hoped they could, because now I had no idea how to proceed, and proceed I must, quickly. If my son and his mother weren't on speaking terms, something in the adoption had gone terribly wrong. If my son had emotional problems, maybe information about his biological family could help. I owed his mother a debt. She had taken in my baby, loved him, and watched him grow. As a mother, I felt greatly distressed that the two of them were estranged, and I wanted to fix this as soon as possible—if it was within my power.

By the time I began searching for my son in earnest, I was forty-eight and had moved to Urbana, Illinois. In the years between my first husband's death and my second marriage, I had worked as a carpenter to support my children. I was co-owner of Working Women Construction, a company that did room additions, roofing, and kitchen and bath remodeling. I took a few days off work and flew down to Phoenix for a Search Triad meeting. The group's leader put me in touch with other birth mothers, many of whom had been reunited with their children. The place to start, they advised me, was with a petition to the court to get my records unsealed. They gave me the name and address of the court, and I went back to Urbana, where Bruce had recently gotten promoted to associate professor. I wrote up the story about my son's father (John) and I marrying and having more kids, and about my being a generally upstanding citizen.

These days, Arizona allows contact between birth relatives, but only through a court-appointed intermediary. At the time I was searching, no such law existed. The records were sealed, and I had no good medical reason to justify my request that they be unsealed. The court denied my petition, and I began to feel the first pinpricks of doubt that I would ever find my child. But the next moment nudged that doubt aside. I must find him and let him know he had always been loved.

The Search Triad advisor—a lovely, warm woman named Karen—suggested I look at high school yearbooks. Since the boy's father and I had married and had three more boys, she felt certain I'd recognize my son if I saw his picture.

That summer, Bruce had a week-long conference at the University of Washington. I asked if I could tag along. First, I needed to tell my other children about their older brother and that I wanted to look for him. Jackie, a freshman at Bryn Mawr and the oldest of the children I'd raised, already knew. Unbeknownst to me, she had told her brothers. Shrugging offhandedly, the way teenage boys often do, her little brothers said, Sure, we knew about this. Go find him.

While Bruce attended his professional meetings, I visited public libraries. Their collection of yearbooks was incomplete. A librarian suggested I go directly to the high schools. I did but found that telling the office staff I was a birth mother looking for her son made me immediately a person of suspicion. Besides, there were more than a hundred high schools in the Seattle area. I couldn't visit all of them in a week.

I decided to concentrate on the other piece of non-identifying information Mrs. Sherron had given me. My son had graduated with honors from an accounting program. I sat down with a phone book and, with Bruce's help, came up with a list of campuses. Cold-calling accounting departments, I soon learned to bypass the administrative assistants and speak directly to accounting professors. I explained the nature of my call—that I was searching for my oldest child, given up for adoption, and that I knew he had graduated as an honor student in accounting.

Two professors gave me lists of names—their top twenty students. Systematically, I worked through campus switchboards or called the phone company, asking for numbers.

By the end of the week, all I had to show for my efforts was a list of names, phone numbers, and arrows going to notes about possible contact points for the people I had not yet contacted. Bruce had been tolerant at first, but by the end of the week, seeing me face down on the bed, a pillow over my head, he said, "What's plan B?"

I didn't have a plan B. All I had was a trip back to Urbana and a backlog of work. I went up to the attic, where I had my office, opened my bid books and spreadsheets, and dug in.

WHEN BRUCE, whom I had met when we were leaders of a Presbyterian church's youth group, invited me to move from Palo Alto to Urbana, I'd told him I would if we bought an 1869 Italianate villa that was in such bad shape the city had slapped it with a NO OCCUPANCY sign. The house was big and boxy: two stories, twelve-foot ceilings, a winding staircase to the attic, and five bedrooms. For years, each of my kids had been clamoring for his or her own bedroom. Restoring the historic structure would give me credibility as a woman in a nontraditional profession, and I could weave in the restoration with writing freelance articles for construction magazines, which, up until the time I'd met Bruce, had provided a secondary source of income.

Bruce's job as an assistant professor paid zilch. The house, which had been occupied by a dozen students, had a coin-op washer and dryer in the basement, and we kept them, shoving in quarters for laundry for the next five years. Between his income and mine, we were finally solvent, but Bruce and I had a prenuptial agreement. We would go halves on expenses, but I was responsible for the kids' education. My daughter had just started college, and every month I wrote out a big check for her tuition.

Seeing no way forward with my search, I was tempted just to burrow down into my various income-making activities. The week in Seattle had wiped me out. Between work and normal family life, I had plenty to occupy my time and suck up my emotional energy. Finally, though, I recovered enough to give it one more try.

I called the Search Triad leader, Karen.

"There is one more option," she said, "but it will cost you."

"How much?" I said.

"Ten thousand dollars."

"Really?" I said, my voice a squeak.

"We use a secret searcher. We don't know who he is or where he lives, but I can tell you how to contact him."

"How long will it take?"

"If he's able to help you, two or three weeks. And he'll want the money up front."

"What am I paying for?"

"You don't want to know," she said. "And don't ask him. We're afraid he'll spook."

What he was doing was illegal. I didn't care. I had just about that much money in my bank account. I borrowed the rest from Bruce and went down to the bank for a cashier's check.

The anonymous searcher found my son's name and phone number. I learned that my son had also been named John, like his father, and that his phone had a Seattle area code. But I did not call immediately. I had to prepare myself.

Sitting in the attic, phone in hand, I called Karen. I had the name. What should I do?

She told me to write out a script. A caller can never know who's in the room with the person they're calling. A mother or father could be sitting right there. Or maybe there'd be something going on in the child's life. People sometimes hung up. Then you'd feel awkward calling again. You didn't want to come off as a stalker.

Karen warned me not to expect much. Boys, particularly, seemed to have a tough time with reunions. My son might not want or need anything more from me than his biological information. I told myself I could live with that. If I had to.

"Would it be better to write a letter?" I asked.

"No," she said. "It's important for your son to hear your voice. It's hard to deny the call of blood to blood."

I wrote out my script and took it up to our house's belvedere, a streetcar-size space above the attic. The little room looked out at the treetops. It was where Bruce practiced his trumpet and where I curled up with a book. Now, it was where I rehearsed the lines that could either lead to a future relationship or cut off the one I hoped to have.

My son's twenty-first birthday had been in January. In March, Bruce and I had gone to Seattle and tried to find him. In August, the searcher had given me John's name, and I'd called Karen to find out how to proceed. But I feared being rejected. By calling him, I would be putting myself out there, opening this trough of feeling that had been running like an underground stream through the years between his surrender and the moment I'd learned his name.

By the time I let my feelings settle enough to make the call, more time had passed. It was October, leaf-raking season in Illinois. Bruce had the three boys—ages ten, twelve, and fourteen—out in the front yard. Through the belvedere's windows, I could see that he was raking, and they were jumping in leaf piles. I sat down on a built-in bench and dialed the phone.

"Hello, is this John?" I said.

"Yes, who's this?" His voice had a deep, slightly nasal ring.

"I'd like you to write down my number in case we get disconnected," I said.

"All right. Let me get a pen." He covered the receiver and spoke to someone in the room. "Okay, got it."

"Were you born in Phoenix on January 13, 1962?"

"Yes," he said. "How did you know that?"

"I was there," I said. "I'm your mother."

He shouted to the other person in the room. "My mother's calling! My mother's calling!"

We spoke for half an hour. Yes, John had been in Little League, but basketball was his sport. He'd played for Sammamish High School. He lived in Seattle, where he had grown up, the third of eight. The oldest four were adopted. He'd skipped second grade and graduated high school a year early.

John's parents had divorced. He described his relationship with his mother as "estranged." When he was eighteen, a friend's family had taken him in, and from then on, he had supported himself by doing landscaping and by working in a grocery store. John hadn't spoken to his mother in two years.

"What about college?" I asked.

His teachers had encouraged him to apply for a scholarship, which he had done, but he'd also needed to work summers and vacations. He'd paid for room and board by working as a resident assistant in a dorm, and eventually graduated as class valedictorian from the University of Portland.

As I listened to all this—how early he'd been on his own, his parents' lack of support for his education—thoughts of *no, no, no, no, no* raced through my head. *Just stop*, I told myself. They were his parents. They were the lot he'd been dealt, and he'd made the best of it.

But when I hung up, my body was shaking. My teeth chattered like joke teeth. He'd promised to write, and I'd said I would, too.

By Thanksgiving, he'd sent me a lengthy letter and a stack of photos. Like his brother Ted, John had once had blond hair, but it had turned darker during adolescence, when braces had pulled in his buck teeth and when he'd shot up to a basketball player's height. How freeing it was to hold these pictures in my hand. To fan them out and see him in a Little League uniform and making a slam dunk. Freeing, and sad. I had not been there to cheer him on.

Then John received family pictures from me, seeing, for the first time, people who looked like him. After more phone calls and letters, he decided to come out for Christmas. Jackie had invited her college boyfriend home for the holidays. The kids' grandfather Bob MacDonald decided to fly out, too. It would be a full house for the reunion.

In preparation for the holidays, I delegated the housecleaning tasks. "Make sure you put clean sheets on Jackie's bed," I told her brother Bob, sixteen. He'd promised to deal with the second-floor bedrooms. If we were lucky, Ted, fourteen, would wash the mountain of clothes on his floor and clean the downstairs bathroom. My youngest, also named John, volunteered to move in with Bob. We assumed our "guest" would appreciate having his own bedroom. To fuel our vintage ivory-and-green kitchen stove, as well as our two other wood-burning stoves, Bruce split logs and kindling.

I ordered a turkey and hoped that the house, with its period wallpaper, cornice moldings, chandeliers, and cozy nooks would show who I was as a carpenter, mother, and head of household. Houses often surfaced in my dreams, a metaphor for my identity, and I counted on this house to speak for me.

CHAPTER 5

REUNION

*I*n December 1982, the airport in Champaign-Urbana looked like a Greyhound station. Small planes flew down to central Illinois from Chicago or up from St. Louis. John, striding across the frozen tarmac, fought his way through the windblown snow. He was six foot five, with a loping walk and most of his height in his legs. Between his sock hat and his muffler, I saw a narrow, triangular jaw and a patchy beard. He was his father reincarnated.

Shaking, I thrust out a hand. "I'm Marylee."

He looked at my hand and smiled. "What's with that!" he said, pulling me into a hug.

Grandpa Bob MacDonald, John's grandfather, stood in his long khaki coat, a carry-on in his hand.

"It's colder than a witch's tit," he said.

Trust Grandpa Bob to tell it like it is. "John, this is your grandfather."

"I introduced myself on the plane," John said.

"How did you know it was me?" Grandpa Bob said.

"Marylee said to look for 'the businessman with laugh wrinkles.'"

Bob MacDonald hadn't always been laughing, especially right

after he'd found out his son had gotten me pregnant. It wasn't until after John's death that he found me admirable.

"Let's get you home," I said to John. "Everyone's eager to meet you."

"Can we stop by a liquor store?" Bob asked.

"We have wine," Bruce said.

"With this cold, I was thinking Johnnie Walker," Bob said. "And then maybe you can just drop me at the hotel. It was a long flight. I need a nap."

What was going on with Bob? His eyes were bloodshot. They kept going from me to John and back again. Was he just now realizing that this was the baby I'd given up, largely at his behest? That the baby was now a man who looked very much like his father, Grandpa Bob's oldest son?

Bruce put the luggage in the back of my Suburban. It was the vehicle I used for construction. Chunks of joint compound had hardened on the rubber mats, and as John climbed in back, I saw an amused smile. Bruce drove, with Grandpa Bob in the front seat, turning around to look at John. I had thought Bob, an entrepreneur and self-made man, would add to the favorable impression I was trying to make. I wanted John to feel connected to the web that was the extended MacDonald clan, the web that had supported me during the seven years of my widowhood, but I was beginning to realize that although John (the son) had been real to me all these years, to his grandparents he was a disquieting stranger.

The wipers were barely keeping up with the snow. Bruce eased out onto Neil Street, the country highway that led to town.

John looked out the car window at the fields and occasional barn. "What happened to the mountains?"

Grandpa Bob turned. "If you stand on a stepladder, you can see to the curvature of the earth."

John laughed.

"I didn't move here for the view," I said.

"Why did you, then?" John said.

"Bruce's job."

We reached the outskirts of town, with its mounds of dirty snow.

Bruce pulled up next to a liquor store. Bob went inside. The car finally warmed up. I leaned forward and tapped Bruce on the shoulder. "Tell John what you do."

It annoyed me to have to prompt him, but if I didn't, he'd sit there in silence, like the shy, slightly younger grad student I'd first asked out on a date.

Bruce shifted into park and threw his arm over the seat. "I'm a professor of environmental engineering."

"What's that?" John said.

"I study microbial communities," Bruce said. "I harness them to provide services to society."

"Oh," John said, frowning.

"He does research on drinking water and sewage," I said.

"Ah," John said.

"On our honeymoon," I said, "we visited a sewage treatment plant."

"A good one, too," Bruce said. "It was just transitioning from an old Imhoff tank. Marylee got some great pictures of condoms."

"Condoms?" John said.

"They're in the waste stream," Bruce said.

"I see," John said, his brow furrowing again.

"Condoms get flushed down the toilet," Bruce said. "You know? And then in the treatment plant, methane makes them inflate."

"Like party balloons," I said, feeling reckless and swiping at the window's fogged glass with my mitten. I hadn't expected the subject of condoms to enter the conversation, but now that it had, either John was going to get on board, or he was going to think we were all a little cuckoo.

Grandpa Bob came out of the liquor store with a brown bag. John hopped out of the car and opened the door. *Good manners,* I thought. We dropped Grandpa Bob off at Jumer's Castle, a German-themed hotel next to Urbana's shopping mall. It was just a few blocks from our house. With two bathrooms, we didn't really have room to accommodate everyone, and besides, family chaos had always made Grandpa Bob eager to get away.

Our house in Urbana, Illinois was an 1869 Italianate villa.

As Bruce pulled into our driveway, John said, "Oh, wow. Is this where you live?"

"It is," I said.

"When we moved in," Bruce said, "the building was condemned."

"I put back the belvedere—that little room on top—and the porches."

"Don't forget the shutters," Bruce said.

The shutters with the arched tops. Those had been a real pain, but now the house, with its hip roof and eyebrow windows, looked stunning.

The kids, bundled up in jackets, came running out. Jackie was the first to greet John. "I always wanted a big brother," she said, "and now here you are. The biggest of the brothers."

John Michael, eleven and soon to be dubbed Little John, jumped up and tried to touch John's head.

Inside, the kids pulled off their socks and compared the length of their toes. They played Scrabble. They napped on the living room floor, climbing on, or curled up next to, their new sibling. His booming laugh echoed through the house.

On Christmas Eve, I retrieved Grandpa Bob from his hotel and

Bruce put on his "Chef Cat" apron and a starched white toque. John hung out in the kitchen, watching me light a fire in the green-and-ivory wood-stove. Bruce cooked a whole pumpkin and filled it with French onion soup. Ted set the table with my grandmother's Haviland china. I lit candles. While we ate the first course, Bruce stayed in the kitchen, making chicken-and-mushroom crepes, and Grandpa Bob, playing the paterfamilias, regaled us with stories of R. F. MacDonald Co.'s boiler business, where John, my husband, had worked to pay off his debt for my time at the home for unwed mothers.

On Christmas, I gave John a red photo album with a picture I treasured: his father's West Point portrait. There were other photos, too. Pictures of John's high school friends. Pictures of proms and our wedding. A photocopy of my medical records at the time of John's birth. Also, the "birth announcement" I'd recently sent out as my Christmas letter, telling my friends how happy and proud I was to have found my oldest son.

While the other kids tore into their sweaters and board games, John, sitting apart in an armchair, slowly turned the album's pages. I watched him nod and tear up. Finally, he raised his eyes.

"I wish I'd met him," he said.

John Michael—Little John—sitting on the floor, looked up. "I never met him either."

My son Bob said, "The only memory I have is him standing in the doorway, saying, 'Night night. Don't let the bedbugs bite.'"

"How about you, Ted?" John said.

"Nothing at all."

"I remember him," Jackie said. "He used to put us all on a sled and pull us along a path by a river."

"The Isar," I said. "There was a path right by the institute he was working at when he was killed."

"In Germany, right?" John said.

"Yes, it was," I said. "In Garching, just north of Munich."

"Have you been back?" he asked.

"I couldn't bear it."

My eyes flicked over to Bruce, long-haired and with a full beard.

His bangs had the bowl-cut look—early Ringo Starr. He was smiling. Since we had no children of our own—he thought I'd done my bit for the survival of the species—he viewed his contribution as picking up where John had left off.[1]

~

OVER CHRISTMAS DINNER, which all the kids pitched in to cook, we discovered John didn't like Brussels sprouts but ate most anything else. He learned that Jackie went to college on a partial scholarship and that his brother Bob, with 800s on his SATs, was applying to Princeton and Brown.

"In my family, I was always a superstar," he said, "but here, I'm just average."

That was true. For the first time in his life, he was meeting blood relatives, all of whom were driven to excel.

The day after Christmas, snow continued to pile high. The kids made a snowman in our front yard. It was so cold that neither my Suburban nor Bruce's VW Beetle would start. Grandpa Bob came and went by taxi. John bundled up and, with the other kids, pulled sleds to the nearby grocery store.

He fit into our family as if he'd never been gone. But then, I had always known about him, known he was out there somewhere, whereas he had never even imagined he would see people who looked like him and brothers whose voices had the same deep timbre. When you haven't known someone for twenty-one years and suddenly that person is part of your family, it's easy to spot the genetic similarities. But I'd begun to notice John going quiet when his siblings talked about camping trips and other Christmases. These were experiences he had missed and telling him what had happened only reinforced that this was a family he could have grown up in but hadn't.

Later, when Bruce and I were going to bed, he asked, "Which one of the boys is the most like their father?"

"John Lauer," I said. "He looks like him, talks like him, and blows his nose like him. They even have the same handwriting."

I would have been happy if he'd spent every Christmas with us. I wanted to see as much of him as time allowed. However, I had to face the reality that his first loyalty was to his adoptive family and that he was in the "career-making" stage of life. The best I could do was to try to create a common history and keep the lines of communication open.

CHAPTER 6

THE REQUEST

On March 19, 2013, John sent me a text: "Are you in Phoenix anytime this Thursday night to Saturday afternoon? I'm coming down for business." Come on down, I said, as if he were a contestant on the old game show *The Price Is Right.*

It was not unreasonable for John to question my whereabouts. After our move from Evanston, I often found excuses to leave Arizona. And it was not unusual for our attempts at connection to not quite work out. Despite a good reunion, he'd pull away for months or years, and I assumed that what was going on for him was similar to what I had felt after my own reunion—that the discontinuities between my own lived history (the "nurture" part of my story) and the relief and wonder I felt at finally knowing my birth mother and siblings (the "nature" part of the equation) simply overwhelmed me.[1]

After my reunion, I had listened with a noncommittal smile as my birth family talked about family vacations and camping trips and overnights with their grandmother. Hearing about their memories opened a well of longing and grief. I would pull away, not intentionally but because I couldn't bear knowing how much I had missed.

Some months or years later, I would muster the courage to "go there again." What do I mean by "there"? To the house of pain.

I had not heard from John since Christmas, when my kids, now grown and starting their own families, made a point of renting a big house so that the whole family could spend time under one roof. John sometimes came, but more often did not. Even though I had behaved in much the same way with my birth mother, I never knew how to handle either the silences or the moments when he'd resurface. As I stood in line at a Starbucks now, I fully expected him to bail.

I took my coffee to an outdoor table. Cars zoomed past. Across Scottsdale Road, I saw that a strip club—Les Girls—had opened its doors. Smoking a cigarette, a blonde in shorts and a tank top sat on the front stoop. Hunched over, elbows on her knees, she watched the passing traffic. She might have been thinking, though not with words, *how could my life have been different? Is this where I imagined I'd wind up?* But, of course, I was projecting. Maybe she wasn't thinking that at all. Maybe pole dancing required her to erase all feeling. As I well knew, going numb made it easier to survive. For twenty-one years, I had locked away the love I felt for my absent child, just as I'd slammed the lid on the "crying baby"—anything to make her shut up.

A red car swung into the parking lot. Minutes later, my son, holding a latte, pushed open the patio door. His long legs closed the space between us. Fifty-three, he had put on weight since Christmas. The heavier version of John Lauer gathered me in his arms. One hug, and then another, followed by his fingers giving me a chuck on the chin, a gesture tinged with affection or condescension. I was his mother, but I had not raised him, and, even after our time together, I did not know him well enough to accurately decode the nonverbal clues.

At the tables next to us, golfers and baseball fans down for spring training soaked up the sun. John handed me his coffee and moved a green umbrella to shade the table. Then he sat. With his crisp white shirt and broad shoulders, he looked the way his father might have looked in middle age: eyes so blue you could practically see the sky through his head.

His appearance told me that though he had briefly inhabited my body, everything else about him came from the MacDonald gene pool. His oval face had his father's patchy beard. He also had his father's hands—short fingers with nails the size of quarters—a biological feature his father had bemoaned because his small hands made him less effective playing defense.

I gulped down the rest of my coffee and licked the foam from my lips. It was eleven in the morning. Some feeling in my stomach was trying to announce itself. Hunger. Rage. Oatmeal cookie.

My son checked his Rolex and leveled me with his eyes. "Here we are, together again in Phoenix after fifty-one years."

"Yes," I said. "Here we are."

He pointed to my forehead. "I have those."

"Oh, the oil bumps." My fingers went to the bumpy skin at my temple. "Last time I went to the dermatologist, I asked if he could remove the places on my forehead. He told me no, he had other patients, and if he started, he'd be at it all day."

A laugh came from the boom box of John's chest. Four men wearing Cubs hats turned toward the joke they had missed.

"Do you live near here?" John said.

I thumbed over my shoulder. "On the other side of the ASU campus. Bruce draws a little circle around his office, and I've got to find a house within walking distance."

He nodded. "Your house in Urbana was close to his office. I remember that from my first visit."

His first visit. The best and most joyful Christmas of my life. He'd visited us in Evanston only once.

"We actually have a guest bedroom," I said.

"Okay," he said.

"Short notice works," I said. "I don't care."

"Yeah," he said. "Well."

"The price is the same as good advice. Free."

He laughed. "When I came down here before, the rooms were

sixty bucks. The price shot up. My room's running me three hundred a night."

"Spring training."

He frowned. "I never thought of that."

Why hadn't he called me a week ago? Maybe he wanted to work all the time and didn't want to disturb us. More likely, seeing me triggered the same kind of pain it did for me. I could never reclaim the relationship I might have had if he had grown up calling me Mom. Despite that, he was my son, and I loved him.

"Are you getting adjusted to Phoenix?" he said.

I sniff-laughed. "I doubt I ever will."

"It's not a place that ever called to me, either."

The sun peeked around the umbrella, and I put up a hand to shield my face.

John checked his watch again. His smile faded. A fist of uncertainty clenched my gut, the very place—behind that wall of stretch-marked skin—he had turned his baby back flips. I waited for him to push back his chair. Interview over.

"I wanted to get together so you and I could have some time alone," he said.

"That would be nice," I said.

"I thought maybe we could talk about what happened when you were down here."

"What is it you would like to know?" I crossed my arms and then uncrossed them and tried not to look defensive. Surely, after all his years in corporate America, he could read body language.

He leaned forward and pushed his cup aside. "The story of my birth."

"That's the most compelling story for all of us," I said. "How we came into the world. Who our ancestors were. How the combination of nature and nurture made us who we are."

"Yes," he said. "When you sent me pictures of my dad, it blew me away."

"Do you still have the album I gave you our first Christmas together?" I asked.

"I still have it," he said.

"It's quite the coincidence that you want to talk about this now," I said. "I've actually been doing some work with a woman who's an adoption intermediary. She's sort of a private eye for reunion searches. Here in Arizona, I'm not entitled to my records without going to court. On her first pass, she was able to locate some files from the home for unwed mothers."

"And that was?"

"The Florence Crittenton Home," I said. "And last week I sicced her on Catholic Social Service. Maybe she'll turn up something."

"What do you want to know?" he said.

"I've never understood why they placed you with the family they did."

"It wasn't a bad family."

"It wasn't a good one, either."

"My mom always used to say that they got to pick out their kids," he said, "but my grandma always said, 'If you got to pick him out, why'd you pick one with such a big nose?'"

I bit my lip and shook my head. John had his father's nose, of course. All the children had inherited that. For a nose of such size, it was remarkably inefficient.

We talked about his father's deviated septum and the genetics of John's height and baldness, inherited from the O'Briens, his grandmother Henrietta's side of the family. Specific genes in our DNA are responsible for our facial characteristics. A team of researchers, publishing in the prestigious journal *Nature*, identified facial features that linked to fifteen locations in our DNA.[2] The DNA markers were evident even during the development of a baby in the womb. A team at Stanford University found that, of these fifteen genetic markers, seven were specific to the nose.

But the face isn't the only repository of inherited traits. A predisposition to alcoholism, diabetes, or anxiety may also stem from a child's heritage. I knew from my own reunion that body type and stress-induced eating were part and parcel of my genetic makeup, as was a tendency toward respiratory illnesses. Similarly, certain kinds of intelligence—mathematical ability or musicality—may be partially derived from DNA.

Then the conversation shifted to the odd nature of John's adoptive family: four adopted children and four birth children. The youngest four, biologically related, formed their own tribe. Of the oldest four—the adoptees—John was the only one who'd reconnected with his birth family.

"I'm sorry I'm not better at staying in touch," he said.

"Two years ago, you showed up for Christmas," I said. "That's something."

He nodded. "I know it must seem like I'm in the witness protection program."

"It does."

He leaned back and folded his arms across his chest. "I don't know if I ever told you, but I once told a therapist I didn't need anyone. I said if you put me down in the middle of the Sahara with a book and some drinking water, I'd make my way across the sand to Timbuktu. And you know what my therapist said?"

He'd told me this story before. "No," I said.

"He said, 'That's all fine, John, but you don't live in the Sahara.'"

John laughed.

I did, too. Four years earlier, when he was agonizing about whether to get divorced, we'd had a couple of long phone calls. In any long-term relationship, friendship, not passion, counted for a lot. Thinking of my relationship with Bruce, I'd told John that a determination to wait out the bad patches could reap its own rewards.

"What does your therapist's comment mean to you?" I said.

He frowned and thought. "I discovered I do need people. It gets lonely on weekends."

"What exactly do you want to know?" I said.

"What it was like for you," he said.

"Surrendering you, do you mean? Or living through the years when I didn't know if you were alive or dead?"

"Both," he said.

"That prolonged uncertainty was worse by far than your father's death. You were out there adrift, my own flesh and blood."

"Tell me everything. Tell me from the beginning."

⁓

FOR THIRTY-TWO YEARS, I had told him pretty much anything he'd asked. From the beginning. Again? Yes, again, but with a different twist this time. Not just how I got pregnant and by whom, but how it had been for me.

I had told the story of my life, over and over, to various therapists and even to John, and on all these occasions, I had freely shared the facts of his birth and tried not to burden him with more than he wanted to know. But I had not shown him "me," the girl I was then. The chosen child. The adoptee. The crying baby. The part of me I wanted to pretend had played no part in why I had wound up pregnant.

When I was a young mommy raising my other four, I tried to respond to them as individuals, not as part of a litter. Once a year, on their birthdays, each child came up with a plan for how we would spend the day. My youngest, John Michael, wanted to spend a night at the Cinderella Motel on El Camino Real and watch *The Incredible Hulk* on TV. My son Bob wanted to rent bikes in Golden Gate Park and ride across the Golden Gate Bridge.

If my oldest son wanted to know what it was like for me, I would try to share the story of my own adoption and the peculiar admixture of nature and nurture that led to his surrender. But could I really explain such a complicated story?

I was no longer a carpenter. For fifteen years, I had been steadily working away at becoming a writer, trying to find words to express what is often glimpsed only in one's peripheral vision.

As author Anne Rice wrote:[3]

Writers write about what obsesses them. You draw those cards. *I lost my mother when I was fourteen. My daughter died at the age of six. I lost my faith as a Catholic. When I'm writing, the darkness is always there. I go where the pain is.*

Like anyone raking up a past trauma, I was not certain that taking a walk down Memory Lane would do any good. The thought of opening the door to the crying baby's nursery gave me no pleasure. However, in any childhood, there are moments of beauty, wonder, and joy.

Childhood is the territory of play. Julia Cameron's book *The Artist's Way* leads readers back into those rooms of memory and back into our early longing for lives rich with creativity. By going back into my own childhood, I would have a chance to introduce my oldest son to my roots as a carpenter and writer. In addition, I could introduce him to more relatives, all of whom—if I did my job right—would live vividly on the page. Most important, I could show him his father—walking, talking, and living his life in the full expectation that it would not be cut short.

As I prepared to plunge into this memory pool of sensations and experiences, I was struck by what a daunting task lay ahead. An adult seeking to make sense of the past needs to construct a coherent story. A "self" needs to emerge on the page, just as the self of the real-life person eventually emerges from all the conflicting bits of advice, admonitions, punishments, rewards, and sermons that come down from parents, teachers, and the precepts of one's faith.

PART II

AN ADOPTEE'S CHILDHOOD

CHAPTER 7

THE CHRISTMAS CHICK

When I was young, I believed that God could see inside my very soul, a belief that took root because my adoptive father, despite his own shortcomings, had determined to raise me Catholic. The men who climbed the steps and passed between the pillars of Our Lady of Mount Carmel church wore suits and ties, but my father, a longshoreman, was proud of being a "working stiff." Defying convention, he wore his usual long johns, brown wool pants, and flannel shirt. Pausing at the door, he dipped his fingers in the holy water, crossed himself, and continued down the aisle, his splay-footed swagger clearing a path to the third pew.

While Old Father Cavanaugh, in a subdued and quavering voice, intoned the Latin, my father flipped down the kneeler. It hit with a slap. People turned. Ignoring them, my father genuflected, crossed himself, and slid into the pew. I did the same, careful not to sit on his brown fedora.

He leaned on the pew in front. With his slicked-back, silver hair and wind-chapped face, my father looked every bit his age. Only Mass stilled his restless energy.

After the priest had raised the host and turned it to the body and blood of Christ, my father slid past me and joined the others, waiting in line. When he returned, I sat back. I knelt beside him and did not even mind the scent of smoke clinging to his clothes. Soon, I could walk up the aisle with my father. We could take Communion together. I would finally know what it felt like to hold the body of Christ on my tongue and feel the wafer, thin and stiff. The teacher in my Saturday class said not to chew it. We were supposed to let it dissolve while we prayed for Christ's blessing.

I had already memorized the prayers for First Communion. I knew that God was not just one person, but part of the Trinity of the Holy Spirit. I knew that Christ had been born and died for our sins, but that on Judgment Day, God the Father would send us to Heaven or Hell, or possibly Purgatory, where we would spend a long time atoning for the bad things we had done. Oh, except if we were unbaptized babies. Babies went to a place called Limbo, which was neither so glorious as Heaven nor so cruel as Hell. I pictured Limbo as a kind of orphanage in the sky, the kind of place I came from before my parents took me out of there and gave me a home.

My Saturday teacher also told us what to say in confession: "Bless me, Father, for I have sinned," followed by however many days it had been since our last confession. I even knew the kinds of sin: mortal and venial. Also, sins of commission and sins of omission. Sins of omission were the things you should have done, the things your parents expected of you, such as chores and not lying, but that you had somehow weaseled out of, probably by pretending, as my grandma would have said, to have wax in your ears.

OUR HOME WAS NOT FAR from Our Lady of Mount Carmel. A small, flat-roofed stucco house, it had two parts: a living room, dining room, and two bedrooms in front, and an in-law room in back. All the rooms were small, mine barely large enough for a single bed, the bookcase my grandfather had made, and a child's table and straw-bottomed chair my father had bought down in Tijuana. On Sundays, my mother and her parents, non-church-going Methodists, ate breakfast while my father took me to Mass.

Because my father preferred cold oatmeal to warm, my grand-mother put our bowls in the refrigerator.

Back from Mass, my father picked up the *Chronicle* from the driveway. No one dared touch the paper before he'd retrieved it. Opening the gate, we passed the chickens pecking about in the backyard coop, a mesh enclosure my grandfather had made to keep out the raccoons. In the breezeway, I hung my coat. Daddy sepa-rated the paper. Turning to the right, he went back to my grandpar-ents' room—just large enough for a double bed and the wing chair where my grandfather sat, looking out at the yard. "Here you go, Doc," my father would say, and hand Grandpa the funny papers.

After I'd eaten breakfast, Grandpa read me "Prince Valiant" and "Beetle Bailey." After that, my father took the whole family out for a drive. And after that, the chicken and dumplings would be ready, and we could eat. It was the same every Sunday, the only variance being whether the chicken was stewed, fried, or fricasseed and whether we had dumplings or mashed potatoes.

My father said hello to my mother and grandmother, who stood back to back at the U-shaped counter, and then carried his breakfast and mine to the dining room. He liked his oatmeal with raisins, and I liked mine that way, too. I carried the bottle of half-and-half. My father and I were the only ones who used half-and-half. Before pouring it, he would pull off the paper top and sniff. If it had spoiled, he marched to the kitchen and half-and-half glugged down the drain. My parents and grandparents were trying to make sure I didn't turn out spoiled. Children who had no brothers and sisters were often spoiled, my mother said.

After breakfast, my father took a beer from the refrigerator and went into the living room to smoke and read the paper. Grandma, on the side of kitchen sink used for dish drying, held tweezers. She was plucking pinfeathers from a hen. My mother asked if I'd like to help make Christmas cookies. She was baking them for her class.

"Yes, ma'am," I said.

"Let's start by rolling out the dough." She pulled a chair to the counter and double-tied an apron around my waist. Standing on the chair, I saw that she had taken out the muslin bag that held the cookie cutters and arranged them on the counter. She'd also made up batches of green and pink frosting, and she'd even bought some colored sprinkles.

The dough was thin, the rolling pin floury and hard to hold. The handles felt wet and sticky. I pushed and pushed and spilled flour on the floor. Grandma wouldn't like that. Extra work. My mother finally stood behind me and put her hands over mine. Ragged as an untrimmed piecrust, the dough covered the breadboard. I picked up a loose piece and opened my mouth.

"Put that down." Grandma plunged the chicken into a pot on the stove. "If you eat the raw cookie dough, it'll give you a tummy ache."

Mother pointed to the cookie cutters—a star, a Christmas tree, and a gingerbread man, all made of yellow plastic. "Which one do you want to try?"

I pointed to a cutter made of thin, sharp metal. It was a chick, like the ones that had eventually become our backyard chickens. The cookie cutter had a tiny beak and two tiny feet.

"Can I make the chick?" I asked.

"*May* I make the chick," she said.

"Yes, ma'am," I said. "May I make the chick?"

"Very well. Now that you've asked nicely." Mother dipped the cutter in flour and handed it to me.

I took the cutter's handle, not wanting to hurt the chick, even though I knew it wasn't really alive. I pressed, but each time I lifted the cutter away, either the feet or the beak always stuck, leaving a beak-less, footless chicken. It looked deformed. It had to be perfect. I tried again.

"If you roll out that dough over and over," Grandma said, "it's going to be inedible. Have her use the tree."

"Wait!" I said, pulling up the cutter. "I can do it!" And there it was. Finally, a perfect chick. Every tiny toe. A perfect beak.

"Show your father," my mother said. "He'll be proud."

She lifted me down from the chair, wiped my hands, and, with a spatula, slid the chick onto my palm.

Thin and translucent, the chick looked the way I imagined a Communion wafer might.

In the living room, Daddy put down his paper and stubbed out his cigarette. His brown bottle of beer balanced on an upright ashtray.

"Daddy, look!" I said.

"Say, that's nice." He leaned over, plucked the chick from my hand, and gulped it down.

The raw dough would give him a tummy ache. He would be sick. And if he was sick, it would be my fault. Then he saw my face.

"Hey, don't cry." He pulled me onto his lap. His whiskers scratched my cheek. The wool of his pants rubbed my thighs. He picked up his beer bottle and put it to my lips. "Have a sip."

The beer smelled and tasted sour. It dribbled down my chin. I held my breath and pulled and twisted to get away. He had me in his tickle-torture grip, his hand around my wrist. He jerked my arm behind my back. If he got his other hand on my wrist, he'd give me an Indian burn.

I spat beer in his face.

"Hey!" He released me.

Before he could clamp his knees together, I slid down and crawled under the table and cowered, a hard lump in my stomach.

"Come out from under there," he called, bending down. "I didn't hurt you."

"Rex, what are you up to?" Mother stood at the kitchen door, one floury hand on her hip.

He settled back with his beer. "She's got a hair up her ass. That's all."

"Come out from under the table," Mother said.

I pushed the chairs aside and crawled out.

"Turn around and let me retie your apron," she said.

I pulled it off. "I don't want to make cookies."

"You could frost them," she said.

"No," I said.

"No, ma'am," she said.

"Yes, ma'am," I said.

"Then go to your room."

"Can't Grandpa read me the funnies?"

Grandma, her hair kinked by white curls, looked out from the kitchen. "She's acting spoiled."

My mother's mouth crimped. She looked up at the ceiling. "I can't see the harm. All right. Go ahead."

I hurried through the kitchen to my grandparents' room. I never saw my grandfather—Orville Pitney—in anything but a starched white shirt, and there he sat, the legs of his pin-striped pants crossed, the paper spread open before him. His eyes, enlarged by the half-moons of his bifocals, smiled. From his shirt pocket he took a pack of Wrigley's spearmint gum. "Want some?"

"Do you have any Juicy Fruit?"

"As a matter of fact, I do." The gum would take away the taste of the beer.

In his dresser he found a pack of Juicy Fruit and gave me a stick. "Where shall we start?" he asked, gathering me into his lap.

"How about 'Prince Valiant'?"

What I liked was the way Prince Valiant treated his son, Arn. Every father should be like that, firm but gentle.

The author at fifteen months is shown with her mother and grandmother.

CHAPTER 8

WRONGFUL DEATH

At the time of my adoption, my grandfather had moved from Colorado to California. He'd let his medical license lapse, and anyway, he was an old-fashioned country doctor, often as not paid in chickens or rhubarb pies. He had no retirement, not even social security, but he was well educated and particularly fond of Dickens and Mark Twain.

Until I went to kindergarten, my grandfather had plenty to do keeping me out of Grandma's hair. An amateur woodworker with a few basic hand tools, he made me a stove out of peach crates and coffee-can lids. He carved a menagerie of wooden animals. We played endless games of dominoes and Chinese checkers. When the weather was sunny, we sat side by side on the kitchen steps while I carved a bar of Ivory soap and he whittled a Santa or a cow or a dog. When his and my grandmother's favorite programs—*One Man's Family* and *Fibber McGee and Molly*—came on his vacuum tube radio, I went to my grandparents' room and listened.

However, my going to school changed all that. When I started kindergarten, my father persuaded "Doc" Pitney that he could earn far more as a shipping clerk, working on the waterfront in San Francisco, than he had ever made as a doctor. All Doc Pitney had to do, my father claimed, was walk around with a clipboard and match bills of lading with the container numbers on the ship's manifest. The two of them could commute to San Francisco on the train, and the job wouldn't be physically taxing. If my grandfather needed to walk down to the end of one of the piers, he could hop on a jitney. Hell, he'd soon be driving a forklift! my father claimed.

My grandfather went along with my father's scheme. Maybe Grandpa was tired of my father's lording it over him, bragging about how much he made. Or maybe my grandfather thought that he could put aside enough money so that he and my grandmother could get their own little place.

Then, one morning, my father came rushing in. Out of breath, chest heaving, he put a hand on the counter. "Doc fell under the train!"

REDWOOD CITY, Oct. 27—A 78-year-old retired physician suffered a loss of both his legs this morning when he slipped beneath the wheels of a moving commuter train in front of the Southern Pacific station here.

Dr. Orville Pitney, resident of 504 Roosevelt Avenue, was in a critical condition at Sequoia Hospital after his legs were severed below the knees before the horrified eyes of approximately 20 commuters waiting on the station platform about 6:30 a.m.

According to my father, Grandpa ran for the northbound train, which was starting to move out of the station. He grabbed a handrail on one of the cars but then lost his balance and fell between two cars. A sheriff's ambulance arrived, and the ambulance drivers applied tourniquets.

My grandfather died early in the morning three weeks later, on November 2, 1953. He was seventy-eight. Blood clots had spread from his amputated legs and stopped his heart.

On March 15, 1956, the Superior Court of San Mateo County awarded $36,600 to the "family of a retired Colorado physician who died under the wheels of a commuter train in Redwood City in 1953." My mother, uncle, and grandmother had gone to court asking for $100,000, compensation for the train's negligence. A jury deliberated three hours and twenty minutes before deciding whether there would be any award at all, and if so, how much it would be.

After the verdict came in, my father was irate and blamed the lawyer for not having been more aggressive. Even my grandmother, mother, and uncle looked like they'd had the wind knocked out of them. However, the money, though not as much as they had hoped for, made a difference. It meant they could look for a house where my grandmother could have her own bathroom and kitchen and my parents could have more privacy.

Moving? No! In this house on Roosevelt, I had worn my red straw hat and played cowgirl. I had pushed my pet hen, Maude, in my baby buggy and built forts with my father's army blankets. The house was where Grandpa had read me bedtime stories. And it was where I had learned the story of my adoption.

CHAPTER 9

THE CHOSEN CHILD

From 1945 to 1973, four million women in the United States had children placed for adoption, two million during the 1960s alone. The origin story for all of us, whether we were told early or found out by the slip of a relative's tongue, began the moment we learned we had been adopted.

I was crawling under my grandparents' bed, using my grandfather's fleece-lined slippers to push out clumps of lint. The floor made my tummy cold. In the band of yellow light beneath the bed, I saw my mother's ankles. The bed creaked. She had come into her parents' room.

After I had crawled out, she took the slippers from my hands and passed them to her father, my grandpa. Grandpa had begun reading me a fairy tale my mother had brought home from the library: "The Ugly Duckling."[1]

Thus far in the story, a mother duck had found a strange, large egg in her nest and decided to sit on it until it hatched, but when it did, she was surprised by the peeping baby's size and ugliness. Grandpa opened to the page where the mother duck urged her ducklings to jump in the water and forced her strange hatchling to sink or swim.

The mother duck stared at it and exclaimed, "It is very large and not at all like the others. I wonder if it really is a turkey. We shall soon find out, however, when we go to the water. It must go in if I have to push it myself."

Grandpa paused and looked at his daughter. "Are you going to tell her, or shall I?"

"No, I'll do it," my mother said. "Marylee, you should know you are adopted."

"What's 'adopted'?" I asked.

"It means we chose you," my mother said, smiling and leaning back, her hands flat on the chenille spread. "Other parents don't get to choose their children, but we chose you."

"Oh." I huddled back against Grandpa. Our next-door neighbors, the McHales, had two foster children, Charles and Mikey. Charles, the younger one, sometimes came over to play.

"Is 'adopted' like 'foster'?" I said.

"No," my mother said. "Your real parents are dead."

"Oh," I said.

"After Grandpa finishes your story, it's bath time," Mommy said.

And that was the end of it. The beginning of the story of "me" was not the moment I came out of my mother's womb. It was five weeks later, the moment they picked me out and brought me home.

"The Ugly Duckling" always had great meaning for me, not just because my grandfather had read it to me on the day I learned of my adoption, but because the story itself seemed to be telling me an essential truth. It promised that one day, I would discover where I fit in.

Genetically, an adopted child may be brilliant but feel like a misfit because he's being raised by "good" people who share none of the adoptee's drives or desires. Hans Christian Andersen was raised by "good people" whose highest aspiration was for him to become a shoemaker. For a more contemporary example, think of Steve Jobs.[2] Son of two brilliant graduate students. Raised by a mechanic and his wife. Conflicted. Driven. Repeating the pattern of his own abandonment by abandoning his daughter Lisa.

People who are adopted live in the middle of a psychodrama. They do not know the script, only that they find themselves on a stage, mouthing lines they did not know they knew.

~

PRIOR TO MY ADOPTION, my parents had been living on an avocado ranch in Camarillo, California, my father working on the docks at Port Hueneme, my mother raising rabbits and, with the help of sailors, harvesting avocados. They were late to be embarking on this journey into parenthood.

My mother, who had grown up in Colorado, had worked her way through college by teaching in one-room schools. A sorority sister from Colorado State Teachers College (now Northern Colorado State University), in Greeley, had moved to California. When my mother came out to get a master's degree at UCLA, the women reconnected. Dorothy Lipton worked for the California Children's Home Society (CCHS). That's how my mother, who was forty at the time, newly married after a lifetime of never having had a date, and who had no experience with babies, managed to get me. But even though my mother and the social worker were sorority sisters, the adoption almost didn't happen.

Thinking he'd like to go into business for himself, my father had recently bought an icehouse in Camarillo. The CCHS was undertaking a home study to verify my father's income; however, during that process, the icehouse began losing money. Refrigerators had just come in. Ultimately, my father went bankrupt.

To make up for lost income, my mother needed to go back to teaching. The CCHS wouldn't approve the adoption unless she came up with a suitable plan for childcare. She wrote a desperate letter to her parents, begging them to move out from Colorado and take charge of me. And so, instead of my parents, it was my grandparents who prepared my formula of evaporated milk and Karo syrup, who established my every-four-hours feeding schedule, and who washed my cloth diapers.

When I was six months old, my parents sold the ranch and

moved to Redwood City, a bedroom community on the peninsula with an easy train commute to the docks in San Francisco. My mother resumed her career.

At McKinley School, where she taught fifth grade, she often had yard duty, breaking up arguments about tetherball or keeping boys from heaving kickballs at their enemies.

When we were at school together, she walked around the playground with her customary scowl.

"Is Mrs. Benham your grandmother?" one of the boys in my class asked.

"No, she's my mother," I said.

"She looks mean," he said.

"She's not mean," I said. "Just strict."

"Anyway, you don't look like her."

"I'm adopted," I said.

"Oh, sorry."

In those days, admitting you were adopted was like admitting your parents were divorced. I didn't know anyone whose parents had divorced, nor did I know anyone adopted, at least anyone who'd admit it. Even so, I didn't understand why he'd said "sorry." Adoption wasn't anything to feel bad about. My parents had chosen me. They could have picked another kid. If anything, I should have felt sorry for him.

SOON, HOWEVER, I BEGAN TO understand more about what the word "adoption" meant. My mother signed me up for a Brownie troop. The moms of my friends in the troop wore pastel cotton shirtwaists. My mom had a pear-shaped body and wore a girdle with whalebone stays. The other moms had pageboys. My mother had gray hair, short and permed. The other girls' moms stayed home. My mom worked.

On June 2, 1953, we Brownies sat at a kitchen table, watching Queen Elizabeth's coronation. Our craft project that day was making paperweights. The troop's leader had purchased three-inch-diameter glass ashtrays, and we were going to make Father's Day presents. While we watched the coronation, we pressed our school pictures in the ashtrays' bottoms and filled the void with plaster of Paris. After the plaster had hardened, we glued on red felt circles. When we turned the ashtrays right side up, there were our smiling faces!

This school photo is identical to the one placed in the ashtray and covered with plaster of Paris.

Mothers began coming in before we had finished. They bent over and hugged their daughters. They brought along older siblings or babies in strollers. As I looked from the faces of my friends to the faces of their mothers, I saw the same hair and eye color, the same dimples and curls. I looked from the mothers and daughters to the brothers and sisters and babies in strollers. These other families had more kids than mine did, and the people in each family all looked alike. At the time, I didn't understand that there was any other way to have babies than to go pick one out, sort of like a song that was popular back then, Teresa Brewer's "How Much Is That Doggie in the Window?"

And maybe I should have. At home, if I had been paying attention, I might have seen that my mother looked like her father. They both had the same oval face and narrow chin. Both wore bifocals. Both had protruding eyes, a condition, I later learned, that came from having an overactive thyroid.

My uncle Marshall, whom we saw once or twice a year, looked like his mother. He had auburn hair and a distant stare, like the heads we had seen the previous summer on our vacation to Mount Rushmore.

IF I HAD JUST LIVED with the knowledge of adoption within the bubble of my family, I would not have questioned this notion that I had been "chosen," the fairy tale I had been told from the time I could still slither under Grandpa's bed.

"Chosen" was a simpler word to say than "adopted."

"Chosen" was also a simpler concept.

However, how much choice do adoptive parents really have? Can they choose their children? Sociology professor Christa Hoffman-Riem, the author of *The Adopted Child*, says that the notion of parents "choosing" a child is an inaccurate portrayal of what transpires. Adoption is a two-step, bureaucratic procedure.[3] The adoption agency interviews the candidates and makes a prior selection. According to the author, "The freedom of choice for applicants is reduced to the freedom to reject the offer, a decision that, depending on the 'market situation,' could jeopardize the entire adoption plan." She quotes one adoptive mother as saying the following:

> And then we also said [to the adoption counselor], "If we don't take to this child, you never know, you take to some babies too and not to others, do we get . . . are we then put on the waiting list?" Of course, that's really depressing, and "no," she [the adoption counselor] said.

The stress of accepting or rejecting the child the agency wishes a prospective adoptive couple to take is the flip side of the adoption coin. However, a child—an infant—doesn't know that the parents may have worried about hair and eye color, or whether the child will be a good fit.

> Adoptive mother: "What kind of child are you going to get? If it's, er, if it's your own child, you might also expect certain dispositions. If, say, you're dark-haired, maybe the child will also be dark-haired. In our case, it's what kind of child are we going to get? A red-haired one . . . or a dark-haired one? Are we going to get an absolutely fair-haired child?"

During the adoption process, Hoffman-Riem writes, the prospective parents' anxiety often "revolves around the aspect of hereditary traits."[4]

Very true. I had thick, dark brown hair, which my grandmother trained into finger curls by tying rags around it at night. I had eyelashes so long that Santa, making an appearance at Davies Chevrolet, a car dealership in Redwood City, asked, "Where'd you get those long eyelashes?" My eyebrows looked as if they'd been applied with the kind of stick my mother used to pencil in her pale white ones. People said I looked like Shirley Temple and, later, Annette Funicello of *The Mickey Mouse Club*.

The adoption agency had told my parents that I had Irish heritage, and that my dark eyes would turn blue as I grew older. If I had been a blond-haired, blue-eyed baby, my appearance might have invited fewer comments.

~

EVERY SUMMER we drove down to El Paso, where my father grew up. It was on one of those trips that I began to sense that there was more to the story than parents just "choosing" me.

Tumbleweeds rolled across Route 66. Imaginary lakes shimmered on the horizon. My halter top chafed my neck, and the elastic around my midriff rode up as I leaned forward. I wanted to dip my hand in one of those coolers at a gas station and feel around in the ice cubes and water and pull out a Nehi orange soda.

"When can we stop?" I said. "Is our motel going to have a pool?"

"Swimming, always swimming," my father said, driving one handed, a Camel hanging from the corner of his lip. "Deserters from the Spanish Armada must've jumped ship and swum to the coast of Ireland."

"Hush, Rex," my mother said. "Little pitchers have big ears."

"What's the Spanish Armada?" I asked.

Years later, I deduced that this had been an oblique reference to my appearance, my father's little "ha ha" moment about sailors having sex with an Irish lass. But even then, I knew that it meant *something*.

Adoptees, hyper alert and listening for signals about their behavior or appearance, will pick up on these innuendos, even if they don't understand their full meaning. When my son said his grandmother had commented, "If they got to choose you, why'd they pick one with such a big nose?" I recognized this as the same kind of offhand remark directed at me. We adoptees listen in perplexed silence as our adoptive relatives speculate about our families of origin. This attempt, on the part of the adoptee, to understand the nature of his or her own intrinsic "self" and to somehow bring that self into closer alignment with the norms and expectations of the adoptive family begins the moment a child learns he or she is adopted.

No matter how parents attempt to figure out the right language or come up with an age-appropriate story, adoption arises from the decision of adults to transfer legal custody of a child from its family of origin to a family that does not necessarily have any blood relationship, otherwise known as "consanguinity." Simply put, adoption, in a legal sense, has to do with the transfer of property.

The first modern adoption law, passed in Massachusetts in 1851, sought to protect the interests of the child, not benefit the adults. Prior to the passage of that law, however, children were often adopted to do farm labor, a form of indentured servitude. Between 1854 and 1929, the orphan train[5] movement relocated two hundred thousand orphaned and abandoned children to the farmlands of the Midwest. Often, these children were used as cheap farm labor. Like adoption, this wholesale transfer of young children was done with the best of intentions, the thought that such transfers would give the children a better life.

When I began the search for my birth mother, I learned that in 1945 the legal notices for adoptions were posted in newspapers under "Chattel Sales." The transfer of a baby was, as far as the law was concerned, quite similar to the old practice of transferring the ownership of livestock or of window glass, back in the days when glass was an important indicator of a person's wealth and social status.

Indeed, the search for my own genetic heritage began when I found the legal notice of my adoption in the classified ads of a Culver City newspaper. The news slammed into my gut like a fist punch. I hadn't realized how much of me had gone missing. Now I knew. There had been a "me" even before my parents adopted me. Although it would take many more years to track down my birth mother, this one-inch-by-two-inch notice provided proof that an actual baby had existed. A crying baby, separated from her birth mother and taken to a foster home for five weeks, and then separated from that placement and taken to live with Rex and Lorene Benham on their avocado ranch in Camarillo.

I cannot imagine a way to explain the legal matter of adoption to a young child. Telling a child he or she has been "chosen" makes a lot of sense.

However, adoption is not just a legal matter. It is also a matter of biology, and that, too, is hard for children to comprehend, especially if they have not yet learned the "facts of life."

CHAPTER 10

PEACHES

*T*he moments seared into our memories are often associated with particular places. We all remember where we were on 9/11. Or where we watched the moon landing. Or where we had our first kiss. I learned about sex in the kitchen of our new house, a house we had moved into the summer after Southern Pacific sent a settlement check for my grandfather's wrongful death. The house sat on a stretch of unincorporated county land between Redwood City and the tony suburb of Atherton.

It was Saturday, and my mother had rousted me early. Annoyed at having been awoken from a sound sleep, I dressed in play clothes: shorts and a blouse.

By the time I came into our kitchen, my mother had gotten out a blue-speckled, enamel canning vat. Mason jars jiggled in boiling water, steaming the windows, and a mixing bowl of parboiled peaches sat on the table.

"There are some things you're old enough to learn," my mother said.

I took a bowl of oatmeal from the refrigerator. The oatmeal had developed fissures, like land undergoing desertification. I poured half-and-half and sat down.

"Use your napkin," my mother said, as if I needed to be reminded.

I tucked the napkin into my blouse.

My mother pushed a box of red-bordered labels toward me. "While you eat, write, 'Peaches, 1956.'"

Spooning up oatmeal with my left hand, I set to work on the labels. My chair gave me a view through the laundry room and screen door, and I saw Grandma, already outside. Wearing a flowered housedress that buttoned down the front, five-foot-two and shrinking, she lowered the clothesline so she could hang the laundry.

"Okay, I'm done," I said, tucking the labels back in their box and wiping my chin. "Can I go?"

"Wash your bowl," my mother said. "Then you're going to help me with the canning."

"For how long?" I said.

"Until lunch."

I took the bowl to the sink.

My normal Saturday morning job was to sweep the oak leaves off the patio. While I disliked any chore that seemed pointless, such as crawling under the dining table to dust the table legs, I didn't mind sweeping the patio. Acorns and oak balls locked up my skates. When I grew up, I planned to skate for the Bay Area Bombers, a roller derby team my dad and I watched on television. My dad had recently taken us to the Cow Palace to see the Ice Capades. Maybe I could be Sonja Henie, skating backward with my arms held out and my leg uplifted in an arabesque. I had never skated on ice, but I was pretty sure I could do it, because I was really good on roller skates.

I washed and dried the bowl.

"Where's Daddy?" I asked.

"I sent him down to Sunnyvale for apricots," my mother said. "There are some things we have to discuss before he gets home."

Every spring, my mother and grandmother carried in the empty Mason jars from the shelves in the garage. Once filled with canned produce, the jars would provide all our meals until the next canning season: stewed tomatoes, corn, spinach, and army-green peas. My mother called this "putting up."

And, then she explained how "it"—this putting up—was done. The fruit must first be washed, bad spots cut out with a paring knife, and the jars disinfected in boiling water. She explained the dangers of botulism, and that one must always label the jars and use the oldest first. When I got married and was in charge of my own house, I should check before removing the lid to make sure the "in" button on the lid's center hadn't turned to an "out" button. Fruit wasn't usually a problem, she said. Fruit would keep a year or two. I must be very suspicious of green beans, and even canned tomatoes could kill you.

As she explained the science behind canning, and how necessary it was for girls my age to learn these skills, I perked up. Fifth grade was the first year we'd had science. The idea that there was a science to running a house surprised me. This was a side of my mother I had never seen, this assured and confident woman. My mother taught slow learners, and I had assumed she did that because she was slow herself: tentative, plodding, careful.

My fingers shriveled, and the peach skins slid off. The beautiful, golden flesh of the fruit felt firm and slippery in my palm. I stuffed the peaches down into the Mason jars. My mother brought more peaches. The table filled up with jars. After fitting the jars in a wire rack, she carried them to the canner, lowered the metal basket that held them into boiling water, and returned to the table, tipping her chair back against the refrigerator.

"You may have heard certain things from kids at school," she said, blowing a wisp of hair from her brow. "About what happens to girls."

"No," I said.

"You're eleven," she said. "Girls your age begin to menstruate."

I had never heard that word before. I didn't ask her to repeat it, but she did anyway.

"You will start to bleed once a month, and there isn't anything you can do to stop it, so you shouldn't be embarrassed when it happens."

She was staring at me, her eyes bugged open, waiting for me to say something. I was breathless. My heart thrummed in my ears.

She spoke the cringe-inducing words "penis" and "vagina" and explained that those were the correct words for parts of a man's and woman's body.

I had never seen a grown-up's naked body. When she dressed for work, my mother rolled nylons up to the garters that dangled from her corset. Now, curling her fingers, she showed me how a man put his penis in a woman's vagina.

My mother wiped her hands on her apron. The jars of peaches were ready to have the lids screwed on and the labels affixed. Soon my father would be home with the apricots.

"Do you have any questions?" she asked, as if I were one of her slow learners.

My parents slept in twin beds. I was adopted. It seemed unlikely that she'd ever subjected herself to an act that sounded so yucky and gross. "Did you and Daddy ever do it?"

"We did it once," she said.

I closed my eyes and tried to imagine what that might have involved.

Licking dirt off the kitchen floor would have been easier to understand. *Yes, I licked dirt off the kitchen floor. It was not good, but I did it because there was a black spot and that was the only way to clean it up.*

The "sex talk" is one every parent dreads. Much as we try to convey positive messages, our body language often transmits the subtext of our own anxiety. My mother must have wanted to sound objective and thought she was carrying off the conversation about sex with the same tone she'd used to explain canning and botulism —scientifically factual and devoid of emotion. In both cases, however, her facial expression—scrunched-up eyes, mouth twisted— told me she was "putting up." Never once did her tone imply that if the stuff in the jar didn't kill you—if you followed carefully prescribed rules of timing and cleanliness—the result would be fruit that tasted sweet and good.

Very shortly, a different version of the sex talk, illustrated by a black-and-white movie showing eggs floating down the fallopian tubes, made me realize that the information my mother had given me was correct, though horrifying. The teacher at Selby Lane

School separated the boys and girls for separate talks about the changes in our bodies, and there was a great buzz about it. Afterward, boys giggled and taunted us when we gathered in a kickball circle.

I didn't know what to make of the movie, not just the tadpole of sperm swimming up to mate with the ovum, but the warning that once a month, we girls would turn short-tempered. We had to fight against that and work extra hard to be cheerful. I couldn't imagine any of this would ever apply to me, but puberty would soon hit me hard.

IN EIGHTH GRADE, I became—as my mother would have said, though she had no idea this was happening—completely "boy crazy." I complained that the popular girls in school were all skinny and that I needed to lose ten pounds and make myself some new skirts. My mother bought me *The Teenage Diet Book*, and I put myself on an egg-and-grapefruit diet. For an after-school snack, I made diet root beer floats with a single scoop of ice milk. After a week of hunger headaches, I'd lost five pounds and plunged headlong into the mysteries of adolescent attraction, a roller coaster of lust and longing and fear of rejection that is driven by hormonal change.

That year we middle-school students read *The Diary of Anne Frank*. Thinking the ups and downs of my life might one day have some importance, or perhaps just wanting to talk to someone at a time when it was impossible to talk to my parents, I borrowed a small brown notebook. For the first time, I began recording my unsupervised thoughts. This was a mere two years before I became pregnant.

December 13, 1959, Sunday
Dear Diary,
I say that because I can't think of anything more appropriate. I went to Jonny's house today. He's a lot cuter and nicer than he used to be. I'm glad I have him for my best friend. Dave just called

me once today. Dave is my one and only thought lately, excluding schoolwork. He is so nice to me. When he kisses me, I flip, but even when he's just with me, I feel a companionship I have never felt before. I imagine it is something like I will feel when I get married.

My favorite song is "The Village of St. Bernadette" by Marty Robbins. It is just beautiful. My thoughts are so unorganized lately because all I can do is dream of David.

December 14, 1959

Dear Diary,

I'm so happy I got a 95 on my Geometry test. I want to get an A in Geom. So bad. I won't mention the final I got back in Geography, though. (I got a C.)

In school I do think about my work. As soon as the bell rings, however, my mind races to him dearest to my heart. It sounds kind of sickening when written down, but it really doesn't seem that way when I'm thinking about him. Older people criticize teenagers for getting crushes. I think that if the two kids who were in love matured together, that they would still be suited to each other for marriage.

Like Anne Frank, I had begun to think about "love." However, another change had entered my life, one that would profoundly alter how I saw myself. As boy crazy as I continued to be, I was also an ambitious grade-grubber.

The Redwood City School District had revamped its curriculum and decided to put its smartest students on a separate track. In eighth grade, students would begin a course of math study that did not even have a textbook, as the district had agreed to cooperate with Stanford on the so-called "new math," SMSG math.[1] Gone were times tables, long division, and rote learning.

The administration must have wanted to make sure that only the smartest kids were thrown into the "new math," so the school administered an IQ test. The cutoff line on the test was 135. I didn't make it. Suddenly, I was separated from the kids who had been in the highest reading group, who raised their hands when the teachers asked questions, and who sought out extra credit. In eighth grade, I found myself in a classroom with slackers and hoods. For my entire life, I had been praised for bringing in straight A's. Being smart went along with feeling special, with being the "chosen child." For an adoptee, being "chosen" also meant being worthy of a mother's love. My mother was a teacher. I wanted to live up to her expectations.

Knowing of my distress, my mother found out my test score.

"Your IQ is 126," she told me. "We've always known you were a hard worker."

A hard worker? I didn't want to be a hard worker. That was a demotion. I wanted to climb back to the top tier, rejoin my friends and fellow smart kids in challenging classes. I couldn't accept it, I wouldn't accept it, but there was nothing I could do.

But then something happened that took my mind off school. My father, in what was undoubtedly the high point of his life, won a new car in the St. Pius church raffle, the parish we had started attending after our move. The car was a red-and-white Pontiac station wagon with Naugahyde seats. Winning the car meant he could take his family on a road trip, and where better than Mexico, where he could vacation in style?

CHAPTER 11

VERA CRUZ

I still get excited at the thought of a holiday. Every year when my family rents a Christmas house, we bring along one-thousand-piece puzzles. After meals and present opening and during football games, we kneel around a coffee table, the youngest to the oldest joining in. Piecing together the puzzle's edges is where we start. Once we have the size and shape—rectangle, square, circle —we work our way toward the middle. In sorting out the pieces that define the "nature versus nurture" puzzle, I began with the edge pieces, trying to find the personality-shaping events of my childhood.

In my growing-up years, a defining moment was our 1958 trip to Mexico. My father was proud of being a member of Local 34 of the ILWU, the International Longshoremen's and Warehousemen's Union,[1] led by Australian socialist Harry Bridges, whom J. Edgar Hoover was trying to have deported. To improve conditions for longshoremen, Bridges wanted to organize a strike that would shut down West Coast ports, but the FBI was tapping Bridges' phone. Because my father spoke Spanish, he volunteered to go down to Mexico and speak with the union's leaders in person. With his newly won car and family in tow, he would be above suspicion.

My mother's Christmas letter, run off on her school's mimeo machine, recounted a heavily redacted version of the trip: "It is in Acapulco that the longshoremen have a beautiful building and are paying for it by renting out office space. They also maintain a hospital, not only for their workers but also one for children and women. Mr. Lluch, one of the national officers of that union, is a very likable man, and we had several nice visits with him and his cousin, who lived in San Francisco for forty years."

After Acapulco, we drove down to San Cristóbal de las Casas, forty miles from the Guatemalan border. While changing money in a bank, my father met a man who had won the Mexican lottery and invested in fifty-two coffee plantations. He invited us to stay on one, saying he'd notify his servants that we were coming. Here's what I wrote in the travel journal my father required me to keep.

Long yellow ribbons of sun had just cut through the morning fog of the *finca*, but the Indians had been up for two hours. Coffee pickers must work in the early morning while the air is still bearable. We tourists, too, were up early because we were to look at an Indian's hut before it got too hot.

An Indian mother waited outside with her children, two still naked. One girl was much shorter and skinnier than I was, but about my age. Like other Indians, she wore a clean, patched, white dress, but it was much too small. Her hair was a straight and shiny black, her skin a rich maple color, and her eyes were mahogany and smiled for her whole face. Strutting proudly outside the hut were her two chickens and her pig, which I tried to catch. The pig must have thought it was a new form of tag because he dodged and turned and ran between our legs. Finally, I put my hands on his sides and was picking him up when he gave a big lurch forward, slipped out of my hands, and ran for cover. Despite the language barrier, we laughed at that clever pig. When we walked back to the horses, we were to ride around the *finca*, the Indians were still laughing at the *Norte Americana*.

We stayed three days, a totally unscripted and culturally enriching life experience, and one I owe to my father. He was fearless in approaching strangers. He could talk to anyone and find common ground, and I like to think that the one aspect of my personality that comes from having lived with him is this desire to connect.

I remember nothing of the longshoremen's building or the hospital; what is interesting to an adult is not necessarily interesting to a kid. However, I vividly recall Mr. Lluch, a kind man with kind daughters. The girls were fifteen and sixteen. They wore flats with stockings and did not shave their legs. These girls had long, dark leg hairs matted under their nylons. With their lace blouses, lipstick, and gold jewelry, they looked like grown-ups.

Just as we were saying goodbye, the girls took off their gold earrings and put them in my hands as remembrance gifts.

"Take off your headband and give it to them," my father said.

"But there are two of them," I said.

"Go get your other one."

I had two headbands, one red velvet and the other braided-gold plastic. I wore headbands to keep my hair from falling in my face. Those headbands were irreplaceable. I had tried on a hundred in the dime store and chosen those two because they didn't cut into the soft tissue above my ears.

The twenty-four-carat gold earrings meant nothing to me.

"Go on," my father said. "Give them your headbands."

"I don't wear earrings," I said.

"You can have your ears pierced when you get home," my mother said.

Plunging a needle through my earlobe struck me as barbaric. I felt betrayed, not just by my father, but by my mother, who had always told me she'd never let me have pierced ears.

In the end, seeing the stricken look on the girls' faces, I took the velvet headband off my head and went to my train case for the other. Talking back, speaking up for myself, would have done no good. Even my mother didn't dare challenge my father. His unpredictability could turn violent, particularly if he began drinking.

❦

FROM MEXICO CITY, my father wanted to head east to Vera Cruz to do some deep-sea fishing. Problems started when we arrived at what he called a "Mexican tourist hotel." Because of my repeated questions about whether the place had a pool, he'd gone out of his way to find one that did. But the pool in Vera Cruz was saltwater.

I stood by the pool's ladder, too shocked to move. Acacia blossoms floated on the black water. The ladder into the deep end was all rusty, and there wasn't any shallow end. I had never seen a swimming pool that wasn't blue, and I was scared because the water looked thick and smelled like decaying leaves. It reminded me of *The Creature from the Black Lagoon*. In the eerie pink sunset, bubbles rose to the water's surface. The oily sheen looked like a spirograph.

With a pool net, my father pushed away the leaves and blossoms. "There," he said. "Jump in."

"The water looks yucky," I said.

"They take the water straight from the ocean," my father said. "It's cleaner than it looks."

"Rex," my mother said, "that water hasn't been changed in a year."

"No, Lorrie!" he said. "She wanted a place with a pool. She asked twice, which is against the rules. So, against my better judgment, I got her a pool." He turned, his jaw thrusting out. "Get in."

My mother looked at the sky. "Go on," she said. "It won't kill you."

I turned around and backed down the ladder. Inky water swallowed my legs.

My father put his big hand on my head and pushed. "All the way in."

Gulping tears, I felt my feet slip on the ladder's steps. Salt stung my eyes, and when I surfaced, my hair was full of yellow blossoms. I dog-paddled to the ladder and looked up. My father had disappeared.

After dinner, he headed to the *cantina*. There was a card game. When he returned for more money, he was slurring his words. My mother begged him to come to bed, but he would not. In the room next door, I heard them arguing, a body thumping against the wall. It was not the first time this had happened. At home he rarely drank this much, but on this trip, my father had steadily been working his way up from ordering a *cerveza* or five to ordering tequila and mescal. My mother had rope burns on her arm from where he'd "taught her a lesson."

After the argument, my father returned to the *cantina* and my mother came into my room and sat down on the edge of the bed. She beckoned me to the bed and pulled down the elastic front of her dress. From the top of her corset, where two giant cones pushed her flesh together, she withdrew a tiny cotton sack, cinched with pink embroidery thread and held in place by a small gold safety pin. She took out a roll of bills and told me to pack. We were going to the airport.

I had never flown on an airplane. Back in 1958, people drove or took the train. Her plan was to take a plane from Vera Cruz to Mexico City and fly back from there to San Francisco.

Next to the motel, on a broad *avenida*, traffic and taxis whizzed past. My mother stepped forward and waved her white handkerchief. A taxi stopped, and we got in. She had looked up the word for "airport" in her phrase book, and eventually, far beyond the city's lights, the taxi pulled into the airport's parking lot. In the darkness my eyes could barely make out the single-engine crop dusters along the edges of a narrow runway. The planes looked like toys.

My mother thought we should leave our luggage in the taxi until she'd bought our tickets. The driver said he had better wait, and he followed us inside.

The "airport" was a Quonset hut that smelled of diesel fuel, and in the back of it, four dimly lit work bays held disassembled engines. Propellers leaned against the walls. Toward the front was the snack bar's long counter and men sitting on wooden stools. When I looked their way, they shifted their hips and spread their knees. I moved closer to my mother. The taxi driver asked the bartender when the next flight left.

The man smiled, exposing a silver tooth, and turned to a calendar. He pointed at the day. *"Mañana."*

"Aren't there any flights tonight?" my mother said.

"Runway no have lights," the driver said. "If you want, buy ticket now, go tomorrow."

My mother looked up in her head for a moment, and then her eyes made a circle of the room. Like bookends, a Coke machine and a cigarette machine stood at either end of a grease-stained leather couch. "What time is the first flight?"

The driver asked the bartender, and the man said noon. If the plane didn't break down, the driver translated.

"All right." She started to take money from her purse. She looked at the couch. "We can sit over there."

"You wait?" the taxi driver asked incredulously. He looked at me.

Mother looked at me, too. "I guess you're right. It would be better to go back."

"Maybe we should stay here," I said, a rabbit of fear racing for a burrow. "It might be better too."

"Lady!" The taxi driver folded his arms. "I no can wait all night."

I grabbed my mother's arm. "Mom! We'll be fine here."

Mother shook her head. "Don't worry. We can come back in the morning if he's still bad."

I couldn't form a picture of tomorrow in my mind. The plan, speeding in one direction, toward safety, was now rewinding toward Father. I began to pray for one thing: that he hadn't discovered we'd ever left.

The driver loaded our suitcases in the trunk. "I sorry," he said. "I not know."

I slumped down on my seat. Fifteen minutes later, the driver pulled into the hotel's circle drive and a pink slash of neon cut across the backseat. It was the light of the *cantina*. Afraid my father would see me, I ducked down onto the floor and buried my head, the nuclear attack drill.

"Get up from there," Mother said. "Act like a big girl."

We carried our suitcases down the open corridor to my room, and my mother came into my room and began to unpack.

Someone knocked. Fearing it was my father, I pulled the curtain aside.

Hands behind his back, the manager stood in the yellow bug light. I unlocked the door. The man wanted to close the *cantina*, but my father was arguing that he wanted it to stay open.

"It'll be okay," I said. "Sometimes I can calm him down." The room threw a triangle of light onto the veranda. Coming toward us was Father, his white hair flying back, shirttail out, belt unbuckled.

"Hey, honey," Father called from the darkness, "give your old man a hand with his key."

By his tone, I knew he meant me. His words didn't slur, so I couldn't tell how far gone he was. I prayed this was a beer drunk. Mescal made him mean. Any delay, and he would start acting up. Pushing past the manager, I took the key, and with my father propped on one stiff arm against the wall, his hot, sour breath in my face, I used my nail to find the tiny crescent where the key went in. Then I stepped into the room and let my father pass.

He tossed coins on his bed and went into the bathroom. The faucets squeaked. His belt buckle dropped on the floor. "Turn the light on," he called. "I don't want to bark my shins."

I turned on the light.

"Try to get him to bed," Mother whispered from the doorway. She placed our room key in my hand. "Don't stay long. I don't think he'll harm you but be cautious."

I put the key in my pocket. I closed the door so Father wouldn't go back to the *cantina*. Then, while he was in the bathroom, taking a shower, I turned on the bedside lamp and scooped up the coins. He could go straight to bed.

When the water turned off, I heard a towel sandpaper bare skin. He came out with a towel tucked around his waist, a cigarette dragging down the corner of his mouth. His legs straddled the corner of the bed, and where the towel spread, I could see that thing in the middle like a pink, rolled-up sock. "Pe-nis." The word made me cringe as I thought of the day my mother had told me the facts of life. The word "penis" sounded foreign and ugly, but the way he was sitting, I could not help looking at his.

"You're not scared to be in here with your old man, are you?"

"I'm not scared."

My father had taught me how to approach a mean dog. Stay calm inside, give the dog time to growl or challenge, but never take a step back.

He stubbed out his cigarette in an ashtray. "You remember last year when I took you to the FBI headquarters?"

"Yes, sir," I said.

"Can you name the top ten violent crimes?"

He liked to play games that showed his superior knowledge. The most-wanted posters in the FBI lobby came to mind.

"Murder. Arson. Armed robbery. Assault and battery. Felony theft. Kidnapping. Blackmail. Um, killing a police officer. No. That's murder. Uh, interstate flight. Narcotics."

"You've got nine," he said, holding up nine fingers. "What's the tenth?"

"I don't remember."

"Here's a clue." He stuck up his middle finger, the wave he made to women drivers when they braked on curves.

I got up from my chair. "Are we going deep-sea fishing tomorrow?"

"Give up?" he said.

I was tired of this game.

"Need another clue?" he said.

"No." I put my hands in my pockets. My fingers curled around the key.

"Come over and give your old dad a night-night kiss."

Breathing fast, I looked at the door. He half-stood, grabbed my shoulders, and pulled my lips toward his. His towel fell on the floor.

I socked his stomach. "Daddy! No!"

He grunted and fell back on the bed. I leapt for the door.

Father pulled up the sheet, and his sunburned arm reached for the bedside lamp. "Fair enough. Next time, don't ask for a place with a pool."

Back in my room, the lights were out. The moon, coming through the window, cut checkerboard squares on the floor. My mother had left a nightgown on my pillow. I went into the bathroom and scrubbed my face.

Then I went to bed. The cool sheets made me shiver.

Mother rolled over. "Did he go to sleep?"

"Yes," I said.

"What did you say to him?"

"He was talking about last year's vacation."

"He always gets the last word, doesn't he?" She reached across the divide between our beds.

I turned my back and curled up. My shoulders shook and my knees jerked. To control myself, I hugged my pillow.

"Do you have a fever?" my mother asked.

"No," I said.

"He didn't touch you, did he?"

"He didn't lay a hand on me."

And I would make sure he never did.

The next morning, my mother insisted we go home. Ten days in a car with a man who frightened me, but who I had to pretend did not. I sensed that I had stepped into a battle my parents were fighting, a battle of silences and frowns and raised voices. Nobody had bothered to tell me the rules.

CHAPTER 12

LIFE AMONG ALIENS

We drove across the bridge between Ciudad Juárez and El Paso, where my father had grown up, and headed west across Texas, New Mexico, Arizona, California's Central Valley, and finally chugged up rocky Pacheco Pass and then dropped down into the Bay Area. Lying in the back seat, I felt my body alternately trembling and going numb. It was as if I were levitating above myself, a disembodied spirit hovering the way souls are said to hover above the bodies of the recently departed. I wrote in my diary that I felt as if I had "landed among aliens," and my best friend from those years remembers me wondering aloud why the adoption agency had placed me "with these people." One might naturally suppose that disengaging from my adoptive parents might have been an adaptive response. One might even call it a survival response. However, this was not the first time I had felt misplaced or displaced.

The feeling of "mis-placement" or "dis-placement" is widely experienced by adoptees. Nancy Verrier, author of *The Primal Wound*, an adoptive mother who spent a decade trying to help her adopted daughter weather the storm of adolescence, has written, "Many [adoptees] do not feel as if they were born, but as if they came from outer space or a file drawer."[1] And if I felt detached from myself, I also felt detached from my mother. I hovered above her, watched her, waiting to see how she would react—if she would react—to what had happened in Mexico.

My mother was much closer to the events than I am today, and yet in her Christmas letter, written in December 1958, she was hiding her fear:

> We were in Veracruz and were there for one night. The swim in the Gulf of Mexico was lovely. The sun played a trick and did not set over the water but slipped down behind the hills. The sun set on the wrong side of the world for us that night.

How true that was, and how poetically expressed.

But what was a woman who found herself in an abusive relationship to do? Marriage and advice books suggested ways for women to change their behavior in order to induce their husbands to stop cheating, drinking, or being abusive. One of the 1950s marriage-counseling gurus, a shyster named Clifford R. Adams, offered this advice:[2]

> We can assure wives whose husbands are prone to violence that following a program of avoiding arguments, indulging their husbands' whims, helping them relax, and sharing their burdens would "foster harmony" in the home and make them even "happy wives."

∼

ON LABOR DAY, school began. My mother took on a combined fourth-fifth classroom of "slow learners" at Hawes Park Elementary, and I started my freshman year at Woodside High School. When my father was not working up on the docks, he sat in the living room, watching *The Three Stooges* and *Popeye the Sailor* and downing beer after beer.

One of the boys in the school band—I played clarinet—caught sight of my legs. When the band director went down the roster of names, asking if I was "Mary-lee" or "Merrily," this boy said, "She's neither. She's *Hairy* Lee."

Mortified, I asked my best friend what to do. "Shave your legs," she said.

"But my mother won't let me," I said.

"How's she going to stop you?"

It had never occurred to me to disobey my parents, but I couldn't bear the teasing. In the bathroom, with its pink-and-maroon tile and matching maroon towels, I opened the medicine cabinet and found my father's shaving things: a razor and a box of double-headed Gillette blades. Sitting on the toilet, quaking with fear, I scraped my legs until my shins bled.

The next day, the boy in band didn't tease me. Neither my mother nor my grandmother noticed what I'd done. Pleased with this step toward independence, I decided that as long as I was going to be a rebel, I would stop wearing white anklets with my flats. On the way home from school, I detoured into a drugstore at Woodside Plaza and bought myself some "peds," the skin-colored liners for dress shoes. I unwrapped them and wore them the rest of the way home.

The ironing board was set up next to the front door. When I opened it, Grandma came out from her back room. She went to the refrigerator and brought out a pillowcase of damp clothes. She turned on the iron and reminded me that it was my job to iron the napkins and tablecloths. Then she licked her finger and touched it to the iron. I heard a hiss.

The television blared. My father was sitting on the living room sectional. He was smoking and, as usual, had a beer in his hand. He saw me and did a double take.

"Where are your socks?" he asked.

"I didn't wear them," I said, dropping my book bag on the dining room table.

"You look like a Mexican whore," he said.

I didn't know that word. Maybe it had something to do with the Mexican blouse and three-tiered *fiesta* skirt I'd worn that day. I felt okay with how I looked. Pretty, in fact.

My grandmother picked up the iron and yanked the plug from the wall. She walked toward him. "Apologize," she said, holding the iron out in front and continuing to advance.

"Watch out, old lady," my father said.

My heart thrummed in my throat. "Grandma, what are you doing?"

"Apologize," Grandma said, continuing to advance.

My father stood up. I expected him to knock the iron out of her hand and then grab her arm and twist it up behind her back, the way he did with my mom and me. Instead, grumbling that he was out of beer, he brushed past her, nearly knocking her off her feet.

"Whore," he called to me. "Slut." He slammed the door behind him.

Grandma hurried to the picture window. She pulled back the drape and watched him back out the driveway. If he kept drinking, no telling what he would do. Trembling, I took the iron from her hand.

A black dial phone sat on an end table. Grandma found the phone book, and her finger sped down the page. A moment later, she had a locksmith on the line. By the time my mother returned from school, five locks had been changed and the garage had a new padlock.

We had returned from Mexico the third week of August. On September 22, 1958, four days before my thirteenth birthday, the same lawyer who had dealt with my grandfather's wrongful death case filed the paperwork for a legal separation. My guess is that my mother decided to take this step after that night in Vera Cruz. She must have told my grandmother what had happened. Maybe they, in consultation with the lawyer, decided that changing the locks would be the only way to keep my father out of the house.

To imagine what a bold step this was back in 1958, consider that California did not have a provision for no-fault divorce. Mental cruelty, abandonment, and infidelity were the only grounds by which a spouse could sever the bonds of marriage. In 1958, divorce was rare and shameful: The divorce rate per one thousand married females fifteen years of age and over was 8.9 percent.[3] The language of that era referred to "broken homes," and government policies encouraged "family preservation" at all costs. If a woman moved out, she could be accused of abandonment and lose custody of her children. However, in order for the period of legal separation to begin, one or the other spouse had to leave.

After my father's departure and the changing of the locks, the process server tracked him down. The period of official separation began. But what neither my mother nor my grandmother could have imagined was the way he would seek revenge.

CHAPTER 13

BLOOD MONEY

*W*hen my father came home late that night and tried to let himself in, his key didn't work. He bellowed and lunged against the door. My mother called the sheriff. After that, she boxed up his clothes and put them at the end of the driveway. When the boxes disappeared, we knew he had found someplace else to live.

Although my mother might well have considered divorce long before our trip to Mexico, she would have hesitated because my father was the main breadwinner. Financially, divorce would have looked like a disaster. Women worked as nurses, salesclerks, waitresses, telephone operators, and teachers. My mother would have been earning about $33,450 in 1959 dollars.[1] My father earned twice that.[2]

My mother must have done the numbers and seen that, on her own, she could not cover the monthly mortgage payments, let alone our living expenses. To raise her income, she began tutoring after school. She signed up to teach summer school. She and my grandmother pooled their resources and managed to keep the house, but I remember that first Christmas as a lean one. My grandmother gave me a book I wanted badly: *Gods, Graves, and*

Scholars, by C. W. Cerum. My mom gave me two sweaters from a discount store.

My mother's separation decree asked for $1 of alimony for her and $150 per month for me. My father refused to pay. My mother's lawyer filed a motion for nonpayment, and my father called a reporter and had himself photographed with his fingers around the bars of a cell in county jail. The photo wound up on the front page of the *Redwood City Tribune*. My father claimed the $1 alimony was "blood money."

My mother was so shamed by the publicity that she took a day off work and kept me home from school. She was afraid kids would tease me. Instead, when I went back, even the boy in band said how sorry he was that this was happening in my family. Teachers at my mother's school rallied round, especially her principal, William Morrisey, a gruff, red-haired man with a soft heart.

My mother's attorney advised her to hold firm. There could come a day when she'd need my father's financial support. Without that dollar as a placeholder, the lawyer couldn't go back to the court for more.

To get out of jail, my father eventually wrote a check for the alimony and one month's child support. That was the last check my mother ever received. When she took him to court again, the process server couldn't find him. For weeks, he hadn't shown up on the docks. Fortunately, he kept paying his union dues. Otherwise, our health care and dental insurance would have lapsed.

Periodically, my father came around and banged on the picture window. I was afraid he'd break it and leap through the broken glass. If the phone rang once, it was one of my friends. If it rang for an hour straight, it was him. And if it rang in the middle of the night, which it frequently did, we knew he was drunk and trying to harass us.

Today, there are support groups for women in situations of domestic abuse. The National Domestic Violence Hotline lists several indicators that can help a woman assess her risk of abuse.[3] And what we also know is that even when a woman extricates herself from an abusive relationship, the perpetrator's pleas to be let back into her life—to be forgiven for his offenses—can cause a woman to drop her guard. That is even more likely when the husband is the primary breadwinner. Thankfully, my mother held firm, but the stress of doing so took a great toll on her physical and mental health.

CHAPTER 14

FOG

My mother flicked on the bedroom light. "Hurry and change into your clothes."

I checked the clock. "It's two a.m." I was fifteen years old, a sophomore in high school. "I didn't go to bed until eleven."

"Grandma's sick. I called an ambulance. You need to go to the front door and let them in."

And then she was gone. I hopped out of bed and slipped into a pleated skirt and sweater. Heart pounding, I passed the sewing room. Next to the sewing cabinet, where I had left a half-finished cotton skirt, stood my mother's dress form, and beyond that, the door to Grandma's room. Open. Lights on. Moans. I went to the front door.

The ambulance pulled up, sirens blaring. Two men carrying a stretcher hurried across the living room. They returned with Grandma, swaddled in a flannel blanket. Face gaunt, her normally stoic expression collapsed by pain, she pulled off her hair net and put it in my hand. "Don't worry. I'll be fine," she said.

I hoped that was true.

"Grab a coat," my mother said.

Moments later, we were driving up Bayshore, the new freeway

that had replaced El Camino Real as the fastest route to the city. Kaiser had only a clinic in Redwood City. Grandma's illness was serious, and she needed to go a hospital. Streetlights turned the fog amber, but mere fog did not make my mother take her foot off the gas. In silhouette, this fifty-six-year-old schoolteacher, with her thick glasses and protruding eyes, drove as if pushing a pedal car with her reserves of strength. The corner of her mouth began to twitch, the first sign of what would soon become a much bigger problem.

I remember her saying, "It's a good thing Dr. Konstansz happened to be on call."

"Why's that?" I said.

"He'll drive up to the city and meet the ambulance."

Dr. Konstansz was my grandmother's doctor. My mother's, too. I still went to a pediatrician.

By the time we had found a parking spot on hilly Geary Street and walked downhill to the emergency room, my grandmother lay on a gurney. Her lips, drawn together by purse strings of determination, quivered. My mother took Grandma's glasses, folded them, and put them in her purse. She kissed her mother's forehead. Then she and I sat in the dimly lit, nearly deserted waiting room.

Dawn came, and we went to the cafeteria for breakfast. My mother buttered her toast methodically. She was not one to share her thoughts and certainly not her feelings, but her posture—the downward-sloping shoulders, the quivering lower lip, the working of the butter knife back and forth across the toast, her refusal to meet my eyes—told me that this was but one more trial in a lifetime of them. After breakfast, we resumed our vigil.

My mother, I thought, should have more faith that my grandmother would pull through. Every day, if I hadn't gone to a friend's house, my grandmother and I had been working on sewing projects, she at an old Singer treadle and I at my mother's Viking. Recently, she had started a hooked rug made from cut-up strips of my grandfather's suits. Born in 1880, she had lived through two world wars and the Great Depression and had survived my grandfather's untimely death. This—whatever had caused her to summon an ambulance—would not kill her. Nothing could.

Dr. Konstansz, an internist with a pencil mustache and kind brown eyes, came toward us. Dressed in green scrubs, he had assisted the surgeon. Standing over us, he said, "I knew right away it was serious."

"Why did you think that?" my mother said.

"Your father was a doctor," he said. "A doctor's wife would never call in the middle of the night unless she was in extreme danger."

My grandmother had a blockage in her intestines. Gangrene had set in. They had removed half of her lower bowel, a six-hour operation.

My mother took a packet of Kleenex from her purse and blew her nose. They had taken my grandmother to the recovery room. My mother said she wanted to wait until Grandma woke up.

It was New Year's Eve. I had chores to do. Grandma would be fine.

"Maybe I could take a Greyhound to Redwood City," I said.

"How would you get home?"

"I could call that guy from youth group."

"All right," she said, "but don't let him in the house." She dug out change.

I found a pay phone and called information for his number. The guy—John—said sure, he'd pick me up. My mother put me in a cab to the bus station and gave me money for a ticket.

On the bus ride down the peninsula, I thought I'd made a giant mistake. I had been too forward. Boys didn't like it when girls chased them, and I wasn't even sure I'd recognize him.

I stepped down from the bus, and there he stood—John MacDonald—in the shade of the station's awning. Arms crossed, he balanced on one leg, the other bent with his foot against the wall. He pushed off and came toward me with a loping, athletic walk, a guy comfortable in his own skin. The uncertainty and strain of the night washed through me. Here was someone who wanted nothing from me, whom I didn't have to prop up. On his chin he had a scrap of toilet paper glued by dried blood. A shaving cut.

"You made it," he said.

I let him take my arm. "I did."

As he jingled his keys and walked toward a white Ford Fairlane, I had the unbalanced feeling of a domino about to tip.

∽

In the MacDonalds' sunny kitchen, his mother poured me Cheerios and milk. A barbecue table, covered with Formica and with padded benches for seats, filled a long breakfast alcove in the kitchen. John sat across from me. Henrietta, a former football queen at San Jose State, smiled and asked questions about my grandmother. After that, I lay down on the living room couch and tried to take a nap. John's three little brothers ran down the hall and peeked in at the girl their brother had brought home. John, I'd learned, was the oldest of eight. This was all new to me: a house with other children; a house with a stay-at-home mom; and, most of all, a house with children's laughter.

Late in the day, John drove me over to my house and parked in front of the picket fence. At his house, his mother had been in the kitchen. Her questions had made it easier to think it was okay to impose on this guy I barely knew. Now, the old awkwardness came back, along with the feeling that I should run a comb through my hair.

"Are you going to be all right?" he said.

"I'll be fine." And, of course, I would be fine. I had always been fine. Everyone else in my family might be crazy or violent or depressed, but I would always have to be fine. Fine, fine, and more fine.

I got out of the car and gave him a little wave. "Please tell your mom thank you."

When I pushed open the gate, Grandma's face did not peek out from behind the drapes. What if my father came around? Hurriedly, I looked down the street. John's car had disappeared.

I walked down the driveway to the garage, unlocked the padlock, and raised the door. Except for my bicycle, the lawn mower, and the loft at the far end, the garage was empty. I found the kitty litter and poured it on the oil pan in the carport. My mom's car was eight years old, a '52 Chevy that leaked oil. Now, her car sat parked with its wheels cramped against the curb on Geary Street, just outside the hospital, and I had an odd feeling in my stomach, the way Huck Finn might have felt when his raft began moving down the Mississippi—unmoored, swept along by a rapidly moving current, the destination unclear.

My mother had been nagging me to finish nailing the staves back on the picket fence. Every October she knocked off the staves, loaded them in a wheelbarrow, and took them around back to the patio. It was my job to whitewash them. The staves needed to be put back before the roses started their spring bloom. I found a hammer in the toolbox.

I was just finishing the job when a cloud bank crept down the street. The fog was as thick as the fog at Pescadero Beach, as thick as the fog that blanketed Skyline Boulevard, the two-lane, north–south route that ran along the ridge line of the coast mountains. I went out to the street and stood looking up at the bower of trees. I couldn't see where the branches met. A line from a Carl Sandburg poem ran through my head: *The fog comes in on little cats' feet*. Engulfed by this slowly moving cloud, unable to see the sky but feeling the damp tingle of moisture, I held my breath. For a minute or two, light from the setting sun infused the fog and turned it the color of cotton candy. My cheeks felt damp. I was swimming, buoyant, but able to breathe. I spread my arms. Then the light dimmed, and the fog turned gray, like the scene in *The Wizard of Oz* when Dorothy returns to Kansas.

The day of the pink fog: This was one of the strangest moments of my life, an event as rare as snow in the desert, and it left me both joyous and shaken. Even if I told my mother what had happened, she wouldn't have believed me. Had what I'd seen—stood right in the middle of, spinning round like a dervish—been real or imagined? Maybe, as she had the three little girls at Lourdes, the Virgin Mary was sending me a message. Grandma was up in the hospital. This miracle was a sign that she would come home.

I returned the hammer to the garage, took the key from the dog-tag chain around my neck, and unlocked the front door. To keep from getting zapped, I kicked off my loafers. My mother wanted to rip out the wool carpet with its garish, giant roses, but she had to wait and see if my dad would finally pay child support.

The carpet extended into the hall. To the left stood the master bedroom, with its twin beds. Opposite the master sat the sewing room, the bureau drawer that my mother must have been looking in still open. The bureau held birth, marriage, and death certificates, as well as ration books and air-raid-marshal badges left over from the war. The lower drawers of the cabinet held photo albums from my grandfather's life in Colorado. Before his death, Grandpa had been a great album maker. My "job," when I was three and four, had been to sit on his lap and lick the black corners that held his snapshots.

In Grandma's apartment, a rocking chair sat near the radio. My grandfather had made the rocker so that her feet could touch the floor. I sat down. Small as a kindergarten chair.

In her raffia basket I found the wooden rug hook. I picked up the two-foot-diameter circle she had started. The rug felt stiff and heavy in my lap. I turned on the radio. Back when I was a child and measles and mumps meant a week of boredom, she had snapped down my bedroom's window shades and gone back to her room, the squat black heels of her lace-up, old-lady shoes clomping as she lugged the radio to my bedside table.

My grandmother had gone to the hospital on December 30. Two days later, on January 1, 1961, she passed away. After the funeral, I went back to her apartment and collected the rag balls. They were the size of volleyballs. I pushed them under my bed. Then I rolled up the rug and put it in my closet. Summer would give me time to finish it.

I could not have guessed that by summer, I would be on my way to Phoenix and to a home for unwed mothers, or that this rug would be my one anchor to my so-called "normal" life.

PART III

ROMEO AND JULIET

CHAPTER 15

PUBLIC-SCHOOL GIRL

*J*ohn was the only boy I knew who had a car. Even though he had picked me up and taken me back to his house, I wasn't sure he liked me. Yes, he'd danced with me a time or two at youth group, but mostly we'd talked, and anyway, with guys you could never tell.

A charismatic priest had come to St. Pius. Father Peter Gomez Armstrong, balding, round-faced, and irrepressibly cheerful, had started a youth group. Every Saturday night, the Teen Club held a chaperoned dance in the parish hall. Girls from Notre Dame, Mercy, and Sacred Heart grouped together, and boys from Serra, St. Francis, and Bellarmine—the Jesuit school down in San Jose— stood opposite, a no-man's-land between. Like so many schools of fish, forming and reforming along opposite sides of the dance floor, each school had its own clique, the girls all giggling behind their hands, the boys in a huddle, talking sports or whatever boys talked about when girls weren't present.

Shortly before my grandmother went to the hospital, I happened to be standing on the boys' side and found myself on the periphery of a group of five. The two tallest dressed alike: beige jeans and oxford-cloth shirts. Narrow-waisted and broad-shouldered, they stood with the tentative confidence of boys who had only recently heard their voices ricochet between upper and lower registers. One of the tall ones had a blond crew cut and eyebrows as white as my mother's. The other boy had dark hair and blue-gray eyes.

"Are you twins?" I asked.

"Twins!" The dark-haired guy doubled over laughing. "Why would you think we're related?"

"Because you're tall."

They looked at each other and shook their heads.

"What high school do you go to?" the dark-haired one asked.

"Woodside," I said.

"Are all public-school girls that dumb?"

Heat climbed my cheeks. "Are all parochial-school boys that rude?"

"Hey, no harm, no foul," he said, holding up his hands.

Stupid boys. I had looked briefly at their muscled arms and long legs, but then I got distracted by their penny loafers. At Woodside, only girls wore penny loafers. Maybe this was a parochial-school dress code: penny loafers as opposed to saddle shoes, which was what the guys at Woodside wore to dances.

"Want to dance?" the dark-haired one asked.

"What's your name?"

"John MacDonald."

I hadn't seen him out on the dance floor.

I took a step back. "I'm just a dumb public-school girl. Why would you even be interested?"

"Who says I am?"

He put his hand on my waist and pushed me away from his buddies. I put my right hand in his. Stiff as a mannequin, he shuffled forward. Could he not tell that a simple fox trot, moving his feet in a square, would have kept him from stepping on my toes?

"Didn't you ever have dance lessons in PE?" I asked.

"No," he said. "My sisters tried to teach me, but they gave up."

"It's simple," I said. "Just keep to the beat."

"I can keep to the beat."

"In your dreams."

I loved to dance, and every day when I came back from school, I turned on Dick Clark's *American Bandstand* and learned the new moves. The Mashed Potato. The Frug. The Swim. The Twist. The Watusi.

Halfway through the song, I settled for pushing John's feet sideways with my feet. It was like trying to push bricks out of the way. And as we danced, sort of, I grew more and more annoyed at his robotic moves and at his stupid comment about public-school girls. My mother taught in public school. My father believed that the foundation of our democracy lay in the education of its citizens. I loved my school.

"So, how many public-school girls do you know?" I asked.

John thought a minute. "None, I guess."

"Where do your sisters go?"

"Two go to Sacred Heart. The other's still at Mount Carmel."

"Then I can only conclude you're prejudiced."

"I was only teasing," he said.

"What even made you say that?"

He pulled in his chin and looked down at me. "I'm sorry I hurt your feelings."

"You didn't hurt my feelings. You made me mad."

"Hey, hey! Come on." He stopped dancing.

A mirrored, spinning ball flashed colored lights around the room, and the parent-DJ changed the record to Elvis Presley's "Blue Suede Shoes."

Rather than retreat to his gang of four, John took my elbow and steered me toward the double doors. "Let's go outside and talk."

"Don't you want to dance?"

"I don't know how to fast-dance."

"Or slow-dance."

"Now who's being mean?"

"I'm sorry. This is pointless. You're not going to like me anyway."

"You don't know that."

I felt like saying, *I do know that. I can read the handwriting on the wall*. Why would John like me? My early "love interests," as my mother called them, had wasted no time in asking me to go steady. Then, in baffling reversals of affection, these same guys had asked for their rings back and sent me sobbing to the school bathroom.

"How old are you?" I asked.

"Sixteen."

"What year are you?"

"I'm a junior."

At Woodside, guys went out only with girls in their same grade. "I'm only a sophomore."

"That doesn't matter," he said.

On either side of the doors, chaperones sat on folding chairs. John found two spares and set them up in a corner.

While the music blasted, we shouted. John, determined to justify his stupid comment about public-school girls, said that the public-school curve was a joke. At Bellarmine, an A was 93 and above; a B, 85 and up, whereas at the public high schools, like Sequoia and Woodside, a grade of 90 and up earned an A. To drive home the point, he said that at Bellarmine a grade of 80 would have been a straight C, not a B-minus. To top it off, public schools didn't even offer Greek.

A champion debater, I launched into my defense of public education. Woodside had teachers with stellar credentials: a Jamaican, Oxford-educated PhD who taught Latin and French; my Physiology teacher, Mr. Parsons, who had dropped out of Stanford's med school in his third year; and my Spanish teacher, Moises Macias, a Moroccan Jew with a pure Castilian accent.

"You prove my point," John said. "Spanish is easy. It doesn't even have any declensions."

"Yeah? Well, Greek and Latin are dead languages. Nobody speaks them."

"I guess Spanish is good if you want to talk to fruit pickers. You could study all you want, but you'll never be as proficient as a native speaker."

"My Spanish must not be too bad, because I tied for twelfth in the statewide Spanish proficiency exam. Anyhow, I didn't come here to have a debate."

Back on the dance floor, arms pumped up and down.

Hoping for a reprieve, I said, "Do you know the Watusi?"

He rolled his eyes. "No."

Boys were supposed to take the initiative; at least, that's what *Seventeen* and *American Girl* advised. I was stuck. Mock-plugging my ears, I said, "It's hard to carry on a conversation."

"We could go outside," he said.

"Then we can't get back in," I said.

"We could sit in my car and talk."

"My mom wouldn't like that. She has a thing about boys and cars."

"All right, then," he said. "I guess we can try to block out the noise."

He stood and turned his chair. We sat knee to knee, our foreheads almost touching. I smelled the cinnamon of Dentyne on his breath.

John asked what clubs I was in, if I was in student government, and if I went out for any sports. Although I was good at field hockey and archery, it had never occurred to me to go out for a sport. Girls generally didn't, but, even so, I felt put on the spot, as if this were another instance of my school's failing to meet an artificial standard I hadn't known existed.

This made me more determined to convince him that a public education was every bit as rigorous as his. The music grew louder— the DJ was playing "At the Hop"—and meanwhile he and I were having this quasi-adult conversation, with me shouting about Junior Statesmen and *Robert's Rules of Order* and the Model United Nations.

"The Model UN's a communist-front organization," he said. "You ought to watch out."

"For what?"

"For communists. There's this guy, Archie Brown. He's head of the Communist Party in California."

"So?"

"They infiltrate all these liberal groups."

This guy was either naive or annoying. I could fold my chair and walk away, but if I left, I'd have to go stand on the girls' side all by myself.

What I believed was that every citizen bore responsibility for making the world a better place. I was fifteen, a seedling still buried in the soil, but with a little water and the right amount of sunlight, I'd pop through the surface of my childhood and stretch toward the sun of an autonomous life, one where I could participate in the political process. Vote. Write letters to the editor. Maybe even run for office. John didn't know a thing about me—not a thing—yet he felt entitled to put me down. I was a serious person, not a humorless person like my mother, but serious in the way that it was good to be serious because it meant you were applying yourself and trying to figure out who you wanted to be when you grew up. I pasted on a fake smile. I knew what I knew, even if he didn't, and if I had to prove myself, I would.

John sat back and folded his arms. He looked over my shoulder. Was he wanting to go back to his friends? I turned. A tall redheaded girl was staring at him. Or at us. When I stared right back, she frowned and then gathered her friends in a scrum. I couldn't stand cliquish girls.

"Do you know that redheaded girl?" I said.

Two chaperones held opposite ends of a bamboo pole. The DJ put on a record for the Limbo. The group surrounding the redhead broke apart.

"The girl at the end of the Limbo line," I said.

"Oh, her," he said. "Yeah, I know her sort of."

"Who is she?"

"Ginger Dawkins," he said. "She goes to Mercy."

"Why does she keep looking over here?"

John shrugged. "I heard she has a crush on me. But listen. About the Model UN. It's dangerous. They try to brainwash you."

"Who tries to brainwash me?"

"Not you specifically. Communists prey on idealistic youth."

I should have just excused myself and joined the line of people snaking around the edge of the room. Doing the Limbo didn't require a partner. Instead, here I sat, watching John scowl and twist his athletic ring. His knuckles were large—my mother would have said from cracking them—and patches of dark, wiry hair covered the backs of his hands. The hair reminded me of the Lluch girls with their hairy legs and of my father's friend in Mexico, Señor Lluch.

"Where did you come up with this bizarre theory about communists?" I asked.

"They would do anything to impose a godless society on us," John said. "They're trying to destroy the American way of life."

"You sound like a John Bircher."

"I am," he said.

I was tempted to shake him up and tell him about the time in sixth grade when the FBI visited my house, trying to dig up dirt on my father's union. At one time in the not-so-distant past, Joseph McCarthy and the House Un-American Activities Committee had found communists under every bed. Of course, it was a free country and John was entitled to his opinion, but he was ignorant and misguided, and I had just wasted an hour sitting in a corner, talking to a guy who obviously had no interest in asking me out.

However, a week later, when Grandma woke us up and the ambulance came to take her to San Francisco, I remembered John's having mentioned that he had a car.

CHAPTER 16

TILLIE'S PARTY

*W*hy did I "fall in love" with John when our core values clashed? When he was convinced Goldwater would save us from perdition and I went door-to-door, passing out Kennedy flyers? Pheromones, I suppose—the neurotransmitters of attraction. When I was with John, sitting knee to knee, arguing, even, I felt a frisson of pleasure, a smile rippling down my spine to my fingertips, which came alive when he held my hand. At Mass, as he sat next to me, kneeling when I knelt, standing when I stood, reciting the Latin responses during the Sacrament of Holy Communion, I felt spiritually comforted.

With Catholicism in common, we tabled the debates and went on constituting our own little world. Teen Club dances on Saturday night. The occasional picnic at Blackberry Farm. Sunday Mass. Sunday brunch after Mass, the large MacDonald clan crowding in at the kitchen table where his mother had first offered me a bowl of Cheerios.

Even at that first youth-group dance, I had seen that he was smart, maybe slightly smarter than I was, especially in math and science. Although quiet, he was a natural leader, captain of the football team, and acing all his classes. In ancient Greek, he was reading and translating Aeschylus's play *Agamemnon* from the Oresteian Trilogy, and over the phone, he'd give me updates about what was happening.

"So, Agamemnon comes home from the Trojan War, expecting to be given a hero's welcome, and instead, his wife, Clytemnestra, is pissed off."

"Why is she pissed off?" I said.

"He sacrificed his daughter, Iphigenia."

"For what reason?"

"So that the gods would give him wind."

"And why did he need wind?"

"He had a fleet. Wind was the only way he could return to Troy."

In sophomore English, the teacher wanted us to give a ten-minute talk about a poet. The one he assigned me was E. E. Cummings. I read John the first few lines over the phone:

> *in Just-*
> *spring when the world is mud-*
> *luscious the little*
> *lame balloonman*
> *whistles far and wee*

"What's this even supposed to mean?" I asked.

"Honestly?" he said. "I can't make heads or tails of it."

"Well, I have to give a talk about it, and I have no idea where to even begin."

"Go to your school library and see if they have anything."

"I did, but I can't really copy from *Compton's Encyclopedia*."

"I'll see if we have anything at Bellarmine."

"I wish he'd assigned me Walt Whitman. At least *Leaves of Grass* sort of makes sense."

I wasn't sure why John kept calling, but with Grandma gone and my mom going to bed right after dinner, it felt good to hear his interested, sympathetic voice. Sometimes we'd get tired of talking about classes and quizzes but still not be ready to break off the conversation. For diversion, he'd strike a match and tell me he was lighting a fart. Boys could be so stupid.

"You'd better not do that in my presence," I said.

"Then entertain me," he said.

If my mom hadn't gone to sleep, I'd pick up my ukulele and practice chord progressions or toot out an excerpt from Von Weber's Clarinet Concerto #1, the one piece of clarinet music that sounded good without accompaniment. If John called me on the days that he had band practice, he'd honk out a tune on his baritone sax.

When we talked, I pictured him upstairs, a dormer bedroom he shared with his brother. On his desk, he had a portable stereo and a stack of albums. He'd just bought Bob Newhart's latest, *The Button-Down Mind Strikes Back*, and held the phone next to the stereo so I could listen. When I was a little girl, my grandfather had made me a toy telephone with two tin cans connected by a string. The two foster boys who lived next door had one end, and I had the other, and when we pulled the string tight, we could talk to each other after our parents thought we'd gone to bed.

The phone cord didn't reach all the way into my bedroom, and my mother started to object that I was tying up the line. I didn't see why it mattered. I had my homework done. It didn't cost us to receive a call. I sat on the overstuffed sectional in the living room, my hand cupped over the receiver, wishing John and I were together. I liked listening to his voice—it had a deep, rich timbre—and I liked to make him laugh. He laughed easily and well, and ever since his "public-school girl" comment, I had not heard him make a joke at another person's expense.

He called me three or four times a week, and I still wasn't sure why. Sure, we danced together at Teen Club, but he'd never even asked me to a movie. I felt like one of John's model airplanes, taken down from a shelf but just as easily put back when the novelty wore off. While my life felt complete with a single good friend, John's life was crowded with people, particularly the kids he'd gone to school with at Mount Carmel.

On weekends, he would sometimes include one of his friends in our phone call, and so I'd find myself talking to Dave Morton, his best friend. Then his other good friend, John Tillinghast, a.k.a. Tillie, would show up and John would break off to shoot hoops in the driveway.

One day, John said, "Tillie's having a party. Want to go?"

My mom had a rule: no boys in cars until I turned sixteen. "Who'll drive?" I asked.

"I guess my father could," he said.

"My mom could drive," I said.

"No, he'll do it if I ask."

I had never met John's father, but he pulled up beyond my picket fence and John came in to get me. The whole way over, John's father didn't say one word beyond "hello." No interview. No attempt to see if I was suitable date material for his son. Instead, his eyes, looking back at us in the rearview mirror, flicked from John's face to mine.

In those days, older people often said I looked like Elizabeth Taylor, and people my age compared me to Annette Funicello, one of the leads on Walt Disney's *Mickey Mouse Club*, but I didn't think I was anything special. I was a brunette in an era when blondes were the glamour queens. Sure, I occasionally modeled for my uncle, a serious amateur photographer, but not because I had anything great to wear. I made my own clothes and wore no cosmetics other than lipstick, so why was this old guy with the thinning hair staring at me continuously?

Tillie lived with his mom in a small bungalow in Redwood City. As John and I walked up to the front door, I heard music playing, but I wasn't ready to go in.

"I don't think your dad likes me."

"He doesn't even know you," John said. "How could he not like you?"

"He kind of glared at us in the mirror."

"He's just mad at me."

"Why?"

John opened the screen door. "Because he had to drive down from Burlingame."

"What's in Burlingame?"

"His office," John said, standing aside for me to enter. "Don't let him bum you out. Let's just have a good time."

The lights were low. John's buddies, boys he'd known since elementary school, scuffed across the carpet with their dates. Soon, John's cheek rested on my head. Cocooned against his chest, I inhaled his scent: nutmeg, cinnamon, and cloves. I had never pressed so tightly against a boy that my breasts flattened, and when I leaned my head back, his moist lips met mine. I closed my eyes and let the kiss settle into the stream bed of my soul. Water might ripple overhead, but gravity had drawn me down into the sand, where I wanted to stay forever.

Then his tongue darted between my teeth.

"Ew!" I drew back and wiped a hand across my mouth. "What are you doing?"

"That's French kissing," he said. "I read about it in a book."

I pulled away. "What kind of book?"

"A book Tillie lent me. But we don't have to do it if you don't want."

"I don't!" I said. "If you ever put your tongue in my mouth again, I'll bite it off."

"Okay, okay," he said, pulling me close again. "Don't get all upset."

I wasn't upset. I liked that he was dancing more or less in time to the music. It was just that I didn't quite know what to expect or how to handle his advances: his intrusive tongue or the hard thing in his pants. But I did like the grip of his fingers laced through mine, and the way he curled my hand against his chest as if we were two mice in a nest. For the first time in a long time, I felt secure.

Although the party was nowhere close to breaking up, at nine forty-five, fifteen minutes before my curfew, John's father pulled up outside and honked the horn. I tucked in my blouse and ran a brush through my hair. John climbed in the backseat and put his arm around my shoulders. On the ride home, I felt the pressure of his fingertips, silently communicating that he cared. And it was a good thing we were coming home early. On Monday I was auditioning for a school play, and I was nervous about it because I hadn't been onstage in a very long time.

CHAPTER 17

FRIAR JOHN

From the time I was three, I had been the lead singer and dancer in a troupe of child performers called Dorothy Roberts' Stars of Tomorrow. In elementary school and all the way up to eighth grade, I'd had twice-weekly lessons in singing, tap, acrobatics, and ballet and performed in a Broadway show–style extravaganza every spring.

However, my parents' divorce and my mother's money problems put an end to my child stardom. Eighth grade had been my last performance. At the end of freshman year, after the debacle of our trip to Mexico and my mom's subsequent divorce, she asked if I wanted to rejoin the troupe. I went to one session. At home, with my too-tight tap shoes, standing on a piece of plywood in my bedroom and watching myself in the mirror as I rattled and shuffled , I knew I had fallen too far behind to catch up. But sophomore year, I had a chance to start afresh.

Every fall, my high school's chapter of the California Scholarship Federation held auditions for a Shakespeare play. I wasn't sure I could still stand before an audience and reach the back of the room with my voice, but my mother encouraged me to audition.

In 1951, an elaborate clown costume, worn while performing for the Stars of Tomorrow, doubled as the author's Halloween costume. All the costumes were made by the author's mother and grandmother.

Trying out for the part of Juliet seemed the obvious choice, since by this time I wore John's football ring on a chain around my neck. That meant I couldn't date anyone from my school. Sure, I didn't know him all that well, but under the spell of Shakespeare, I imagined that we were a modern-day Romeo and Juliet, capable of the kind of love no adult could possibly comprehend.

Despite all that, the role that interested me most was that of Nurse. Sitting in a folding chair in the multipurpose room while my competition got up and read, I saw my English teacher, Mr. Nail, a balding man with a high voice and a tendency to point and shout, smile when Susan Mayberry, one of the drama club's regulars, got up to read her lines.

The auditions came down to the two of us. In the end, Sue's dimpled moon face and hip-bumping, bawdy stage presence won the day.

Mr. Nail cast me as Friar John.

"That part has very few lines," I said.

"But important lines," he said. "The audience has to hear them to understand why there's a mix-up at the tomb."

Later, when I saw how many lines our Nurse had to recite, I realized I would have had no idea how to memorize that much poetry. It would have taken me hours of study each day. Instead, I tied a pillow around my waist and hid my long hair under a friar's cowl. I had a walk-on in Act One, and then I said my ten lines in Act Five. Apart from that, I lounged backstage. Ironically, if I had won that audition, I might not have found myself pregnant.

CHAPTER 18

MAKING OUT

My mother had been invited over to John's house for Sunday brunch and welcomed into the extended MacDonald clan. A dozen or more cousins, aunts, and uncles showed up every Sunday and left a mountain of plates to wash, a job that fell on John's sisters and me. So, this was what it was like to be part of a family, I thought: washing, drying, stacking plates. The camaraderie took away some of my annoyance that the boys had gone into the TV room to watch sports.

Although John and I were going steady, my mother's no-boys-in-cars rule still held, although in a modified form. If John and I went out at night, he could drive, but we had to double-date. The rule didn't apply to daytime or dusk. While I was at rehearsal, John had football practice, but after that my mother said it was okay for him to swing by and pick me up. I was not allowed to invite John into the house when my mother wasn't there, so, after play practice, around five or five thirty, just as it was getting dark, we found secluded places to prolong our time together. If we had time, we drove down to the Stanford Arboretum, but the best parking place was a cul-de-sac two blocks from Woodside High. A single house sat at the top of the hill, but otherwise the street had five empty lots.

In the five months since Tillie's party, John had never again put his tongue in my mouth, but his hand often slipped under my blouse. Heat rose in my face and my body shivered, as if held in the grip of a pleasurable fever. Some part of me that had always existed just below the surface of my good-girl docility emerged from its cocoon. This *thing*, this *me*, wasn't a monster I could push back in the closet. It was fundamental to my nature, called to life by John's sucking my breasts and by his fingers stroking my thighs. His tongue was my tongue, his lips mine as well. In his car, as the day dimmed to dusk, he slid the seat back and moved over to my side and waited for me to undo my bra. I undid his zipper and slid my hand down his pants. The steering wheel got in the way, of course, but he moved back enough for me to lie down and receive the warm, full weight of his body. We kissed like drowning people, each trying to climb on top of the other to capture a last gasp of air. One day I said "stop" and he did not.

When I got home, I was shocked to see blood in my underwear. Heart racing and waiting until my mother went into the bathroom to take a shower, I called him and told him what had happened.

"I think that's supposed to happen," he said.

"Are you sure?"

"I broke your hymen," he said. "It's not a big deal."

Fine for him to say. The word reminded me of the time in sixth grade when my mother had first uttered the words "vagina" and "penis" and I had recoiled at the thought of a man and woman "doing it." Now, here I was. I had stepped over a line, surrendering my virginity, a treasure the Church warned me to protect until I received the Holy Sacrament of Marriage.

But none of that ultimately mattered, because once we started, we couldn't stop. To pretend that John and I were not doing what we were in fact doing, we organized our time to make it seem like we were normal teenagers engaged in normal teenage things. On weekends we played miniature golf. We stopped at drive-ins and ate hamburgers and drank milk shakes. We played chess at the dining room table and took tennis rackets up to Woodside High School's courts, lobbing balls back and forth until dusk.

But a trip to the Santa Cruz Beach Boardwalk or a walk along windy Atascadero Beach was merely a pretext. The beach was one of the few places where we could take off our clothes. The water was too cold to swim in, but we hadn't come for that. We carried blankets out to the sand and found a secluded spot between the boulders at the base of a cliff. Then we stripped down to our swimsuits and got under a blanket. The suits went, along with my shame. Here, out of sight of my mother and the Church, I could reveal my true self—not the brainy self, striving for admission to Ivy League colleges, but the dirty, gritty physical self that took me down a parallel path. Crazed with desire, I turned myself loose.

I loved the way the hair on John's chest plunged downward like a spear. I loved the hard ripple of his stomach, and the way I could straddle him and pull back and pull back so that he would beg me to stay glued and let him come. Afterward, I would fall on his chest and hear his labored breathing, feel him reach for the blanket and tuck it around my shoulders. Even now, I can recall my cheek against his, the smell of his Old Spice and Bay Rum, and the scratch of his whiskers against my cheek. In all the years since his death—fifty, now—I've never made love to anyone who had such an intuitive sense of my natural body rhythms. And in the years of our marriage, whatever we might have argued about, we never carried that argument to bed. Sex washed away grievances. As it had from the beginning, it was the glue that held us together.

WHEN WE TOOK John's brothers and sisters to Mass, the other kids filed out, stepping over our feet and leaving us holding hands in the pew. To walk up the aisle, stick out my tongue, and allow the priest to lay the wafer on it, I needed the wet rag of contrition wiped across the blackboard of sin.

More than that, I needed us to stop. Just stop. And I had to figure out the answer on my own. My mother neither shared her own troubles nor asked what was going on in my life. If I got A's on tests and kept up with the ironing, that was good enough for her. My diary became a trusted friend, and when I looked back through its pages, I saw that I had stopped writing about my classes, teachers, and assignments. Neither did I write about friend problems, always such a rich mine of dramatic material for any self-absorbed teen. The reason? I had cut myself off from my friends, not that I had a ton. Worse than that, I hadn't gone to a meeting of the Model UN in months. I also passed on the yearly Junior Statesmen convention in Sacramento because John was afraid that I might meet someone. Thoughts about sex—and the torture of trying to stop—had become repetitive to the point that I was boring even myself.

If I continued on this path, the fever of love and shame burning in my cheeks would strip my life of everything that had previously given it meaning. At Mass, I knelt and prayed that I would have the strength to do what I needed to do.

After the usual post-Mass Sunday brunch at the MacDonald house—sausage, biscuits, hash browns, and scrambled eggs—John drove me home. We sat outside in his car, and I looked down the leafy tunnel of trees, remembering the day he had dropped me off after my grandmother's death. The Day of the Pink Fog. Now, I was in a fog of a different sort. I had a big week of exams ahead. I needed to get my mind back on schoolwork.

"What's wrong?" he asked.

"We're going to hell if we keep on like this."

"We just have to control ourselves," John said.

"We're obviously not," I said.

"I'm going to confess to my Greek teacher, Father Fulco, and see what he says."

"I know what he'll say: 'Just don't do it.'"

John had gotten a 98 in theology. Surely, he knew the Catholic Church absolutely forbade sex outside of marriage. In the Church's eyes, fornication ranked right up there with adultery, one of the Seven Deadly Sins. As far as the Church was concerned, the only reason to have sex was to have children. The Church even defined using a condom as a mortal sin.

If I step back into my mindset at the time, I believe that the fear of committing a mortal sin—the stain it would leave on my soul—

loomed much larger than the abstract fear of having a baby. I discounted the possibility that sex could lead to pregnancy, possibly because I had no notion of having been conceived by an actual man and woman.[1]

My "origin story" was that I had been picked out, chosen, and then brought to live with my mother and father when I was five weeks old. Before that, my history was a blank. Or, more accurately, I had no history. I was like one of those stateless exiles without a passport, fated to wander in perpetuity. (Of course, I had a home. My adoptive home. But I did not feel "at home" there. The place I felt happiest was over at the MacDonalds'.)

John, of course, knew about babies, not just in the abstract, but in the particular. The oldest of eight, he'd watched his mother's stomach grow. He'd been called on to help with the younger children when she went to the hospital. He'd changed diapers and swaddled infants and walked back and forth, holding his younger brothers in his arms. Babies were real to him in a way that they were not to me. Though we never spoke about the possibility of pregnancy, he must have known that babies were not always planned, or welcome.

When John and I were alone on a beach or in a car, it was as if I were standing in front of the freezer, holding a spoon and a tub of ice cream. I had the spoon. I had the ice cream. I knew I should put the ice cream back in the freezer and not stand there until the whole half gallon disappeared, and yet I couldn't help but dig in.

In 1961, the language of addiction had not come into our common parlance, but John was an addiction. Not only was he an addiction, he had become my entire world. When we were apart, I ached. When we were together, I tried to figure out how to go back to a celibate life.

Coincidentally, and because he knew I was interested in why he thought a Jesuit education so superior to mine, John had loaned me a book about the writings of Thomas Aquinas. I had pored over the *Summa Theologica*. Aquinas wrote that intellectual virtues perfect the intellect but do not always dispose a person to make good choices. Aquinas claimed that the passions associated with food, drink, and sex "result from the sense of touch," and that to break a pattern of intemperate behavior, one had only to institute new habits. To do that, one needed to engage the will and direct it. Even if John couldn't stop, I could. I would go to confession, and then I could resume taking Communion. A day at a time, I would clear my conscience and regain my sense of purpose.

But then, just when I'd determined to stop having sex, my mother surprised me.

"I've been talking to one of the new teachers at school," she said, picking up the sheets I had ironed. They needed to go in the linen closet, and she had her own system for arranging them. "Sybil has three teenagers, and she's convinced me that I've been too strict."

Too strict? If only she knew.

"From now on, you can go out with John without the need to double-date, and I'm moving your curfew up to eleven o'clock."

"Thank you," I said.

"You don't look as happy as I thought you'd be," she said.

"No, I'm happy," I said, forcing a smile.

In my desperation to be with John, I had begged for exemptions to the rules. Could I stay out until ten fifteen, just this once? Would it be okay if John drove me over to Tillie's, where we would pick up Tillie and his girlfriend? What about John's junior prom? It ended at midnight. It was down in Santa Clara. If I had to be home by ten, then there was hardly any point in going.

My mom had succumbed to the drip torture of boundary testing and my unrelenting reminders that John and I were good students who had never given her any reason not to trust us.

I did not see John all week, nor did I have time to talk to him on the phone. I had a big history test coming up, and I spent the week reviewing my class notes and writing practice essays. On Thursday night, exhausted from the effort it had taken to keep my mind on my studies, I picked up the phone—not something I ordinarily did, because girls who chased boys were thought to be overly forward.

"Are we going out this weekend?"

"Yes," he said. "How about a movie?"

"As long as it's not a drive-in."

Expecting that we would have to be back by ten, always a challenge, he left the phone on his desk and loped downstairs to find the entertainment section of the *Redwood City Tribune*. For three months, John had been pressuring me to convince my mother to amend the rules. And now, just when I needed her to lock me in my room and forbid me ever to lay eyes on him, she had decided to trust me. He came back upstairs, and we settled on a movie. Then I told him the news.

"Finally!" he said.

My stomach sank. I would have to find my own way to erect a wall.

On Friday, I walked from my house to St. Pius, a half hour that allowed me to firm up my intentions. Aquinas called temperate behavior—moderating one's desires for food and sex—one of the Cardinal Virtues. The habit of temperance was what separated us from the animals. I sat in the pew and waited for a turn in the confessional.

A smoker departed, and I took his place on the box's wooden kneeler. During the low mumbling of someone else's absolution, I cleared my throat and tried to breathe. The smoker's lingering smell reminded me of my father. Even pulling a sweater up over my nose didn't help.

At last, the panel separating the priest's cubicle from mine slid back. Hoping for the new assistant priest, I looked at the wire mesh. Father Armstrong's bald head and stocky shoulders were dimly silhouetted. He would recognize my voice.

"Yes, go on," he said.

"Bless me, Father, for I have sinned. It has been eight weeks since my last confession."

"Go on."

Closing my eyes and making the sign of the cross, I said, "I let a boy put his hand inside my blouse."

"Is that all?" he asked.

"Yes, that's all," I said, because even here, alone with my conscience and seeking a priest's absolution, I could not confess what John's fingers felt like on my breasts, how it felt when he cupped them in his hands and sucked them.

"Go, then," Father Armstrong said, "and avoid the occasion of sin."

The car was the occasion of sin. I couldn't avoid the car. "Yes, Father," I said.

"And for your penance, say ten decades of the rosary."

That would take half an hour. John had gone to confession down at school, and he would be here soon. I had time, though. Saying a sincere penance was the only way to wash away a sin, and I applied myself to the task. I had sinned in all three categories that would damn me to hell. First was thought. I had to stop my lustful thoughts. The second category was word. I had to stop telling lies. And then there was deed. I had to stop the deeds that led to the lies. The solution was simple, really. Stop the thoughts that led to the deeds. Stop the deeds that led to the lies. Tonight, John and I would make a fresh start.

I BOUNDED FROM CHURCH, saw John's car idling at the turnaround, and hopped in the passenger seat.

"Guess who was hearing confession?" I said.

"Father Armstrong," he said.

"Yeah."

"Did you tell him?"

"Not everything."

"We're going to stop at the pharmacy," John said.

"Won't that make us late for the movie?"

"We have time."

John drove to downtown Redwood City, then a zone of shuttered stores and Chinese takeout. He stopped at a pharmacy with a neon green mortar and pestle out front.

"I'm going to run in and buy condoms."

"But that's a mortal sin!"

"Father Fulco said it's okay."

"You told him?"

He shrugged. "He's a Jesuit."

"So?"

"He has a more sophisticated understanding of theology than the diocesan priests."

"Oh, sure he does!"

"It's not all black and white." Leaving the engine idling, he opened the door and hopped out.

I turned on the radio. The Top 40 countdown was on KFRC. I had listened to two songs before John opened the door and slid in.

"Asshole!" He pounded the steering wheel.

"What's the problem?"

"The guy wanted to see an ID."

"But you've got a driver's license."

"I'm not eighteen."

In 1961, condoms were sold by the pharmacist, not over the counter. The first oral birth control pill, Enovid, had just come on the market, available through a family doctor, but not to teens. Planned Parenthood existed as an organization, but it did not open its first clinic until 1963. Back then, married couples used condoms and diaphragms; however, Catholics weren't allowed to use any form of birth control, apart from the "rhythm method," and teenagers were only beginning to get instruction on sexuality and family planning.

Despite political opposition and in conjunction with Planned Parenthood's efforts to improve access to contraceptive information, New York City's Health Department allocated $305,000 to care for six hundred teenage unmarried mothers. The city's hospital commissioner allocated money so that "18,000 women [could] receive free contraceptives in the first ten months of 1964."[2]

According to Rickie Solinger, author of *Wake Up Little Susie*, "public officials . . . felt strongly that unmarried mothers, especially teenagers, should not be engaging in sexual relations and should, therefore, not be provided with birth control. Some who took this exclusionary position were Catholics opposed to all contraception."[3]

Solinger writes that Milwaukee alderman Richard Nowakowski voiced his opposition to five federally funded birth control clinics that had been set up in the city. "We will have 'sexmobiles' moving around the streets passing out birth control to whomever wants it—just like popcorn wagons."

To someone like the Milwaukee alderman, it would have looked like John and I couldn't keep our hands out of the popcorn box, but not for want of trying. Rereading my diary, I see that I broke up with John many times (though not officially—just in my head), and then he would drop by the house, or I would call, and it would start all over again: the sneaking around, the vows to quit, the remorse.

As the end of my sophomore year approached, I felt little desire to study and wrote about feeling tired and sick to my stomach. My mother had encouraged me to run for a class office. She said it would help me get into college and that it might even help me get a scholarship from her sorority, Delta Zeta. Knowing how much my achievements meant to her and thinking she was probably right, that serving as a class officer would look good on my college applications, I let myself be persuaded. Although my heart wasn't into pandering for votes, I walked the open hallways with a rictus smile, taping up campaign posters made from sheets of colored paper snitched from my mom's classroom. Short on time, I hastily ate my pimento-loaf sandwich and then had to leave Spanish and throw up.

Trying to stop having sex was making me confused and ill. Or maybe something else was wrong—an intestinal disease. Maybe I'd picked up a parasite in Mexico that had gone dormant until now. For weeks, I had been dragging through the day and was almost constantly sick to my stomach.

CHAPTER 19

DISASTER

My mother still had one of the paisley aprons my grandmother had made from chicken-feed sacks. She stood at the stove, a spatula in her hand. "What's for dinner?" I asked.

"Liver and onions," she said.

Oh no—my least favorite dinner. The taste made my stomach turn, and now the smell did, too. I opened the refrigerator and took out a pillowcase of sprinkled laundry. After my grandmother's death, the ironing board had become a permanent fixture in the living room, but even trying to do forty minutes a day, I couldn't keep up with the tablecloths, napkins, and sheets.

At least play practice had ended. The performance had been a big success, and I could get the ironing out of the way before I sat down to write the speech I had to give to the school assembly. My heart was not in it, but the vote for junior class secretary was coming up in another week.

As I ran the iron back and forth, the smell of mildew nauseated me. I raced for the bathroom, locked the door, and threw up. I flushed the toilet, brushed my teeth, and opened the door.

Yikes! There stood my mother, eyes bulging behind her trifocals, white hair frizzed.

"Is it possible you could be pregnant?" she asked.

Holy Mary, Mother of God.

"I don't know," I said. "I guess I could be."

"I knew it." She stood aside.

A chill ran down my spine, and I turned. "What do you mean?"

Fists balled, she leaned forward. "You're *just like your mother*!"

Moving away from her, I wiped spit from my face. This was a fever dream, the alternating waves of heat and cold, my burning cheeks, my mother shouting at me.

She backed into the living room and sank down on the couch. Then she leaned forward, elbows on her knees, hands covering her face.

I followed her and stood like a parent shaking a finger at a child caught in a lie. "You told me my parents were dead."

"They're not," she said. "At least, they weren't at the time of your birth."

She looked toward the front door, as if she expected my parents to knock.

"What did you mean when you said I was just like my mother?"

"She was the same age as you when she got pregnant."

"Fifteen and a half?"

"Yes," she said, spitting out the words. "And you're *just like her*."

A fist slammed into my solar plexus. My father's old game. Anticipating another sock in the stomach, my muscles tensed in anticipation of the blow.

What words could I even use to express the flood of questions that welled up in a white heat behind my eyes and that threatened to spill out in tears? If I said "real mother," I would sound ungrateful and disloyal. Would saying "the woman who gave birth to me" be any better? I might be pregnant, but my pregnancy was no big deal compared to finding out who I was, the *me* I had been groping for all these years.

My fingernails dug into my palms. "Do you know anything else about my biological origins?"

"Your parents weren't married. The boy, your father, was nineteen."

Finally, the truth.

The inside of my mouth felt dry. Swallowing hurt. My parents were real people. They had ten fingers and ten toes. They'd had sex. Behind me, I smelled burnt starch. I turned off the iron and took the pillowcase of mildewed clothes out to the washing machine.

When I returned, my mother, forearms on her thighs, sat hunched forward. Spasms made her right leg jerk. She looked down at the floor and made little hiccup cries.

Standing before her, I was tempted to smack her cheek, which is what my father would have done. One blow would collapse her carefully stacked pile of cards.

"What exactly do you know?" I asked.

"Your mother was a good student. Just like you."

"And my father?"

"He was a carpenter."

"A carpenter!" I said, thinking of how I'd once built a two-story backyard fort. How easily sawing and hammering came to me, almost as if I'd been born with tools in my hands. Aptitude. A second truth. The missing puzzle piece dropped into the pie-plate-size hole at my very core.

"Do you know what they looked like?"

"Both of them had blond hair and blue eyes."

"But that can't be. Brown is dominant."

"Your father apparently had one brown eye and one blue. Maybe it came from him."

That still didn't make sense. If he had one blue eye, his genes, plus my mother's—if she was indeed blue-eyed—should have made blue dominant. The third truth did not explain the dark chocolate of my eyes, but it did make me remember my adoptive father's offhand comment about Spanish sailors jumping ship off the Irish coast.

"How did the girl who gave birth to me get pregnant?"

My mother took off her glasses and rubbed her eyes. "The same way you did." After she'd put her glasses back on, she looked straight at me. "What I want to know is, how could you do this to me?"

It's not about you, I wanted to cry. My mother was the last person I wanted to hurt. In all the times John and I had found ourselves tangled in the front seat of the car or under a blanket on the beach, the fever of his touch had caught me up in a tornado of pleasure. I could no more put my feet on the ground than I could think of anyone outside that whirlwind of desire.

Until now, this moment, when my mother had pointed out the obvious. The shame of the divorce had nearly crushed her. My unplanned pregnancy would be the *coup de grâce.* I had spent my entire life trying to be the daughter she wanted me to be—smart, artistic, talented, and popular with boys. My mother could bring her skills as teacher to a gifted child, and the more that child succeeded, the greater the reflected glory. She had wanted nothing more than to give me a good life.

Nancy Verrier wrote about the phenomenon of adoptees who do not act out. Rather than show their anger, they became people-pleasers, sending all their adoptee rage underground. To these people-pleasers, the baby that had once yearned for its birth mother and cried when she was not there had died.

> As children, they [the adoptees] were very polite, cooperative, charming, and generally "good." But locked inside them was pain and fear that the unacceptable baby who died would come back to life if they were not vigilant.[1]

Verrier wrote that "awakening the baby would lead to nothing good." And, for a single instant with my mother, I had nearly allowed the rage to spill out. In the moment she told me I was just like my mother, I wanted to say, *Hey, you lied to me!* But I couldn't scream at her or argue, nor could I, in an instant, overcome the decades of conditioning that had me raising a hand to ask a question.

I was a child. Still, she had lied about the facts of my birth. Not only had she withheld information about my parents, she had withheld information I needed. The chosen child had been swiftly "unchosen" in the very moment I might have hoped for unconditional love.

CHAPTER 20

A VISIT TO THE DOCTOR

*B*efore, I was the chosen child. After, I was the child of a sexually active teen. Before, my hymen was intact. After, I could never claim to be a virgin. Before, my doctor was a pediatrician. After, I went to an ob-gyn.

My mother took me to the Kaiser clinic in downtown Redwood City. She and I sat with a bunch of women—pregnant ones, with their hands resting on their bellies, and old women flipping through *Women's Day* and *Redbook* and *Ladies' Home Journal*, looking at recipes or whatever they were looking at, their eyes so focused on the page that all the while I felt my face burning and shoulders stiffening under their fake disinterest.

My mother bent down and ran her fingers up her stocking to straighten the seam. Then she picked up the magazine she had been reading, *Woman's Day*, probably an article about a Jell-O mold with fruit cocktail, or green bean casserole with mushroom soup and dried onion rings, recipes popular in the day.

"Marylee Benham," the nurse said.

My mother got up, too, and my stomach flip-flopped. The last time she'd seen me naked, I had been six or seven, but beyond that, I didn't want her anywhere near me. Since the day she had asked if

I could be pregnant, I had not been able to stop thinking about what she'd said: *You're just like your mother.*

"Your mother can wait out here," the nurse said.

"All right," she said, staggering back to her chair. "But call me if you need me."

It was going to be all right, I felt like telling her. I probably had a stomach flu, and then she could take back her words and make me her daughter again.

In the examining room, a poster on the wall showed a woman's internal organs: the ovaries, the fallopian tubes, the uterus. In Human Physiology, I had dissected a pregnant cat. I knew the names of the organs. I also knew how conception occurred. When two gametes joined, a zygote (from the Greek, meaning "joined" or "yoked") formed. The zygote contained the DNA of both individuals, twined together in a new combination, and this tadpole traversed the fallopian tube. On the wall hung a medical drawing of an upside-down baby. I had seen babies in grocery stores, but never up close, and this hypothetical baby, floating in its sac of amniotic fluid, reminded me of babies in Limbo, the place unbaptized babies went. Limbo, the dance. Limbo, a period of interminable waiting. I was in Limbo, waiting for the doctor to make a diagnosis, but, on the plus side, at least Limbo wasn't Hell. I still had a chance.

The nurse unrolled paper from a giant roller and tore it off on a serrated blade. She handed me a sheet and a cotton gown. "The tie goes in back," she said, closing the door.

After I changed, I hopped up on the table and covered my knees.

The nurse came back, picked up my clothes from the chair, and hung them on a hook.

"So," she said, sitting down, the questionnaire balanced on one knee. "Your name is Marylee Benham. Can you tell me why you're here?"

"I'm throwing up all the time," I said, testing the queasiness of my stomach. On a scale of one to ten, it was an eight. "I think I might have an intestinal worm."

The nurse frowned. "Do you have dogs?"

"No," I said. "We have a cat."

"Okay," the nurse said. "Can you tell me how often you throw up?"

"Just about every day, but especially if my mother makes me a pimento-loaf sandwich."

The nurse smiled. "I guess that would make me throw up, too."

"Even the smell of it gets to me," I said, recalling the time I'd had to flee Spanish class and throw up in the bushes.

"When was your last period?" the nurse asked.

"I don't keep track."

"I'm going to put down 'not sure.' Does that seem right?"

"Yes, I'm really not sure."

"And have you had relations?"

"My grandparents are dead," I said. "I have an uncle in Oakland."

"Sexual relations," she said.

"Oh," I said.

"How old are you, honey?" the nurse asked.

"I'm fifteen and a half," I said. "I just got my learner's permit."

The nurse looked up from the questionnaire. "And when did you start your menarche?"

"My period, you mean?"

"Yes. When did you start menstruating?"

Gross! Yuck! "Seventh grade," I said.

A moment later, the doctor, with a goatee and ears that reminded me of Mr. Potato Head, came in. The nurse handed him the chart.

He flipped through it, read what the nurse had written. "Okay. Let's see what we've got here. Have you ever had a pelvic exam?"

"No," I said. The room felt cold. I hugged myself.

"It's okay," the nurse said. "You'll get used to them."

"I don't want to." I shook my head *no no no* and covered it with the sheet.

"Honey, it's the only way he can tell what's wrong. Something's making you throw up."

"Can't he just give me an X-ray?"

"No," the nurse said, "it wouldn't be good for——"

"Lie down," the doctor said.

I didn't move.

The doctor washed his hands and took a pair of rubber gloves from a drawer. They went on with a squeak.

"Well?" he said. "Are you going to cooperate, or are we going to have to get your mother in here?"

"I'll cooperate," I said.

Paper crinkled beneath my hips. The examining table felt hard, and my feet hung off the end. The nurse told me to scoot down. I did, and she said I had to scoot more. My feet were bare, and she put them in stirrups. I put a hand over my eyes. I heard a snap and opened my eyes to see her unfurling a second sheet. It was the size of a tablecloth. I had ironed a bunch of them before coming over. She pushed the stirrups apart, spreading my legs. A floor lamp scraped across the floor. The light clicked on. A sensation of heat came next.

There was a vent in the ceiling. Looking up, I could see the louvers in the vent and the blackness inside. The room had the same ceiling tiles as my school, and I thought of how when you looked up at the ceiling in the girls' bathroom, there were always spit wads of toilet paper.

"This may hurt a little," the doctor said.

I heard a squirt, like a mustard bottle.

"It'll feel cold," the nurse said.

I gripped the edges of the examining table. A cold metal tip and two spoons spread me open. The doctor hunkered down. His fingers probed. Then the metal thing came out. The gloves snapped off and dropped in the garbage can. The lid clunked. The doctor turned off the light and pulled the sheet down between my knees.

"Have her come into my office when she's dressed," he said.

The nurse handed me a Kleenex. "You can wipe yourself off."

She went out, leaving me alone with the medicinal smell. I hopped off the table and rushed to the little sink. I sounded like a cat with a hairball. Green stuff burned my throat. I turned on the faucet and rinsed my mouth. At least it wasn't chunky and hadn't clogged the drain.

Finally, I got dressed.

The nurse poked her head in. "Ready?"

This was going to be bad.

On the doctor's desk sat an ashtray and an anatomical plaster model of a woman's internal organs. My mother, her cheeks drawn in as if she were sucking on a lemon, sat in the office, her purse in her lap.

Squaring his shoulders, the doctor said, "Your daughter is eight or nine weeks pregnant."

The floor fell away. I wanted to shout or weep, and scream, *No, this can't be happening!*

"Are you sure?" my mother whispered.

"We'll have her give us a urine sample," he said, "but yes, even without that, I'm sure."

He pushed the Kleenex box toward my mother. She removed her glasses and blotted her eyes.

"What year are you in school?" the doctor asked.

"I'm a sophomore," I said.

"A sophomore." He picked up a pen and, with the tip, turned the calendar pages of his Rolodex. "When does your school year end?"

"June twelfth," I said.

"June twelfth." He frowned. "You can probably make it till then without showing."

"She's a straight-A student," my mother said. "What does one do in this situation?"

I wasn't a straight-A student. I had an A-minus average. My mother was lying. Again.

"What about her father?" the doctor asked.

"We're divorced," my mother said. "We have no contact."

Another lie. They had contact. Occasionally, she took one of his midnight calls. And, I saw that we were alike after all. From her, I had learned to bend the truth.

The doctor picked up his pen. "You may want to ask around to see what other people do in this situation."

My mother tore a Kleenex into little pieces. "No one can know about this," she said. "If people find out, my daughter's reputation would be ruined."

"In that case," he said, "I don't know what you're going to do."

Turning to me, and in the same tone of helpful neutrality a school counselor might have used when offering me the option of Physics or Chemistry, he asked, "What do you want to do?"

I thought of John the day he had picked me up at the Greyhound station, standing there in the shade, one foot against the wall, arms folded across his chest.

"I want to get married," I said.

If John and I were to get married, we wouldn't have to sneak around. On the other hand, if kids at school found out, I would be branded forever, a modern-day Hester Prynne, forced to wear the scarlet A while the hypocrite—Dimmesdale—got off scot-free. Of course, that was an unfair comparison. John wasn't Dimmesdale. Whatever happened, he would stand by me.

CHAPTER 21

HOMEWORK

*W*hen I returned from the clinic, I took off my girdle and tossed it on my bed. Finally, I could breathe. John knew my mother had confronted me. He knew I had a doctor's appointment. "Call me as soon as you know," he'd said.

I uncurled the phone cord, took the phone out to the patio, and sat on a picnic bench. It was a beautiful day, and everything that anchored me to this place was still here: my old tetherball pole with its deflated ball; the pear tree in the middle of the lawn, starting to bear fruit; my mother's gladioli shooting up from behind the curving border of the flower bed; the intense blue of the sky just visible through the oak tree's sun-pierced umbrella. My index finger in the phone's rotary dial pushed past its resistance—and my own. I pictured the Formica-covered breakfast table in John's kitchen and the Princess phone on the wall. The news that I was pregnant stretched like a taut string between two tin cans.

The phone rang. One of John's little brothers answered, and I heard him shout, "John, phone's for you." Faintly, John's deep voice echoed down the hall. "I'll take it in my bedroom." Then the receiver banged against the wall and, against the tick-tock of my pulse, seconds passed.

John reached his bedroom, lifted the receiver, and shouted down for his brother to hang up. I heard his bedroom door swing shut and the squeak of bedsprings and pictured the black-and-yellow-checked bedspreads on the twin beds in his room, the stereo where, on any other day, he might have held the phone's receiver and put on a Bo Diddley LP, the music a placeholder for the deeper conversations we did not yet know how to have.

"How did the doctor thing go?" John asked.

The doctor thing. Jeez.

"I'm pregnant."

There was a long silence on the other end.

"What are we going to do?" I asked.

"Let me go talk to my mother," he said. "I'll call you back in a few minutes."

"All right," I said, "but how's talking to your mother going to help?"

The line went dead. He'd hung up. I nested the receiver in the phone's cradle.

Hearing a knock at the window, I turned. My mother stood pointing to the yard. Although it was May and the oak tree had just leafed out, oak balls and dead leaves had fallen to the ground. It was my responsibility to keep it swept, and I had not done it.

I went to the garage and found the push broom and cleared a path between the kitchen door and the clothesline so my mother wouldn't trip. When John still hadn't returned my call, I found a tarp and pushed all the debris onto it, and when he still hadn't called, I gathered the corners of the tarp and, like Santa Claus delivering presents, threw the bundle over my shoulder and carried the leaves to the compost pile.

I returned the tarp to the garage and knelt to wash my hands at the spigot. The phone rang, and when I picked up the receiver, the silence told me it was John.

"Well?" I said.

"Her immediate response was 'Poor Marylee.'"

"You know what my mom said?"

"No. What?"

"'Why did you do this to me?'"

"That's ridiculous," he said. "We weren't out to hurt anyone, least of all her."

"Thank you," I said.

"Actually, my mom's not too happy about this either."

Her oldest son, the honor student and football hero, had done something beyond her comprehension. She had told him that her last three pregnancies had filled her with despair. She'd thought there would be no end to babies. "And now this," she'd said. Still, she instantly forgave John and pitied me. She said she'd tell John's father and that the families would meet to discuss what to do.

"We could get married," I told John.

"I know," he said. "I'm thinking about it."

He was thinking about it. God, it was like being back at Teen Club, where the girls waited on pins and needles for the guys to cross the floor.

MY HUMAN PHYSIOLOGY class had almost reached the end of the textbook. Even though the academic year was almost finished, Mr. Parsons had loaded on the homework: excerpts of important bodily processes that we should commit to memory before the final. Sitting at my desk, the unfinished furniture I had saved up for with my allowance and that my mother had shown me how to stain and varnish, I reviewed the key elements of the Krebs cycle, a cellular process that breaks down sugars and begins the process of transforming them into amino acids. I studied the illustration, the little arrows going in a clockwise direction, each step in the process given a name. The harder I tried not to think about being pregnant, the faster the arrows in the circle whirred.

As a child, I had watched my grandfather repair a clock. It was a Seth Thomas clock in a wooden case, and the clock required winding with the key. Carefully, he unhooked the pendulum, thus removing the weight, and, with a small screwdriver, made some adjustments. He wound the spring. When he removed the key, the minute hand spun madly until he stopped it with his finger and reattached the weight.

Everyone must have thoughts like this. Spinning thoughts. Even my mother. After Vera Cruz, she must have spent many a night wondering how to escape. Looking for a way to get rid of my father and take back control of her life. That was all I wanted: to have a say in whatever happened next.

Sometime later, when I put a rubber band around my index cards and gave up on the memorization, I decided that the best thing I could do under the circumstances was to go to bed early and try to get some sleep. Because of my nausea and attempts to hide it, I had slept very little.

I opened the bedroom door and called out, "I'm going to hit the sack."

"Me, too," my mother answered. "It's been a long day."

I changed into my nightgown, turned back my bed, and found my old sock monkey, one my grandmother had made and that I had thrown in the back of the closet because I had outgrown it. The record I played when I needed to calm myself was an LP of Brahms's Piano Concerto #2 in B-flat Major. I put it on the portable stereo next to my bed and, after turning out the light, hugged the sock monkey to my chest. I wiggled my toes against the cold cotton sheets.

Why hadn't John immediately said, "Yes, let's get married. We love each other, and I'm sure it will work out"? He and I were Romeo and Juliet. Unlike the Montagues and Capulets, our parents were modern people. They would let us marry, and we would find some way to finish school. Then we would live happily ever after because we were happy now—happy, that is, when we weren't trying to stop having sex.

Aquinas was right. Sex in the context of marriage was a good thing, God's gift. John and I had been torturing ourselves too long.

The way I saw it, John was a star student, as well as an athlete. He could get an academic or football scholarship. Santa Clara,

Stanford, and San Jose State were all driving distance from my house. We could live in the back room, my grandma's room. It had its own bathroom and kitchen, and we could come and go by her back door. If John loved me the way I loved him, we could make it work.

CHAPTER 22

THE MEETING

The two mothers—John's and mine—set up a family meeting. My uncle and aunt were the first to arrive. Uncle Marshall, a structural engineer, took the armchair and checked his watch. "I need to get back across the bridge before traffic." I brought out Grandma's rocker for Aunt Louise, half Cherokee and with circle braids above her ears.

There was a knock on the door, and my mother told me to stay seated. She would let them in. I expected that John would grab a dining room chair and scoot it next to mine and that we would then hold hands and give each other the gumption to get through whatever kind of ordeal this would prove to be. The main thing was to put up a united front. But, John, in a pale blue oxford-cloth shirt, shuffled in like a prisoner invisibly shackled between two guards.

John's father, in a navy sport coat and red striped tie, the knot loose and the neck of the shirt unbuttoned, shook hands with my uncle, whose look of grim determination sent a chill down my spine. When my uncle sat down, the three MacDonalds moved to the sectional couch. I saw that John's mother had worn not her usual skirt and sweater, but rather a beige suit and the veiled pillbox hat she often wore to Mass. This was the first time she had ever been in my house.

Once seated, John unbuttoned the cuffs of his long-sleeved shirt, and, in what looked like an attempt to avoid my eyes, methodically folded each sleeve to just below the elbow.

My mother began the conversation by repeating what I'd told her on the way back from the doctor's office, that I thought maybe we could get married.

"Out of the question," John's dad said. "He's too young. He'll be trapped."

John's eyes, pleading for understanding, sought mine. He looked like a rabbit, briefly startled before hopping away and disappearing into its burrow. I wanted to get away, too.

My uncle, a manager for Bethlehem Steel and used to tough negotiations, raised the issue of a paternity suit and insisted that, at the very least, John take financial responsibility.

I raised my hand.

"Yes?" my mother said.

"Financial responsibility for what?"

"For getting you pregnant," my uncle said.

Like an eighth grader brought to the vice principal's office for acting up in class, John sat with his head bowed, forearms resting on his knees. The small pops of his cracked knuckles filled the moments of silence.

John had broken the law. He was seventeen. I was almost sixteen, but my uncle kept saying that John could be arrested for having sex with a minor. As far as the money was concerned, Bob MacDonald, ever the businessman, said he hoped they could avoid a lawsuit. Dragging my name through the papers would only give me a bad reputation.

He looked pointedly at my mother. "And I'm sure you wouldn't want that. Apparently, from day one," he said, "Marylee has been pursuing John. She called him from the bus station and has been after him ever since."

I reeled back. My jaw dropped. I waited for John to speak up, but he continued to crack his knuckles. I thought of John's father on the night of Tillie's party. His eyes flashed with the same hostility. "I'm not saying John should be let off the hook, but I don't want my son's life wrecked."

At that moment, I began to understand that the dream I had been harboring—of a happy, cheerful wedding, followed by whatever that would lead to—was nothing but an illusion, fostered by the fairy tales I had grown up reading.

Bob MacDonald had a solution for the issue of financial responsibility. He'd go thirds on the cost, with my mother and John paying the other third.

"Don't forget I have football practice at the end of the summer," John said.

My uncle exploded. "Then you'd better get your debt paid off before then."

"How much is it going to cost?" John said.

"We're trying to find that out," my mother said.

"I contacted the principal at Sacred Heart." Henrietta, John's mother, sat primly with her knees together, purse in her lap. "She gave me the name of a home for unwed mothers in San Francisco."

"She can't go there," my mother said. "There's too much risk Rex would find out."

"Doesn't he have visiting rights?" Bob MacDonald asked.

"Not until he pays child support," my mother said.

"Where would she go, then?" my uncle asked.

"Phoenix," my mother said.

John looked up. "Why Phoenix?"

"Because I can say I'm going there for my health," my mother said, the right side of her body twitching as if to prove the point. "People often go to Arizona for their health, and, as you can see, I am having some neurological problems."

My uncle took a notebook from his pocket. "You'll need moving costs, plus money to replace your salary."

"And rent," my mother said. "Even if Marylee goes in a home, I'll need a place to live."

"You understand, young man, you're going to have to pay for this?" my uncle said.

John hung his head. "I guess I'd better get a paper route."

"You can work at the company," Bob said.

"For how much an hour?" John said.

"Minimum wage."

All this time, my aunt Louise had sat quietly rocking in my grandmother's chair. Clasping her hands, she leaned forward. "What about the baby?"

I looked at John. His baby. My baby.

"*All my fortunes at thy foot I'll lay,*" I said, looking at John, "*And follow thee my lord throughout the world.*"

"What's that from?" he said.

"*Romeo and Juliet.* Act two, scene two."

"Oh, yeah," he said. "Your play."

"Not my play," I said. "Our life."

My mother stood up and went to the kitchen. The faucet came on. She was getting a drink of water.

Henrietta looked at Bob. "Maybe we could take the—"

"I don't need one more mouth to feed," he said.

"If Marylee goes into a home," my mother said, returning to her seat, "I believe the home will arrange for the baby to be adopted."

Buckets of hot and cold water splashed on my face. The room spun and the floor dropped away. I covered my stomach.

"But what if we got married?" I said.

"Pregnant girls can't go to high school," my mother said. "I looked in the district manual. If they find out you've had a child, you'll get expelled."

In the book *Birthmothers*, author Merry Bloch Jones outlines the difficulties of the negotiations surrounding unplanned pregnancies, in which some minors are included, and others pretend to go along with "the plan."[1] I was in the "pretending to go along with the plan" category, even though I didn't fully understand what the plan entailed, but in this moment, the small episodes of our young lives were each coming at me in a rush of contentment and confusion: the bowls of Cheerios, miniature golf, movie popcorn, freezing

Atascadero Beach, the roller coaster at the Santa Cruz Beach Boardwalk and the roller coaster of emotion.

"Do you want to marry Marylee?" my uncle asked.

"I think we should wait," John said.

"How long?" I asked.

"Until we graduate," he said.

"From high school?"

"No. College. I want to get into West Point. There's a qualifying exam, and after that, it'll be up to my congressman."

"What if you don't get in?" I asked.

John shrugged. "Then we'll see."

"John can't get married without my permission," Bob said, "and I won't give it."

What it came down to was that there were no good alternatives for kids like us. If we'd been marginal students, an unplanned pregnancy might have led to a shotgun wedding and John working as a pipe fitter in his dad's plumbing business while I was a stay-at-home mom.

As to whether I could have terminated the pregnancy, abortion was illegal. My mother would have had no idea where to find an abortion provider. Even though she was angry and shamed by my behavior, she would not have wanted to expose me to a dangerous, possibly fatal, pregnancy termination. This was 1961. The Supreme Court did not decide *Roe v. Wade* until a dozen years later.

The MacDonalds said their formal goodbyes, John looking down at the carpet, rather than at me. Tears welled in my eyes at seeing him so unmanned. My uncle, furious at being strong-armed by Bob MacDonald, took my mother's elbow and helped her to her feet. At last, my little Cherokee aunt Louise, with her circle braids above her ears, rose from my grandmother's rocker and approached me, reaching for my hands and holding them. Her dark eyes teared, and she touched my cheek with the backs of her fingers. "I'm so sorry," she said.

"Me, too," I said, choking back a sob.

I stood on the steps of an escalator. Where it would take me, I didn't know, only that it was moving me from the place I stood, there on the flowered carpet of my living room, to a place I could not yet imagine. I must submit to the will of the adults, for there was no other choice. But the cloud hanging over me had a silver lining. Lying was gone and the pretense was gone, as well as thoughts that John might rescue me by taking a firm stand on my behalf. There were limits to love, not just love that I thought my mother owed me, but love that John owed me, too. He had stripped me of my virginity without a second thought, and it was I who would have to bear the consequences.

CHAPTER 23

PAPERWORK

On July 3, 1961, my mother wrote to Lois Clark, superintendent of the Florence Crittenton Home in Phoenix, Arizona.

Dear Madam:

Sister Mary Bernadine, directress of girls, Good Shepherd School for Girls, suggested I write you. I am the mother of a 15-year-old unwed girl who expects a baby in January. We are coming to Phoenix, where we know no one, and where we hope to keep her secret. This is the first time that she and the boy, age 17, have given either family any trouble. We will be in Phoenix in August. What are your rates and how soon must reservations be made?

Sincerely yours,
    (Mrs.) Lorene Benham

Mrs. H. E. South, director of the Florence Crittenton Home, wrote back on July 7, 1961.

Dear Mrs. Benham:

We have received your letter of inquiry dated July 3, 1961. Your letter indicates your daughter is in approximately the third or fourth month of her pregnancy. It is the policy of this Home that all arrangements must be complete for a girl's entry on or before her sixth month.

We have a waiting list well into August. Therefore, it would be wise for your daughter to complete the enclosed application and return it to us at the earliest possible date.

Our fees are $135.00 per month for board and room, and $125.00 delivery fee. We have three schoolteachers (commercial, home economics, and academic), so your daughter would be able to continue her high school studies while she is in our care.

Since you are moving to Phoenix in August, it would be advisable for your daughter to contact us so arrangements can be made for her to be seen in our Tuesday clinic. Please advise us when you would like to have your daughter enter our Home so we may place her on our waiting list.

Sincerely yours,
Mrs. H. E. South
Executive Director

On my application, I wrote that I had been referred to the Florence Crittenton Home of Phoenix, Arizona, by Catholic Social Service of Arizona, 1515 East Osborn Road, Phoenix. I filled out the form on July 12, 1961. Under insurance, I wrote, "Carrying $10,000." In retrospect, I believe that was a life insurance policy my mother had taken out in case of my death. Under savings, my mother wrote, "$1,500 in joint account with mother." This was a savings account my mother had set up through the Redwood City Teachers' Credit Union. She said it would help me establish credit in case I one day needed to buy a car, and, indeed, she was prescient. When John and I eventually married, I went to the credit union for money to buy our first car, a used VW Beetle.

While the details pertaining to insurance recall aspects of my life that I would not have remembered in any other way, it is what I wrote in response to the question "Why do you wish to enter Florence Crittenton Home?" that really floors me. I do not remember having the level of fear that this brief note telegraphed.

> My parents are divorced, and I live with my mother. If my father were to learn of my condition, which I hope to definitely avoid, he would make our lives very difficult. His mind is rather mixed up, as evidenced by his actions and letters, and I would be scared to death to be in his care. If I could enter your home, there would be little chance of anyone finding out, and I could resume school without anyone being the wiser.

The expected date of my child's birth was January 18, 1962. In response to the question "What plan, if any, have you for your child?" I wrote the following:

> All of us believe that it would be best for the child to be adopted. I was adopted when I was five weeks old and know that it has many advantages and is a good life. Since I was adopted when five weeks old, my descent is different from that of my parents. I am Irish, mostly.

The form asked for information about the family, and I wrote, "My father recently completed a term in jail and is now beginning a new one, for drunk driving."

My mother made two small corrections. The first jail term was for failure to pay alimony. She wrote the word "adopted" before my father's name and underlined it twice. I wrote that he was born on September 12, 1905, in Waterloo, Iowa, and that he "usually worked as a longshoreman." She amended that to "shipping clerk." As for his employer, I put down "ILWU," but she changed that to "Pacific Shipping." He was a member of the International Longshoremen and Warehouse Union, but it was not his employer.

Under dependents, of whom I was the only one, I wrote, "He will not accept his dependents." I'm pretty sure my mom coached me on that one. My father had not sent one penny of child support in the two years since he'd moved out of the house.

Under "Mother," she amended what I had written to say, "adopted Mother."

As for her, Elsie Lorene Pitney was born on September 14, 1902, in Forest Green, Missouri, and taught elementary school for the Redwood City school district. She listed her salary as $550 per month. She amended the form to add, "Mother has sick leave from Redwood City Schools (nervous and anxieties)."

The condition she described as "nervous and anxieties" was, in fact, we learned much later, a condition called *hemichorea*. The doctors did not know then what caused the involuntary jerking of the limbs on the right side of her body.

While I had noticed her facial twitch the night of my grandmother's illness, the full-body jerking had started soon after our visit to the obstetrician at Kaiser. Now, neurologists, seeing this condition in postmenopausal women, believe it may be brought on by undiagnosed diabetes. I thought my pregnancy had caused it, and my mother's pained expression told me that she thought so, too. But the jerking and a letter from her doctor that recommended she take a leave from teaching gave her a cover story. She told people we were moving to a warm climate for her health.

SO MUCH FOR MY PARENTS, but what about us, the teenagers at the center of this drama? On the application to the Florence Crittenton Home, a section asked about the baby's "alleged father." John, I said, was born March 28, 1944, a square on the calendar that I still experience with a feeling of searing loss. Of Scotch-Irish descent, he worked during the summer as a plumber's apprentice. He was a junior at Bellarmine as of July, the date of the form. He would be a senior in the fall.

How long had I known him? "Since last summer," I wrote. Does he admit paternity? "Yes." Will he pay for your care here? "Yes, he, my mother, and his parents," for that was what they had settled on.

The form required me to write a brief description of him (height, weight, coloring, personality):

6′ or 6′ 1″, 175 lbs., brown hair, light skin, green eyes, excellent personality, is studying to be an engineer, has seven brothers and sisters. We plan to get married when we graduate from college.

The plan to get married after college aligned with my mother's desire that my reputation not be ruined and John's father's wish that his future not be compromised.

Filling out the forms gave me a chance to state my case—that John and I were good people, college bound, and sharing a common faith. I was trying to imply that we weren't like "the others," for whom, I imagined, sex did not involve fidelity and faith.

CHAPTER 24

GOING AWAY

I was two people. The first was me, trying to cope with day after day of prolonged nausea that I feared would continue the whole nine months. The other girl pretended to be normal and sat for her final in Human Physiology. Behind her teacher's desk, jars of fetal cats, pigs, and sharks floated in formaldehyde, and as she sat there with five sharp No. 2 pencils next to her lab partner, the Nobel Prize winner's son with whom she shared memories of a dissected cat, she recalled the adventure this class had been, how, at the beginning of the year, she had known nothing about DNA and RNA or about the inner workings of the body. Now, she knew how bodies evolved from our genetic ancestors and how remnants of those ancestors lived on in the very makeup of our mitochondria.

On the day school let out, that girl—the one thinking she might like to become a biochemist—disappeared. I took off my girdle and let my stomach muscles relax. My mother, uncle, and John's parents had mapped out a life-altering path that I, from then on, would have to keep secret. No bike rides and no swimming. Trapped indoors, constantly nauseated and heartsick, I lived with a woman who rarely spoke and whose shoulders sagged with the weight of what I'd done. But even in such circumstances, my mother was never one to tolerate idleness.

I had outgrown all but one of my blouses, a white boat neck that had always been two sizes too big. If I wore a regular skirt and safety-pinned the waistband, I could pull the blouse down over my hips, the sailor's "midi" look. "You're not going to fit in that much longer," my mother said. "You need to make new clothes."

She took me to the fabric store to find fabric and a muumuu pattern. I devoted my mornings to spreading fabric on the dining room table and pinning the pattern pieces. After lunch, I vacuumed up the threads and did the ironing. By three or four, I was tired and sat in Grandma's rocking chair, listening to her radio and hooking the rug she had left unfinished. Because my mother told me I could not leave the house, I had to content myself with Reader's Digest Condensed Books. The shortened versions of *Marjorie Morningstar* and *Green Mansions* ended too quickly and were dumbed down, leaving me longing for a library where I could browse the stacks and pick a book at random.

To pay his share of our moving expenses, John had started at his father's company; his dad had him working six days a week and moving pipe from one side of the warehouse to the other. On Saturdays, the office closed at 3:00 p.m., and then John drove down from Burlingame.

On the last Saturday before my mother and I were to leave for Phoenix, John's Fairlane pulled up beyond the picket fence, half an hour later than I'd expected. He came up the front walk, hitching his khaki pants and looking toward the open door. As if he were my brother and not the love of my life, we sat in my living room, our knees chastely touching.

"Sorry I'm late," he said. "I went home and showered."

"That's okay."

"I think my big problem is I have you on the brain." He threw an arm across the back of the sofa, a gesture that in the privacy of his car would have invited me to turn sideways and slide my fingers down his pants.

I didn't dare.

"I'm glad you're thinking about me," I said.

"I had a dream last night."

"What about?"

"I can't remember the details, but you were in there someplace." He leaned forward, took my hand, and caressed my thumb. That was his signal. A week was a long time for both of us, and it had been three weeks. John must have been climbing the walls.

Hearing a noise from the kitchen, I yanked my hand away. "I got my grades."

"How'd you do?"

"A's in everything except Algebra II."

"What'd you get in that?"

"B-minus."

"I thought you took that before."

"I did, and I got a C. I needed to get an A this time to bring up my GPA to a 4.9, and I'm mad at myself."

"Actually, it's all a big joke," he said.

"What's a big joke?"

"All this worry about college. I'm going to join J. D. Salinger and write some haikus."

"Learn to dance first."

"After you get back."

My mother stopped on her path from the kitchen to the bedroom. Her deadpan gaze settled on us. Like a cloud of gnats, weariness and disappointment followed her from room to room. "Since you're here, John, could you mow the lawn?"

John looked at me. "Sure. When?"

"Now," she said.

"Can't it wait?" I asked.

"The tenants are coming over."

"All right," he said, and stood.

"I can sit on the porch and keep you company," I said.

"Someone might see you," my mother said. "You can sit out on the patio while he mows the back lawn."

I went out the kitchen door, opened the back door of the garage, and showed John the rusty push mower. "Wait, wait," I said. "Let me hit it with some 3-in-One Oil." I brought the yellow metal can from my father's tool kit and squirted oil down around the wheels. Now, when John pushed it, the mower would hum.

While he tackled the front yard, I raked leaves off the grass in back. The tenants, a young couple with two kids, came outside to take a quick look at the yard, and I knelt in the flower bed and pretended to pull weeds. After they'd gone, I washed my hands in the hose and held it while John took a drink.

My mom was boxing up the kitchen. This whole move thing was like the Cave Train ride at the Santa Cruz boardwalk. You stepped into the moving car, an attendant strapped you in, and then the little car clanked forward, slamming through the big wooden doors and plunging into the dark. Phoenix, straight ahead.

"Marylee," my mother called from inside, "can you have John carry boxes to the garage?"

"We want to spend some time together," I said. "I can do it later."

"No!" she called. "I don't want you lifting heavy things."

"Where do you want the boxes?" I asked.

"In the garage loft."

John brushed his thighs with the backs of his hands. "Grass stains. My mom's going to kill me."

"Every time you show up, my mom has something for you to do."

"I don't mind helping her out, but if I'd known, I would have worn jeans."

He made twenty trips carrying boxes out to the garage, where the previous owners had built a loft. To the right of the loft were narrow shelves where my mother stored canned fruit, vegetables, and jam. Below the loft sat a wooden barrel that contained my grandmother's Haviland china. I pulled up the lid, picked up a gravy boat, and held it to the light.

"Grandma left me this in her will," I said. "It's part of my trousseau." The porcelain was so thin, you could see through it.

He took the gravy boat, returned it to the barrel, and tamped down the lid. Then he swiveled me around, hiked up my muumuu, and thrust into me from behind.

I leaned over the barrel and held my breath until he came, and then wondered why I had let him do it. The garage smelled like the tidepools, salty and damp.

John zipped up his cock and smoothed my skirt. Then he turned me around. What if my mother had walked in?

I covered my face and, already grieving, let out a sob.

"Come on, now," he said, pulling out a handkerchief. "The time will fly."

What I wanted—desperately—was to fix what had just gone wrong, namely, my deep disappointment in how he had chosen to spend our last hour together, but I didn't really know why I was so upset, and told myself not to be so stupid.

He put his arms around me and rested his cheek on my head.

A few steps away, the screen door ratcheted open.

"Marylee, could you or John give me a hand?" my mother called.

I pushed him away.

"Be right there," I said.

"I'll fly down there for Christmas," John said. "Cross my heart and hope to die. When do you go to the home?"

"November."

This might have been the moment to talk about the baby, but the home wasn't real. The baby wasn't real. Besides, my mother needed help.

We went inside. The kitchen smelled like Magic Marker. More boxes. On them my mother had written, "Pots and pans," "Fruit-cake pans and cookie cutters," "Fragile," and "This side up." I took the light boxes, John, the heavy ones. By the time we were finished, it was five forty-five. My mother was putting a Pyrex dish of maca-roni and cheese in the oven.

"I should get home for dinner," John said, washing his hands. "Looks like you're going to eat before too long."

"It's just leftovers," she said. "I'm too tired to cook."

"Well, take care, Mrs. Benham."

She sighed and used her apron to wipe her forehead. "Say hello to your mother."

John looked at me and shook his head. My mother hadn't even thanked him.

In the living room, he sidestepped the ironing board.

"I should put that in the garage."

"Want me to do it?"

"It's not heavy."

"Whatever you say." He slid the chain from the door.

"Wait," I said. "One more hug."

He opened his arms, and I stepped into his embrace. His cheek rested on my head, and my hands met behind his back.

"I'm going to miss you," he said, his voice cracking.

"Write," I said.

"I will." He broke free. "Call you later."

I wiped my nose with the back of my hand. Five months until I saw him. An eternity.

As I helped my mother with the last of the packing, I could not have imagined that I would never again live in this house, but that is the way it turned out. When we returned from Phoenix, my mother rented an apartment. After I left for college, she moved back to the house, renting out my grandmother's apartment so that she would have company and could afford the house payments. She lived there quite happily for five years.

Then, on September 21, 1970, in the middle of the night, I got a call from her renter. My mother had had a massive stroke. For a week she was hooked up to a ventilator, unable to talk, the right side of her body paralyzed. When I spoke to Dr. Konstanz, the same mustachioed doctor who had cared for my grandmother, he told me he had put a DNR order in her chart. The daughter of a doctor wouldn't want her life prolonged.

A week later, she had a second stroke and died. As I cleaned out the house, I found the barrel of my grandmother's Haviland. By that time, the uneaten jars of peaches would likely have caused botulism, and I threw them out.

PART IV

PHOENIX

CHAPTER 25

HEAT

We arrived in Phoenix on July 17, 1961, and my mother rented a one-bedroom stucco bungalow in a motor court of identical small dwellings. Our unit, next to the alley and the garbage cans, had a green door with a little peephole.

"Always look out before you open it," my mother said.

"Do you think Daddy could find us?" I said.

"I hope not, but he's very resourceful."

Resourceful or not, I didn't see how he could possibly know where we were. Until today, even we hadn't even had an address. Plus, my mom had arranged to pick up her mail at the post office, using general delivery. Inside the bungalow, she told me to take the bedroom.

Our place would have been unbearable without the swamp cooler, but its day-and-night racket, its glass-rattling whir, made it hard to concentrate.[1] What I remember of that place is how yellow light came through the window shades and fell on the living room's hide-a-bed.

John wrote every couple of days. He'd just learned to use the pipe threader and driven over to Modesto to help install a boiler.

Dear Marylee,

I received the letter you wrote Monday. The letters sort of keep you close to me. Although time goes by fast here, it seems like a million years ago that you were home taking it easy. You can't realize how much I appreciate your letters. I've been getting one just about every day. I've been thinking about college. What I'd like to do is get married, not wait until I graduate. I guess that's not too cool, though. Anyway, it would be nice. I told my parents I was going to fly down there and see you at Christmas, and my dad said how was I going to pay for that? I have so much on my mind, sometimes it feels like my brain's about to explode.

Love,
    John

I wrote back that I'd love to get married. The sooner the better, and maybe it was just being apart that made him feel overwhelmed. We could work our way through school. He could get a scholarship. I could study for a GED and go to De Anza Junior College. I had money from my grandfather's train accident to cover my books and tuition. As far as money to live on was concerned, we didn't need much. "I understand about your brain feeling like it's going to explode," I said. "The only way I can calm myself down is with food."

"Don't get fat," he wrote back.

I promised I wouldn't, although ever since I could remember, I had been battling the same five pounds, and in my current state of perennial nausea, snacking was the only thing that took away the queasiness.

One week went by. Then another. Still John did not respond to what I'd said about marriage. Maybe he'd spoken to his parents or shown them my letter. I prayed he had not. His father would think this was another instance of Marylee being too forward. What I'd put down in print, an actual plan that might have allowed us to keep our child, simply disappeared.

As to how John was spending his time, he wrote that on weekends he went over to Santa Cruz with Tillie. He and another friend spent a week hiking in Yosemite. He sent me postcards of Half Dome and El Capitan.

Seeing those postcards enraged my mother. "He ought to be sending us money," she said. I didn't understand why she was upset. John earned only minimum wage. Taking one week off for a vacation didn't seem like a big deal. Sadly, I had no idea how money worked: that the roof of our sweltering little bungalow didn't magically appear over our heads; that the allowance my mother doled out was money she had to earn. I didn't understand that come September, when her health leave officially began, she would have no money coming in, apart from whatever her tenants paid in rent.

Before Labor Day, school and football practice got under way. John played in the Catholic Athletic League, in which Serra High School was Bellarmine's big rival. He was Number 86 and played defensive end. He wrote that football was "keeping him out of trouble," whatever that meant.[2]

As far as I could tell from his letters and our brief phone calls, John's life back home was pretty much a repeat of his junior year, except that now he was a senior. To keep his mind off "what was going on down in Phoenix," he was taking various fitness and aptitude tests required by West Point. He asked what I was up to, how I was spending my days.

"I'm basically doing nothing except reading," one of my letters said. "We live in something called a 'motor court,' except there aren't any cars because barely anyone lives here. My mom says people from the Midwest don't come down until December, and that's why we got the place for cheap."

I normally read until 1:00 or 2:00 a.m. and woke up at noon, when my bedroom became unbearable. Then I made toast and drank a 7-Up. Nothing else tasted good. I pretty much subsisted on toast and saltines.

Knowing that I would miss the first semester of my junior year, my mom had ordered high school extension courses from UC Berkeley: history, Spanish, art, and English. After I finished breakfast, I sat at the kitchen table and tried to do the assignments. They were deadly dull and, with my mother hovering over my shoulder as if I were one of her slow learners, I made almost no progress and would in fact return from Phoenix with three incompletes, classes I forced myself to toil away at the following summer.

Responding to my request for research materials to complete a history assignment, my mother lifted the ban on my going out in public and took me to the Phoenix Central Library. I reread *The Brothers Karamazov*, but I did not like it nearly as much as when I'd read it in eighth grade, and my mother soon made it clear she didn't approve of me reading all the time. "You'll ruin your eyes, and it's not good for you to stay holed up in your room."

I knew that, of course, but in case my father had somehow gotten wind that we were in Arizona, she didn't want me outside until it was dark, at which point I was allowed to go swimming.

The problem was, we had no television. Reading was the only way I could calm myself, and the books had to be long and emotionally complex, or my mind would drift. I reread Hawthorne's *The Scarlet Letter* and asked a librarian if she knew of other books like it. She directed me to Thomas Hardy's *Tess of the d'Urbervilles*, Victor Hugo's *Les Misérables*, Gustave Flaubert's *Madame Bovary*, and Jean Des Vignes' *Forever Amber*. All were novels about women who defied society's sexual norms, either by having children out of wedlock or by having affairs. The women paid a price for their defiance. And it wasn't just the women who suffered—their children and parents suffered, too. I understood the many facets of this suffering and saw that my mother was paying the price for what I had done. Every morning I awoke to hear my mother grunting and struggling to lift the hide-a-bed's metal frame.

Wanting to redeem myself in her eyes and believing she must want company, I unfolded a TV tray to hold my propped-up book. In the living room's only chair, I held my Grandma's ever-expanding rug and stabbed my wooden hook.

My mother stretched out on the sofa. "You should eat more," she said. "You look like a scarecrow."

By this time—the first week of October—I *was* eating. Too much, in fact. But then I would throw up. My body reacted negatively to whatever my mother put in front of me: liver and onions, canned spinach—things she said I needed because of their iron content.

"I can't eat a big meal at night," I told her.

"If you don't like what I'm making," she said, "then cook for yourself."

"I don't have any money."

"I'll give you fifteen dollars a week."

"Will that be enough?"

"If you budget," she said. "You need to learn some responsibility."

What that meant, exactly, I didn't know. For a person my age, I was very responsible. I got good grades. I did my homework without having to be reminded. I made my bed and did the dishes after dinner, even when she got every pan in the kitchen dirty and when the can of congealed bacon grease on the stove top overflowed.

The refrigerator in our stucco bungalow was smaller than the one at home, and an inch of ice quickly formed on the freezer compartment. "It's going to be your job to defrost that," my mother said, putting a saucepan of water on to boil. I was to remove the contents of the freezer, stack everything on the kitchen table, and cover the frozen food with dishcloths. Then I was to put the saucepan in the freezer and slam the freezer door but leave the refrigerator open. As soon as the ice melted on the freezer's sides, I could slide a pancake turner between the metal and the ice. If I removed the ice chunks before they melted, then I wouldn't have to mop up a mess in the refrigerator.

"Any questions?" she asked.

"No," I said.

"Don't use a knife, whatever you do."

"I wasn't even thinking about it."

"Well, don't. You could damage the cooling coils."

I was to do this chore once a week, on the afternoon before we went to the grocery store.

When the air temperature fell to ninety or whatever the evening low might be, we drove to the grocery store and picked up food.

Back home, my mother put away her food, and I put away my soda crackers and jugs of milk and Cheerios and fish sticks. She put away her chicken and hamburger and pimento loaf. I stocked the fridge with TV dinners; Swanson's turkey dinner with a dollop of cranberry sauce was my favorite.

My responsibility in the evening was to take out the trash before I went swimming. I crumpled the aluminum TV tray and carried out the bucket, then soaped it and left the lid open to dry. I did that to make sure she didn't have another reason to fault me or to feel aggrieved that I wasn't the daughter she thought I was. But that didn't mean I had to talk to her.

Over the course of a day, my mother and I said maybe ten words to each other. "Do you want . . .?" "Are you ready to . . .?" Two prisoners sharing a cell might have spoken more.

The thing was, my mother didn't read, not the way I read. It struck me as strange for a teacher to go to the library and not check out a single book, not even the Reader's Digest Condensed Books that came regularly to our house. My mom never wanted to play chess or Chinese checkers, and after a time or two, I stopped asking. When I wasn't doing my homework, she sat in the kitchen and, for an hour or two, occupied herself with solitaire or writing letters to her friends back in Colorado, the people she'd known since before her marriage, back when she was Doc Pitney's daughter.

After dinner, my mother unfolded the sofa bed and, arms beneath her head, rested under the swamp cooler. I read for forty-five minutes, the time required for me not to die by getting a stomach cramp, and then I changed into my swimsuit—one of the gathered kind. My stomach stretched it out.

In my high school pool, I had earned my junior lifesaver certification and taught swim lessons for the Red Cross. During my freshman year, I had gone out for swim team; backstroke was what I was best at, but good enough only for the relay. Besides my weekly trips to the library, the motor court's bean-shaped pool was the only place I could get away from my mother and escape into a familiar, buoyant world.

I swam between nine and ten o'clock in the evening. Drained as I was by the day's heat, I would hang in a dead man's float or swim underwater, holding my breath, trying to see how many laps I could do before I had to surface. I swam from the shallow end, where my belly scraped the bottom, to the deep end, where a single glass eye shone through the fogged water. Breast-stroking, I touched my fingers to the light's ferocious heat. When I surfaced, gulping in mist from the sprinklered lawn, thick black bugs floated on the surface. They weren't beetles, exactly, or sow bugs, which were smaller and curled in the fetal position, and they weren't cockroaches scuttling up the walls or out by the garbage cans, where it was now my job— my *responsibility*, as my mother was so fond of reminding me—to take out the trash.

The bugs had thick bodies and segmented carapaces. They reminded me of blackened almonds, each with a hard nub of a tail. Their front legs were shaped like a crab's and circled together in pincers, struggling frantically to grab my finger. Three bulbous eyes reminded me of my mother's. Then came two vestiges of legs, bent like clothes hangers and sticking straight out. Behind those legs, not even halfway back, two more crablike legs turned toward the rear, the pushers that helped the bugs scuttle away from the filter's intake.

The Phoenix library didn't have any books about bugs, and so even today, I can't place these creatures in any taxonomy. But they were there: complex, interesting beings that populated the pool at night. My friends.

Shortly before ten, my mother limped out and stood beneath the yellow light, her arms crossed, her mouth an upside-down horse-shoe. Fighting against the water's downward pull, I hauled my body up the ladder.

"It's your birthday tomorrow," she said. "I thought we could go out to dinner."

My birthday. God, not how I'd ever pictured it, not that birthdays ever gave me much pleasure.

"It might be easier to just eat at home," I said.

"No," she said. "I want to take you out."

What I wanted to do, in the deepest sense, was get out of here—out of Phoenix; out of the "situation"; out of watching my belly get bigger by the day. But I didn't want to disappoint her when she was making a clumsy attempt to do something nice.

In fourth grade, right after we'd moved into our new house, she'd invited over the girls from my old Brownie troop, the girls I'd made paperweights with the day the queen was crowned. I hadn't seen them all summer, and they acted like they didn't know me. After their parents picked them up, I went to my room and cried. My dad stormed in and said I shouldn't act like a baby.

In *The Primal Wound*, Nancy Verrier writes that adoptees often sabotage their birthdays, which "commemorate an experience, not of joy, but one of sorrow and loss."[3]

Verrier's point is that even children adopted as infants carry a sense-memory of separation from the mother they expect to meet when they emerge from the womb: the heartbeat, the voice, the breast. Babies destined for adoption were not brought to their mothers immediately after birth. They were cared for in the hospital nursery and often taken to a foster home.[4] The "memory" of this displacement lies below the level of conscious thought. Adult adoptees are often left with a horrible, visceral sense of abandonment and displacement on the day of our birth. When I look back on my life in its entirety, birthdays were—and are—the worst days of my year.

I picked up my rubber thongs from a pool chair and dropped them on the pool deck. Then I bent over to towel-dry my hair. My mom wouldn't let me go to bed with a wet head—it would give me a cold—and in this heat, I couldn't bear to turn on a hair dryer. The whole time, she was watching me with that look she called her eagle eye.

I wrapped the towel around my waist and tucked it in. She looked me up and down.

"I'm so thankful my mother's not alive to see you like this," she said.

"You're glad Grandma's dead?"

"If she wasn't dead already, this would have killed her."

"Mom! Please!"

She was right, of course. Oh, and by the way, happy sixteenth birthday.

"Let's go to the IHOP," I said. That shouldn't strain her budget.

"Are you sure?"

"Yes," I said.

"Can you still fit into your blouse?"

"I think so."

My sixteenth birthday should have opened a mini portal, giving me a foretaste of adult privilege. For most teens, sixteen is the age when the outlines of adult identity begin to firm up. Instead, my puzzle pieces had gotten jumbled and I was having to start from scratch. Still, it was a mile marker. I should find a way to mark the occasion, something that would be meaningful to me.

Back in the apartment, I looked in the cupboard. Duncan Hines' spice cake was my favorite. We had a box. There was cream cheese in the fridge and powdered sugar in the cupboard. I could make myself a cake. Sixteen years earlier, I had entered the world, born to a girl who was, according to my mother, just like me. In my peripheral vision, I saw a shadowy female figure, the silhouette of a young woman who had given birth sometime around her own sixteenth birthday. I longed for her and wished I could speak to her about being pregnant and unwed. She would understand.

Mary Kathryn, the author's birth mother, was sixteen in 1945. Just visible beneath the cat is the slight bulge of her stomach. She was five months pregnant. She was, indeed, a blue-eyed blonde and of Irish descent, but her mother and aunts had dark hair and brown eyes.

CHAPTER 26

LINGERIE

To keep from running the oven during the heat of the day, I got up at seven and had a cake in the oven by seven thirty. While it baked, I made the frosting and put it in the refrigerator. From the lady who collected our rent, my mother had found out about the Park Central Mall. We would go shopping to buy me a bra. Then we would have pancakes at IHOP. By the time we came home, the cake would have cooled, and I could decorate it and add the leftover sprinkles from the one I'd made for my mother's birthday. Finally, we had a plan.

"Does that sound good?" my mother said.

"Yes, perfect," I said.

At Goldwater's, we took the elevator to the third floor and found Ladies' Undergarments, which was where my mother said I needed to go to be "properly fitted." Ladies' Undergarments was where she bought her corsets. Her back was bad, and her legs were thin, the only part of her that looked remotely like the flat-chested flapper in my grandfather's photo albums.

She stopped at a rack. I slid around to the opposite side.

"May I help you?" A clerk in a peach-colored cotton dress boxed me in against a column.

My mother peered over the top of the rack. "She needs to be fitted for a bra."

"I need underpants, too," I said.

"Let's start with the bra." The woman took a tape measure from her pocket.

Like a mummy's arms, mine crossed over my chest.

"Hold your hands above your head, dearie."

I did.

Her tape measure circled my breasts. "A thirty-six should do," she said. "C cup, I think."

"Try a D," my mother said.

"Would she like an underwire?" the woman said.

"No!" I said. "Just a plain bra."

"Cotton or nylon?"

"I don't know," I said. "Just make it plain, with no lace or anything."

It wasn't like John was going to see it. And even if he did, he'd have it off in two seconds. What I wanted was the bra I'd seen in a sack at Walgreens. Anyway, I didn't want to wear an old-lady bra with wires. I didn't even want to shop in this department.

The clerk led us to the fitting room and said she'd bring bras for me to try on. My mother sat down in a chair and whispered through the curtain, "Make sure you keep your blouse pulled down."

I tugged the hem of the white boat-neck blouse down around my hips. It had taken three large safety pins to secure the waistband of my skirt. Having done that, I leaned back against the wall and waited for the clerk.

She brought five bras. "Remove your blouse, dearie," she said. Then, seeing my face, she added, "Would you rather have privacy?"

"Yes," I said.

She handed me the bras, each dangling from its own small hanger. "Try one on, and if it doesn't fit, hand it out and I'll bring another."

I unclipped a bra.

Outside, the clerk and my mother were talking about the weather. How hot it was this late in September. How unusual this was. My mother talked about the weather in California. "The city motto where we're from is 'Climate Proved Best by Government Test,'" my mother said.

"Wait till November," the woman said. "You'll be glad you're here."

November. I would be in the home.

I pulled off my blouse and looked over my shoulder at the straining hooks and eyes of my old bra.

"Doing okay in there?" the woman shouted.

I grabbed for my blouse. "Fine. Don't come in."

"Are any of them fitting?"

"I'm just on the first one."

"I can come in if you like."

"No!"

"She's at a difficult age," my mother said.

"Sometimes they . . ." The clerk lowered her voice.

A water balloon of a breast. How gross! One at a time, I put them in the cups. Then I fastened the hooks on my new bra. The bra size was right—it wasn't binding. I felt like Jane Mansfield. From a B to a D. The price tag said $21. I didn't understand why a plain bra with no lace cost that much, or why the one in Walgreens that looked just like it cost $5. At least I knew the size. I'd take just one, and when I'd saved enough from my allowance, I'd buy another at the drugstore.

I started to get back into my old bra, but it was too small, and when I lifted the straps over my shoulder, the safety pin at my waist unsnapped.

"Yeow!" I said.

The curtain flew open. The clerk looked at me, her eyes going down my body, then up to my breasts. They paused there. I spun around to face the wall and, in the mirror, saw her looking at the safety pin on my skirt. Her face reddened.

"You're bleeding," she said. "Let me get the first-aid kit."

"Please, no," I said, "but would it be okay if I wore the new bra home?"

"Surely," she said. "Let me go get scissors. I'll cut off the tag."

She slid the curtain shut, and as I put the bra back on, I listened to my own ragged breath. I redid the safety pins and slid the blouse over my head. Then I looked in the mirror.

From the shoulders up, I looked like myself—same pageboy as always, same oblong boat neck resting on my shoulders. But below my shoulders, the blouse compressed my boobs so much that my nipples showed through the fabric. The hip-length hem contained a bulge half the size of my tetherball. I turned sideways. From deep in my abdomen, I felt a flicker of movement. Had I imagined that? I smoothed my hand over my belly. There it was again, the signal of a finger tapping out Morse code. My God, a baby. This couldn't be real.

The woman returned with scissors, and I turned my back so she could cut off the tag. My mother never let me wear new clothes home from the store. I hoped she wouldn't be upset. Also, the bra cost a fortune, and I hadn't asked permission before I'd said I'd buy it.

CHAPTER 27

THE CRITTENTON MISSION

We all have different layers of self. The person I am in my seventies—mother, grandmother, former carpenter, writer, and wife—has age-spotted hands; graying, wispy hair; and osteoarthritis. This person—this version of me—reluctantly went along with her husband's move to Phoenix, sensing that his career rightly took precedence over her wishes and that, apart from the "crying baby," she had no good reason to justify staying in Evanston. Since that move, when driving the date-palm-lined historic neighborhoods of old Phoenix or catching glimpses of the red double humps of Camelback Mountain, that older, wiser self had sat silently, listening to her husband natter on about his research, a passenger overcome by sorrow.

I speak of "she" because it is easier to see myself from the outside—competent, caring, successful in many dimensions of life, not the least of which is being an empathetic listener and booster of this man who has made an extraordinary contribution to saving the environment. In a water-short state and a water-short world, an environmental engineer whose specialty is cleaning up contaminated groundwater is everybody's hero, and I was glad to be the canoe that bobbed along behind the ocean liner of his career.

But that was not the only me. As with the many tiers of a cake, there was a middle layer, the sixteen-year-old girl stuck in the endless loop of trying to figure out what, exactly, had contributed to her signing the surrender papers, consigning her son to being an ugly duckling—the smart boy with the big nose and deep laugh. And the very bottom layer, out of reach of her conscious mind, lay the bassinet of the crying baby, who, over the years, has made her infrequent and futile protests.

To untangle the interwoven strands of loss and identity, this older me needed to confront the bogeyman of the past. John and I had married, and I had graduated from Stanford, so, clearly, the moving escalator on which I had set foot the moment we arrived in Phoenix had taken me to my desired destination. In Phoenix I had been "re-virginized," and after I gave birth to my son, my life started all over again. And yet. And yet. Inside me lodged a lava-like knot of humiliation, shame, and rage. This might very well have been the same rage that welled up decades later in Jim the therapist's office, but it might also have everything to do with what had happened in my teens, when I had no power to direct my own affairs. Today, I would call this *agency*.

To untangle the strands of this history—the tiny, crying baby being drop-kicked into the universe and landing in the home of Rex and Lorene Benham, and the teenage girl emerging from a pupa-like state into the butterfly of adolescence, I needed to have a better understanding of why the adults in my life had decided I should go to Phoenix in the first place. I wanted to understand the Crittenton Home's mission and why I wound up there.

In combing through old issues of Arizona newspapers, I discovered that businessman and evangelist George N. Crittenton had purchased the land for the Crittenton Home for Wayward Girls in 1897. An article in the *Arizona Republic* said that "the generous-hearted, far-seeing women of the community of Phoenix got behind the movement to establish this shelter for the girls in need and distress. Charles N. Crittenton, a New York businessman, visited the state of Arizona and gave liberally of his wealth to help build the Florence Crittenton mission."

A CRITTENTON HOME DEED – Among the documents filed with the country recorder yesterday was a deed from Charles N. Crittenton, trustee for the Florence Crittenton Rescue home [sic] for this city, to the National Florence Crittenton mission of Washington, D.C. The deed conveys lots 21 and 22 of block 8, Dennis addition, the location of the Crittenton home. The deed is made, as it states, for the purpose of carrying out the original intent of the trust.

The Florence Crittenton Home's original purpose was to help unmarried women learn skills that could help them support their children. Placing children for adoption was not part of the founder's mandate. Residents of the Crittenton Home kept their babies with them until they could get on their feet again.

By 1898, a seven-bedroom brick building had replaced the site's original structure, described as a wooden firetrap near the railroad tracks. Women's groups from as far away as Yuma held candy and crafts sales to furnish the place.

After World War II ended and soldiers came home, the number of unplanned pregnancies skyrocketed. Another building campaign began, with money coming from the community chest, Kiwanis clubs, and churches. According to an article in the *Arizona Star*, the new building cost $133,000 and opened October 1, 1954.

> The building has a capacity for 50 women who live in a dormitory separate from the hospital and nursery facilities. It also has a recreation room, dining room and multi-purpose room (which serves as a chapel, meeting room and work room) as well as the administrative offices.[1]

In 1961 there was no nursery, nor even any room large enough to use as one. In fact, there were no babies, but there were plenty of girls and women waiting to give birth, and, as the director had written, there was a waiting list.

CHAPTER 28

THE WAITING ROOM

Finally, November 12 arrived, and it was time for me to enter my seclusion. My mom said I should leave my skirt and boat-neck blouse in the closet. She'd bring them after I delivered. I folded a robe, nightgown, and muumuus into my suitcase, and on top piled coursework from Cal, library books, art supplies, and rag balls. Plopping my butt down on the suitcase, I squished it shut and then checked the drawers. Oops! I'd almost left a photo strip from a booth on the Santa Cruz boardwalk: me and John, our heads together, then kissing, then putting our faces right up to the camera so that our noses looked big. Of course, his looked big anyway. Half the time it was stuffed up, and he breathed through his mouth. Gosh, the things we knew about each other.

Outside, I threw my stuff in the backseat and squeezed behind the wheel. My mother, in a black jersey dress and veiled felt beret, locked the door and came around to the driver's side.

"Get out," she said. "I'll drive."

"Are you sure that's a good idea?"

"I need to get back in the habit."

After a few fits and starts, we were on our way.

Phoenix's wide, palm-lined streets were laid out in a grid, and from the valley's flatlands, the humps of Camelback Mountain were always in view. Ahead of us, a Good Humor truck slowed. Just in time, my mother lifted her foot off the gas and slammed on the brakes. I covered my eyes. God, I hoped she wouldn't rear-end the truck.

"Please be careful," I said, looking between my fingers. Tire shops, taquerias, and motels with names like the Log Cabin and Indian Country lined Van Buren. "And if you're shaky, don't drive."

"I'm okay," she said.

She didn't look okay to me, but I guess she just meant she wasn't getting worse.

At Thirteenth, she turned north, into a working-class neighborhood of motor courts and small stucco houses. Much as I wanted to get away from her, moving to the home was like moving to a new school. Surely, she'd offer some advice about making friends or keeping up with my assignments or not feeling anxious, because the home would look after me.

Instead, after she had pulled over to the curb, she lifted her veil and flipped down the visor. From her purse, she dug out a tube of lipstick and her compact and began powdering her cheeks. "You go on in. I need to put on my face."

Makeup wouldn't help, and anyway, who was she trying to impress? Next, an eyebrow pencil came out of her purse. Two brown arches. Wasn't she going to say anything? Cry? Break down and tell me she loved me?

She spun her lipstick out of the tube and applied it. With one of the used tissues in her purse, she blotted her lips. "Remember to watch your things. A place like this is certain to attract a bad element."

A bad element. Gosh. People could probably say that about me. I opened the door. Better get this over with.

A high concrete-block wall and ten-foot-high oleander hedge hid a one-story building made of sand-colored brick. The gate squeaked open. Carrying my suitcase and rolled-up rug, I stared at three girls coming toward me—a brunette with a pixie haircut, a year or two older than I was, and two other girls—high school or college age—

in smocks. The girl with the pixie haircut was pretty in an Aubrey Hepburn–ish sort of way, but her face was marred by acne. Two or three years older than I and a hundred pounds heavier, she walked as if a cannonball were about to drop from between her thighs. One of the girls walking toward me was nearly as tall as John—six feet. Except for being pregnant, she could have been a model for *Seventeen*. The third girl, with a ratted pageboy stiffened by hair spray, looked less pregnant than the others. Talking among themselves, the girls did a quick up-and-down of my body and smiled. How strange to be pregnant and smiled at. Even librarians gave me the old hairy eyeball.

I opened the screen. The waiting room had two chairs beneath a window on my left; on the right were two doors labeled VISITORS. I propped the rug in the corner and put my suitcase where my mom wouldn't trip. There she came, opening the screen, her gait steady for once. I had expected the opposite.

A sliding glass window opened into the home's office where a woman with an erect posture forced by a secretarial chair sat typing. We'd had those same chairs in my typing class. She opened the window.

"You must be Marylee," she said. "Wait just a moment. The director's on a phone call."

We sat. To calm my jitters, I picked up a dog-eared *American Girl* and read an article about oily skin and how a paste of water and oatmeal—if you let the paste get thoroughly dry—would draw the dirt from your pores. I should take better care of my complexion. I didn't want to leave here with a bunch of zits.

"Next time you go to the grocery store, could you pick up some Quaker oats?" I asked.

My mother sighed. "They provide meals."

I patted my cheek. "For my skin."

"Your complexion's perfectly clear. Oh, and make a list of books you want from the library."

"I don't know what books I want until I get there."

She looked sideways at my stomach. "You can't go like *that*."

"Like what?"

"You're big as a house."

I studied her: the tinge of violet in her newly permed hair; the powdered cheeks; the fingers nervously twisting an opal ring. She had been born in 1902, practically the turn of the century, and with her faint white mustache and powdered cheeks, she reminded me of Miss Havisham, the wealthy spinster in Dickens's *Great Expectations*. All she needed was a wedding dress.

A door across from us opened. The woman who stood there had steel hair that flew away from her face like the blades of a spinning metal fan. Mrs. South introduced herself.

Pushing off both arms of the chair, my mother stood. "I brought your letter."

"I don't require it," Mrs. South said, smiling at me. "We're expecting her."

"I thought I might come in and see her room," my mother said.

"Nonresidents aren't allowed back in the living area." She indicated two side-by-side door, each labeled VISITORS. "If you'd like to visit, call a day ahead and talk to Karla."

"I don't have a telephone," my mother said.

"Call from the post office," I said.

"Yes, I suppose I could."

No point prolonging the goodbyes. "If you don't mind, I'll walk my mother out," I said, taking her elbow. This would be our big moment of reconciliation. She could apologize and say how sorry she was that I was having to go through this, and I could say how getting pregnant wasn't something I had planned.

I accompanied her down the walk and stopped at the gate.

She held out my car key. "Do you need this?"

"You keep it."

"Can I have a hug?"

"If you take me to the library next Saturday."

"All right. I will, but I'll stay in the car."

"Fine," I said.

I forced myself to endure her embrace and a dry peck on my lips. I wiped off her lipstick with the back of my hand. My face felt hot and my forehead pinched. This had not gone at all how I'd expected. With no phone at home, my mom had no way to reach me if her condition got worse. Also, I forgot to mention I was low on Prell.

Then the gate creaked. At home, I would have hit it with some 3-in-One Oil, but here, the gate was someone else's—God, I hated this word—*responsibility*. I turned and went back up the walk. My mom started the car.

Inside, Mrs. South invited me into her office. Bookshelves lined the walls on the right. The late-afternoon glare from the falling sun shot through the window behind her, and the light on her hair made her look like a haloed saint. With her elbows spread and shoulder pads bulking up her dress, she made an imposing, official pyramid.

"I gather from the form you filled out," she said, looking at a paper on her desk, "that you and your father are estranged."

"That's sort of true," I said.

"Where is he now?"

"The last I heard, San Francisco," I said.

She made a note.

"And the father of the child?"

"He's alive," I said.

"No." The silhouette of her head shook. "Do you know who he is?"

I had put his name down on the form. Of course, I knew who he was. I wasn't some slut, not that I knew anybody else who was having sex. But, just to be certain, I told her again. My boyfriend was John MacDonald, an honor student at Bellarmine Academy.

In her 1963 testimony to Congress, Annette Baran, a social worker and researcher studying the long-term effects of adoption, said, "Information given to adoptive couples at the time of adoption is scanty and usually describes immature, confused, adolescent unwed mothers and fathers."[1] On that intake form, John and I were frozen in time. But I wanted to make sure there would be no later misunderstanding, and that my child would know—that the people in the home would know—this pregnancy was not the result of a casual relationship.

"My boyfriend and I are in love," I said, "and when we're old enough, we'll marry."

With a perky smile, Mrs. South said, "Of course you will, my dear. Now, let me show you to your room. All of our girls feel off balance when they first arrive, but in a few days, you'll feel right at home."

I doubted it. I didn't have a home. Renters had moved into my mother's house, and like in *Goldilocks and the Three Bears*, a stranger was sleeping in my bed. On the plus side, my mother had left. Over the silent summer and fall, tension had baked into my body. Now it melted.

CHAPTER 29

PAM

*T*he waiting room opened onto a wide, dark hall. I didn't have my watch on, but it must have been about three, and the lights were out. Same rule as at my house: No lights until six o'clock; eight thirty in summer. The room I was to occupy was just across the hall. I stood in the doorway, holding my rug and suitcase, and looking at four identical beds, two on each side. Thin bedspreads, a color between pink and beige, had cardboard-like ribbing.

"You're A," Mrs. South said, pointing to the first bed on the right. There were yellow built-in closets, two on the left and two on the right.

"Excuse me," she said, squeezing past. She opened a closet door. "Here's where you can hang your clothes."

A tennis racket and swimsuit would fit in, but not much else.

"It's pretty small," I said.

"Do your best. As you can see," Mrs. South said, indicating the neatly made beds, "we strive to keep a sense of order. In the morning before you go to breakfast, you will make your bed and put away your nightgown. If you take anything out of your locker, make sure you put it back."

"No problem." I heaved my suitcase onto the bed and unsnapped the locks.

"I'll go see if I can find Pam," Mrs. South said. "I think you two will hit it off." She pointed to the bed opposite mine. "That's Gloria's. Just so you aren't surprised, she's a Navajo. Gloria's quiet and doesn't talk much, but then, that's typical of Indians. Any questions?"

"How old are they?" I asked. "My roommates."

"Nineteen," she said.

I'd been hoping for someone closer to my age.

"Any other questions?"

"No," I said.

"Then I'll leave you to unpack."

I rolled the rug as tight as I could and stuffed it lengthwise in the closet. There were five wire hangers, just enough for my muumuus. A tier of drawers formed a sort of dressing table between the lockers. Embedded in the yellow paint were circles the size of nail polish bottles. I set out Grandma's brush, comb, and hand mirror. It wouldn't look good to have my rollers sitting out, so I found an empty drawer for them, my shower cap, and my Clearasil.

"Hi there!" said a reedy voice. "I'm your roommate Pam."

I turned to face a blonde with short, wavy hair and a swan's neck. To counterbalance the weight of her belly, she stood with her hands on the small of her back, and when she came toward me, extending a hand, she walked like a duck.

"You're Mary," Pam said.

"Marylee," I said, feeling my face turn warm. "All one word. Like 'M-a-r-y-l-e-e.' My last name is Benham, with a silent 'h.'"

Pam lowered her voice. "We don't use our last names. Karla blacks them out before she hands out our mail."

John would find that amusing. It was straight out of "Spy vs. Spy" in *MAD* magazine.

Pam looked at the workbooks, binder paper, colored pencils, pens, glue, and watercolors spread out on the bed.

"I see you brought art supplies," she said.

"I'm supposed to be taking a drawing class."

"My mother's an artist."

"Mine's a teacher."

"What grade?"

"Fourth," I said. "Her specialty is slow learners."

"Mine's an art teacher. No surprise." She looked up at the ceiling and made a clicking sound that reminded me of the geckos in Mexico. "We'd better do the tour. Grab your suitcase."

I followed her into the hall.

Across the way was a phone booth. She opened the bifold door. "The first thing you need to know about is phone etiquette."

Phone etiquette. Miss Emily Post.

"If you're expecting a call, make sure you're around so we don't have to run all over, trying to find you."

Where else would I be? Unless the place had a pool.

"Does your boyfriend call you?" I asked.

"Yes," she said. "We have a schedule."

"That's a good idea."

Continuing down the corridor, we passed a room in which two long couches and a couple of armchairs had been crammed. In the center of the circle sat a console TV with short, splayed legs. The room reeked of smoke.

"Do you smoke?" Pam asked.

"No! Yuck!"

"You won't be watching much TV, then."

"I'd rather read."

"Me, too," Pam said.

We had come to the end of the hall. She opened a door on the right. It was filled with suitcases—blue ones and pink ones and brown leather, all stacked on top of each other. A small bookcase and a card table stood in the corner.

"Is the luggage room always unlocked?" I asked.

"Don't worry about theft. You won't need your suitcase until you leave."

I added my suitcase to the pile.

Pam closed the door and crossed the hall.

"So, this here on the left," she said, pushing open a door, "is the sewing and ironing room. Oh, hi, Marianne. Meet the new girl."

A roly-poly plain Jane with squint lines and strands of silver hair stood arranging dresses on a clothing rack. "The Ladies Auxiliary keeps bringing in maternity clothes," Marianne said, checking the size tags. "I don't know what we're going to do with them all."

"What are maternity clothes?" I asked.

Marianne, her eyebrows shooting up, looked at Pam.

"Clothes for pregnant women," Pam said.

Marianne lifted a hanger and showed me the cutout of stretchy fabric on a pair of capris. "If you need pants, these might fit."

"I didn't bring any blouses," I said. "If there's a sewing machine, I might want to make another dress."

"We have two Singers, but first you should take a look at the clothes rack." Marianne beckoned me into the room. "I'm only five foot two and a petite. Otherwise, you could have my clothes."

"That's all right," I said. It made me feel weird thinking about wearing some other girl's clothes. Like wearing the clothes of a dead person. "I'd rather make something new."

"Atta girl," Marianne said. "Stay busy."

"Busy hands are happy hands," Pam said.

"That's the mantra around here," Marianne said. "Involve yourself in constructive activities. Less time to mope."

"I'm not moping." I was just reading a lot.

Pam was looking over her shoulder, and I could tell she wanted to finish the tour. This was like being back in seventh grade and having an eighth-grader take you from your locker to the gym to the lunchroom; all the while, you're staring at the inked-in numbers on the back of your hand and thinking you'll never remember your locker combination.

"If you ever want to talk," Marianne said, "my room's the single down near the clinic."

"Thanks," I said, backing from the room.

Out in the hall, I said, "But why would I want to? She seems nice, but I don't even know her."

Speaking from behind her hand, Pam said, "Marianne's sort of like an RA."

"What's an RA?"

"A resident advisor. They're seniors who live in freshman dorms. My boyfriend's one."

"What's his name?"

"Doug, but I call him Dougie."

"Dougie," I said, trying out the name. It sounded infantile.

I turned and looked back at the sewing room. "How old is she?"

"Marianne? Thirty-two."

"That's really old."

"She's not the oldest," Pam said.

"But why would someone her age be in here?" I asked.

"For the same reason we are," Pam said. "She's not married."

"Couldn't she *get* married?"

"Everyone has a different reason," Pam said.

"Is your boyfriend—Doug—paying for you to be in here?"

"He's going halvsies with my parents. Now, up these steps"—Pam indicated a narrow staircase that bent to the left— "is the schoolroom."

From above us, I heard giggling and chatter.

If this was a school, how did they get any work done with that racket? And besides, it was Sunday. Was school in session seven days a week? I followed Pam.

The room had four tables that made up a square. Around the square sat two dozen girls my age, all of them wearing maternity smocks. To fit their stomachs under the table, they had to slouch. Textbooks lay open. A woman Marianne's age handed out worksheets. Smiling, she looked up. "Oh, hi, Pam. Is this the new student?"

"This is Mary," Pam said.

"Marylee," I said, drawing out the syllables. "It's all one word."

"Welcome, Merrily," the teacher said.

I pronounced my name again. "Mary-lee." Under the circumstances, I shouldn't care what she called me. Every class started with the teacher mispronouncing my name, and I had to either sit and listen to it be pronounced "Merrily," as in "Merrily We Roll Along," or head that off at the pass.

"You're welcome to join us as soon as you get settled," the teacher said.

I didn't want to be rude, but this was Sunday. "Do you always have school on weekends?"

"I'm doing a makeup session," the teacher said. "I was out sick last week."

"She's for the high school students," Pam said. "I'm taking correspondence courses from the University of Wisconsin, but I work up here."

"My classes are from UC Berkeley," I said.

"Mrs. South told us you were in high school," Pam said. "Did you skip a grade?"

"They're high school courses from UC Extension."

"What grade are you in?" the teacher asked.

"I'm a junior," I said.

"Then you can sit next to Rhonda." She pulled out a chair next to a girl with a horse face and mounds of black curls. The curls ended in an inch of straight hair that looked like she'd gone to the men's barbershop. Rhonda's pencil was poised over a math worksheet, and her eyes went to my lip. The sun had given me a cold sore. Rhonda probably thought it was a zit.

"I'm here four hours a day," the teacher said. "You're required to be in the schoolroom during that time."

I couldn't concentrate if there was a lot of noise. The only way this made sense was if I gave up my correspondence courses and started in on whatever they were learning, but then that would have wasted my mom's money. It was November. I would be far behind. I didn't have all that long until I delivered.

"I'd rather just work in my room," I said.

"You should take that up with Mrs. South," the teacher said.

I was sure Mrs. South would think it was okay. After all, I was smart. Plus, I didn't see why she'd care, as long as I wasn't running up and down the corridor, making a nuisance of myself. My mother had not explained what this place was. She just talked about it as "the home" that I would go into when it got close to my "time." I guess I was enough my father's daughter to bristle at arbitrary rules.

Back downstairs, the corridor continued. Along the hall were more rooms, each with four beds. I thought of Ludwig Bemelmans's *Madeline* books. *In an old house in Paris that was covered in vines lived twelve little girls in two straight lines . . .* Pushing the panic bar on a door marked EXIT, Pam stood aside so that I could see the backyard, planted with Bermuda grass, its centerpiece an octagonal clothesline where girls could hang their hand washables.

We backtracked past our room and the director's office. Pam pointed out a dining room with cafeteria-style tables and an aluminum tambour that pulled down to hide the kitchen. We came to the end of the hall. Marianne's room, the only single and the only room painted blue, was tucked into the corner next to the visiting rooms, one of which could be entered from the hall. Pam turned into the clinic/hospital wing. This wing was half as long as the other wing. White molded-plastic chairs were pushed up against the walls. The hall ended abruptly at frosted-glass double doors.

"Let's say hi to Gloria," Pam said, taking my hand.

I found myself in a room with two beds and hospital curtains hanging from the ceiling. One bed was empty. The head of the other bed was raised, and a moon-faced girl with blue-black hair sat propped on pillows. From the bulge beneath the sheet, I could see that Gloria had not delivered.

"Hey, Gloria," Pam said. "I want to introduce our new room-mate, Marylee."

"Pleased to meet you," Gloria said.

"You, too," I said.

Pam went around to the far side of the bed and took Gloria's hand. "Did they say how much longer they're keeping you?"

"Until I deliver," Gloria said.

"Are you sick?" I asked.

"They want my blood pressure to come down." Gloria held out the arm nearest me and looked at the needle taped to the crook in her arm. It was attached to an IV. "I can't eat salt."

"Why is that?" I asked.

"Preeclampsia," Pam said.

My Physiology teacher would have known what that meant.

Pam and Gloria talked about Gloria's condition and the likelihood of her having something called a C-section, and then a nurse came and kicked us out. She had to check Gloria's blood pressure.

Pam pointed to the clinic at the end of the hall. That was where we would come for our weigh-ins and weekly exams. There was a nurse at the clinic twenty-four hours a day.

"When it's your time, the nurse will prep you and call an ambulance," Pam said.

"An ambulance! For what?"

"To take you to the hospital," Pam said.

She crossed the hall. "These are the rooms they put us in after we deliver."

A nurse in a white uniform, a starched hat, and squeaky shoes pulled a curtain around a bed.

"Why don't we stay in the hospital?" I asked.

"Because they don't want us in the maternity ward."

"Oh," I said, not sure who "they" were and why "they'd" care. The only time I'd been in the hospital was when I had my tonsils out. A nurse gave me ice cream, and it set my throat on fire.

When we returned to our room, our other roommate, Diane, had returned from her job in the kitchen. She tore off her white hairnet and threw it on the nightstand. This girl Diane was very pregnant. Her stomach was huge, and, unlike me in my muumuu, she wore a maternity top that reminded me of a throw cover over a sofa. Her thin brown hair was pulled back in a ponytail, and the skin of her forehead looked as taut and shiny as scalded milk. Washed out. Washed up.

She fell back on the bed and put her hands on her belly. "Bending over the dishwasher is killing my back."

"Why are you washing dishes?" I asked.

"We're all assigned chores," Pam said.

"The kitchen has a commercial dishwasher," Diane said, massaging her belly and moving so she could see me. "It steams and sanitizes the dishes, but you can also get a steam burn from opening it too fast." She held up her forearm. A burn ran the length of it. Her skin had blistered.

"My grandma would have put Crisco on a burn like that," I said.

"The nurse put bacitracin on it," she said.

That was good. For a minute there, I was beginning to think this was some kind of slave camp. We were supposed to come in here to be cared for, yet here was Diane, operating a commercial dishwasher like the lowliest busboy in a restaurant kitchen. If my father had known about this, he would have mounted a protest.

CHAPTER 30

THE CARD TABLE

*L*ate Monday afternoon, I squeezed into the phone booth and stacked piles of nickels and dimes. I needed to call John and tell him I'd moved in.

Mrs. South came out of her office. "I understand you wanted to speak to me."

"I need to talk to you about school," I said.

"Are you trying to call someone?"

"My boyfriend, but he doesn't answer."

A week earlier, when I'd called John from the library, he'd said he'd come straight home from football practice. I was using up my allowance and annoyed that his little brothers kept picking up the phone.

"Why don't you come into my office for a minute?" Mrs. South said. "I was in a rush yesterday, trying to figure out where we're going to put two more new girls."

I scooped change into my hand and put the coins in my pocket. When I made these muumuus, I had never dreamed the big pockets would come in so handy.

"Have a seat," Mrs. South said. She started to go around behind her desk but hesitated. "Would you like something from the kitchen? A chocolate milk?"

"Thanks," I said. "I would."

She left, and a moment later returned with a chocolate milk and a straw.

At home, my mother kept a canister of Nestle's Quik on the counter. I sucked up a mouthful. Too sweet, but chocolate was chocolate.

Behind her desk, Mrs. South had stacked three cardboard boxes of books. "I went to a yard sale last week. The teacher said we need some reference books."

"Is there a library here?" I asked.

"That's something I wanted to do when I came," she said. "I hoped the volunteers might set one up, but they had other priorities."

What other priorities could be more important than books?

"Pam said I should talk to you about the schoolroom," I said. "I spent the morning trying to study, but I couldn't concentrate."

Mrs. South opened a manila file. "Your mother wrote that she'd signed you up for classes through the University of California Extension Service, but wouldn't it be better for your transcript to say Central High? Your classes would transfer with no questions asked."

Would that be better? If the office staff at Woodside found out I was pregnant, the principal could kick me out. "I don't think my mom would go for it."

"I could talk to your mother."

"No! My mother has this chorea thing."

"Are you referring to the jerking?"

"Yes," I said. "Half her body jerks. 'Chorea' is a Greek word. 'Choreography' has the same root."

"And because she has this jerking, you don't want to switch schools?"

"First of all, I'm pretty sure she's already paid for my classes, and second of all, I'm pretty sure they wouldn't give her a refund."

She smiled. "Is there a third of all?"

"They sent me the workbooks. I should just get it done."

I had these courses, each one as thick as a phone book. I was supposed to send in the assignments at whatever intervals I wanted. With a table to study on, I might be able to make progress.

Mrs. South made a note. "The rules here are that anyone in high school must be in the schoolroom during normal class hours."

"I know, but it's noisy up there," I said. "I can't concentrate."

"It is noisy," Mrs. South said, "but that's because the girls are helping each other. It's a good time to get to know the other residents."

I didn't want to get to know the other residents, and I didn't need help.

"I'd rather study in my room."

Mrs. South made another note. "Unfortunately, we don't have desks."

"There's a card table in the suitcase room. I could use that."

"Oh, sure, the card table." Mrs. South smiled. "The only time that gets used is at Christmas. The Ladies Auxiliary puts the tree on it."

"It must be a pretty small tree."

"It has to be. We don't have that much space. Anyway, if you can study on a card table, I can't see the harm in it."

She made another note. "Girls like you are what make this job a joy."

Girls like me. I was no kind of girl.

"Thanks so much."

I closed the door, walked down to the kitchen, and dropped the milk box in the trash. Then I returned to the pay phone. Diane was in there, doubled over her big stomach and making a call. From her whispered "I love yous," I knew it had to be her boyfriend. We all had our guys.

CHAPTER 31

DIANE

*T*he best part of Phoenix—the only good part, besides the library and the pool—was the sky at sunset. The sun, hovering above the date palms, left them silhouetted against swaths of salmon light. Diane, her ponytail swinging, barreled through the slips hanging from the clothesline and set off toward the clinic wing. She reminded me of the leggy forwards in field hockey, girls running up and down while I bent over with a stitch in my side.

"So, how do you like Phoenix?" she asked.

"What's to like? I've been cooped up with my mother since July." At least here I felt normal. Everyone else was in the same boat, and even though we were all strangers, no one looked at me with that soul-shattering mix of disgust, pity, and chagrin.

Diane lengthened her stride. "Let me know if I'm walking too fast."

"If you want exercise, why don't you just walk on the sidewalk?" I asked.

"We're only allowed to sign ourselves out on Sundays between two and four," she said. "Besides, I live six blocks from here, the oldest of thirteen."

"I'm an only child," I said.

"Must be nice," she said.

"I'm adopted."

"I always wished I was adopted."

"I hate it."

"What's wrong with being adopted?"

"Hard to say." In fact, that had just popped out, and I hadn't understood until that very moment that I did hate it. I hated the circumstances that led to my being raised by my volatile and sadistic father, certainly, and really hated my mother—a complicated hate, because I could not help feeling its opposite, a well of sorrow for a woman who had martyred herself, partly on my behalf.

In *The Primal Wound*, Nancy Verrier writes that adoptees who do not act out in childhood "speak of having a sense that the baby they were had 'died,' and that the one that they became was going to have to be different, to be better, so that it would not be abandoned again. As children they were very polite, cooperative, charming, and generally 'good.' But locked inside them was pain and the fear that the unacceptable baby who had died would come back to life if they were not vigilant. They related an inability to show how they felt about things, especially negative feelings."[1]

At this point, the height of my teenage rebellion, I was kind of sick of people telling me what a good thing adoption was. I had spent years living with a terrifying father and months living with a mother who could not forgive me. I understood why she'd felt betrayed. Of course, I did. But, like the next person, I needed to be loved.

We rounded the clinic and arrived at the front of the building. Through the oleanders came the sound of male voices. One kid was smacking gum. A bubble popped.

Diane put a finger to her lips, grabbed my wrist, and hunkered down. I tried to quiet my breathing.

Then one boy said, "Is O'Brien starting?"

"Coach says he'll sit out another week."

"I heard the scout from the U of A's coming to the game."

The boys passed the gate, their shadows falling on the walkway.

"Yeah, but his concussion . . ." The voice drifted off.

When they were safely down the block, I stood, took Diane's hand, and pulled her up. "Did you recognize the voices?"

"One," she said. "The team manager. They're coming from football practice."

"Is O'Brien your baby's father?"

She hesitated a moment and looked at the ground. "He's my fiancé."

Maybe I should call John my fiancé.

But something in Diane's hesitation made me think O'Brien wasn't the father. That maybe he didn't even know about her pregnancy. We started off again, with me following. Maybe she and O'Brien weren't having sex. Or maybe she'd had sex with someone else. Or maybe she just meant she wanted to get married, and saying he was her fiancé was a way to make the sex part sound okay in the eyes of the Church. In any case, I'd figured out one piece of her story. She came from a family even larger than John's, and that probably meant she was the oldest and a kind of second mother.

When we came around to the backyard, I saw that someone had hung out maternity blouses and a pair of turquoise shorts. I wished I had something besides muumuus.

Diane tagged the clothesline's pole. "One down. Fifty-one to go. I walk a mile."

"How do you figure that?" I said.

"I know what pace I walk. I know how long I walk. Therefore, I know how many laps."

A "distance = rate x time" problem. Gosh, I hated those. "Are you a math person?" I asked.

"Math and science, yes," she said. She didn't even sound winded. "But as soon as I get my diploma, I'm going straight to secretarial college. We're going to put our baby in foster care. I'll get a job. We can get married, take the baby back, and tell everyone we're adopting. He'll be old enough then that I can put him with a babysitter and work while my husband finishes school."

"Good grief! That's complicated." Such a scheme would never work.

"Yes, but it's better than the alternative."

Diane was a tugboat, hauling O'Brien behind her. I had never met a girl so forward. Men were supposed to set the pace.

The sun had dropped nearly to the horizon. By the time we came back inside, it was almost dark. Diane's cheeks had turned neon pink, but even though her heart was obviously pumping, she climbed on her bed and began to bounce up and down, as if on a trampoline. Grandma would have had a heart attack.

"Isn't there a rule about jumping on the bed?" I asked.

"I have to deliver," she said, throwing her arms into the lift. "I need to get out of here by Christmas."

"You can always take some castor oil," Pam said, sitting on her bed. She reached around her belly and lifted up her foot, pressing a thumb into her ankle. "Edema," she said. "I'd better elevate my feet. Can you hand me Gloria's pillow?"

"Sure," I said, not sure what edema was or why putting her feet up would help. I tossed her the pillow.

"I've heard the weekend nurse will break your water," Pam said.

"What are you talking about?" I asked.

"It's another way to get your labor started," Pam said.

Diane, panting, reached out a hand, and I helped her down. She took a towel from her locker. "I'm going to wash my face, and then I'm going down to see Gloria. She's bored out of her gourd."

"If she wants a library book . . . ," I said.

"I'll ask," Diane said, heading out.

Pam turned on her side, her back to me. An unfolded letter lay on the nightstand.

I sat on my bed. The baby's foot pushed out. I cupped it in my hand and gave a gentle push.

Pam rolled over slightly and looked in my direction. "It's Dougie's birthday."

"What do you think he's doing?"

"He's out drinking."

"Why do you think that?"

"It's what Phi Delts do."

The Phi Delts must be a fraternity. If he was twenty-one, he didn't need to ask his parents' permission. He could have taken the initiative. Quietly, I opened the drawer in my nightstand and took out John's most recent letter.

Dear Marylee,

In the past three days, I've received about five letters from you. It really lifts my spirits to get a letter from you.

You asked if I minded it when you send a "mushy" letter. I don't mind it at all. I can't think of anything that sounds nicer than an "I love you" coming from you. I'm sorry that my letters aren't more sentimental. Football, working at my dad's, and school takes most of the sentiment out of a person. I don't love you any less or anything like that—in fact, I love you more—but being in a continual rat race takes a lot of sentimental thoughts out of my mind when I sit down to write a letter.

You're never out of my thoughts, honey. Are you in the home yet? I hope everything is all right.

I love you.
John

I kissed the letter and pressed it to my heart. He and I might not marry until later, but we were committed—he was committed—maybe even more than when we'd been physically together, tortured by trying not to have sex.

I found my notepaper, plumped my pillow, and flopped down on the bed. It was five thirty. Today had been like the first day of high school, when I was running around, trying to find my locker, smiling at strangers, and wondering how hard my classes were going to be. After I finished my letter, I licked the envelope. It was hard to describe in a letter what went on here. The rules. The schedule. The need to stay hidden. At least my roommates talked, and I could talk to them. From July to November, apart from five-minute phone calls with John, I had hardly spoken to a soul. Before I came here, I had been lonely.

CHAPTER 32

ROONAY

I don't know why I let Diane talk me into another walk. Chugging along behind her had worn me out, and I still had time to kill before dinner and then bed, when I could finally fall asleep and forget about all this. Putting fifty new names to fifty new faces was wearing me out. I propped my pillow and took out my rug and a ball of rags. While Pam lay on her side with her back to me, I stabbed the foot-long wooden hook in and out. The door was open. Coming from the director's office were voices I didn't recognize. "Daddy, I love you." "Be a good girl," a man's voice said. "Write, you hear?" a woman's voice said. Southerners, I thought. My grandma's sister lived in Baton Rouge, and she had slapped my face when I dared drink at a coloreds-only drinking fountain. I prayed the new girl wouldn't be a bigot. I might not have the guts to speak up for myself, but when it came to prejudice, I couldn't keep my mouth shut.

Mrs. South entered the room. "Girls, meet Roonay. She's taking Gloria's bed."

Roonay, a black girl a year or two older than I was, had massive thighs but had barely started to show. Though stylishly dressed in black slacks and a sweater, she was what anyone would have called "big." She flopped her giant suitcase on the bed.

Pam sat up and took the pillow from beneath her feet. "Here," she said, tossing it. "This belongs to you."

Roonay caught the pillow. "You all have a clean pillowcase?"

"Certainly," Mrs. South said. "I'll bring one."

"I was trying to elevate my feet," Pam said. "Should I clear out Gloria's stuff?"

"Karla did that already," Mrs. South said. "Pam, would you mind showing our new girl the ropes?"

"Sure," Pam said. "After dinner."

Let her get her bearings, I thought, and continued hooking my rug. Roonay began putting her clothes away. She smoothed out pleats and gathers. She shook out maternity smocks and turned the hangers so the fronts of her blouses faced the same direction. She arranged her tops by color.

My nose was stuffed up, and I blew it. The air was dry here. Out came a clot of blood. Then more blood poured from my nose. I grabbed a handkerchief from the drawer.

"Where's the bathroom?" Roonay asked.

"Across the hall," Pam said.

"I'll get you some toilet paper," she said.

She returned with a roll. "Make yourself some little swizzles and stick them in your nostrils. Ten minutes, and you'll be fine."

Seeing me fumble, she sat down on my bed and rolled me a nose tampon.

"Hold still, and I'll put it in for you," she said. "Now, pinch the bridge of your nose." She applied pressure just where my sunglasses sat.

"Are you studying to be a nurse or something?" I asked.

"Dental assistant," she said.

Everyone in this place had a story, and Roonay's was that she had been a freshman at Spelman and gotten pregnant. She and Pam talked about taking incompletes and rescheduling exams. It seemed that Pam had gotten pregnant early enough for the dean to buy into her medical excuse: a severe case of mono. Pam was taking the entire semester by correspondence, whereas Roonay had already started school, and by the time she figured out what was happening, she had to leave campus.

My high school, Woodside, had only a couple of black students. Ravenswood in East Palo Alto had the most, and MA, Menlo Atherton High School, over in Menlo Park, had a few. I knew this because of my school clubs—the Model UN and Junior Statesmen —and because I'd carpooled down to Asilomar for a weekend training session sponsored by the Quakers. Led by civil rights activist James Farmer, the workshop wanted to train people in nonviolent protest and bus them to Alabama and Mississippi. I wasn't old enough. Over John's protests, I'd done the next-best thing: worked with the local NAACP chapter to pass out anti-discrimination flyers in the apartment buildings of Palo Alto, where landlords typically discriminated against graduate students from the Middle East, Latin America, and Africa. Roonay came from an all-black college. If moving into the home felt weird to me, she must have been double weirded out.

According to Rickie Solinger's book *Wake Up Little Susie*, "The Florence Crittenton home in Phoenix was pointed in its exclu-sionary policy. A 1952 visit to the home revealed that this facility has served Spanish Americans, Indians, Chinese, Japanese, Koreans, and Philipinos [*sic*], but [the staff] say they don't serve 'colored' which means they really only exclude the Negro."[1] Fortunately, by 1961, that had changed, although I suspect Roonay might have been the first.

The smell of dinner was strong now. I pictured mashed potatoes and thinly sliced beef laid out on Wonder Bread.

Roonay sniffed. "Smells like dorm food."

"It's not as bad as that," Pam said. She checked her watch. "I'd better get going."

"Should we come, too?" Roonay asked.

"No, you wait fifteen minutes and then come down." Pam took a hairnet from the drawer. "I need to eat early. My job is to do the dinner dishes. We all have jobs."

"I thought Diane ran the dishwasher," I said.

"She does lunch. My work-study job in school was doing the dinner dishes in the dining hall, and they came on a conveyor belt, so, in comparison, this isn't too bad."

"Do we have assigned seating, or can we just sit anywhere?" Roonay asked.

I immediately thought of lunch counters in the South.

"Anywhere except the diet table," Pam said.

"Which one is that?"

"The table against the far wall."

Roonay wanted to put on her makeup, and by the time we arrived, a dozen girls stood in a line. Women, actually. One, who stood alone with her arms folded, had hollow cheeks and weather-beaten skin, like women in Dorothea Lange's photos of the Dust Bowl. Another had pronated ankles and wore black corrective shoes. With her heavy eyebrows, straight bangs, and wooden crucifix on a leather thong, she had the look of a nun. While the average age of the girls in line was nineteen or twenty, many had graying hair. Marianne, behind me and talking to another girl, was not the oldest, and yet all of us, young and old, had gotten here the very same way. It was astonishing. I'd never imagined that so many other women could be having sex.

The first ones through the food line collected their plates from the stainless-steel counter and filled in the table next to the diet table, first the side next to the diet table and then the side across from that.

The plate coming toward me was meat loaf, canned peas, and mashed potatoes, just like a Swanson TV dinner. The girl serving it was the tall one I'd seen the first day—Joanie. Most of the day, she went around in rollers covered by a gingham roller cap. Tonight, her bouffant was mashed down by a hairnet.

The cook, Ruby, in a gravy-stained white apron, smiled warmly at the new arrival and squirted extra ketchup on Roonay's plate.

Roonay took a seat. I pulled out a chair.

"Can I sit here?" Marianne asked, patting the table.

"Sure," I said, sliding over against Roonay's warm thigh.

"Do you like meat loaf?" Roonay asked.

"Beggars can't be choosers," I said.

"This is Rhonda," Marianne said.

I'd met Rhonda, the girl who'd gone to the men's barbershop, in the schoolroom. "Hi again."

"Pleased to meet you," Roonay said, then turned to Marianne. "What did you do before you got knocked up?"

Marianne laughed. "I taught kindergarten."

"Gosh, really?" I tried to picture her sitting on a floor with building blocks. At her current size, no way could she get up from the floor. "My mom's a teacher. She took a health leave."

"Me, too," Marianne said. "I have mono."

"I have mono, too," Rhonda said, smiling. "It's highly contagious. Ruining my senior year."

Marianne turned to me. "How are you liking this place?"

I didn't know how to answer and wasn't sure why Marianne even cared. I looked around the room. Four dozen pregnant women, all in varying stages. Roonay picked at the meat loaf. From the way her personality had filled our room, I wouldn't have pictured her so subdued, but then, she was the only black girl in a sea of white.

"My first day was tough," I said.

"How long you been here?" Roonay asked.

"This is my third day."

"After a week, it'll feel normal," Marianne said.

"In five months, the walls close in," Rhonda said.

"Why's that?" I asked.

"They just do."

Marianne lowered her fork. "I shouldn't have taken a plate. I think I'm leaking." She felt her crotch.

"She's almost due," Rhonda said.

"The day after tomorrow." Marianne winced. "But I may not make it till then."

"How come?" I asked.

Marianne wiped her fingers on a napkin. "I had a bloody show."

"What's that?" Roonay asked.

"Blood, plus some other stuff, in my underpants. Do you kids know what a cervix is?"

"No," Roonay said.

"It's the opening of the uterus. Do you know what the uterus is?"

"Yes," I said, thinking of my dissected cat. She had been pregnant with six worm-size kittens.

"When the cervix softens, it means it's not going to hold the baby in for much longer." Marianne laced her fingers together in a way that reminded me of "Here's the church, here's the steeple." She continued, "After a bloody show, it's not long before you go into labor."

"Oh, God." I let my face drop into my hands.

Marianne patted my arm. "You're young. You'll survive this."

"Lord have mercy," Roonay said. "I don't know if I will."

CHAPTER 33

CLINIC

Tuesday was clinic. By the time I returned from the shower room, Roonay and Diane had made their beds. Roonay had wanted to go down early, and Diane had volunteered to show her the ropes.

Pam unbuttoned the flannel shirt she wore instead of pajamas.

"What should I wear to clinic?" I asked.

"Your robe and slippers," Pam said.

"Can I wear a bra?"

"No, just underpants."

"Does the doctor stick that thing in you?"

"The speculum?" she said. "Sometimes he just sticks his fingers in and feels around."

My summer robe was more like a slip, and it didn't come all the way around me. I couldn't imagine traipsing down the hall in just my robe and slippers, especially not with my big, floppy boobs.

Pam rubbed oil on her belly.

"What's that?" I asked.

"Coconut oil."

"What's it for?"

"Stretch marks."

"Does it work?"

"Since I started using it, I haven't got any more."

"I've got a ton," I said.

"They'll put you on a diet." Pam changed into an XXL T-shirt, tied her robe, and picked up her knitting. "I'm going to poke my head in and say hi to Gloria."

"Say hi for me, too."

I stopped in the bathroom to pee. Lately I'd been having to pee all the time. Also, I felt like a turkey wishbone. My pelvic bones were spreading apart. The sooner I got this over with, the better.

I turned the corner into the hospital wing. The overhead lights were off. A gauntlet of girls filled the chairs. Some wore their hair in rollers; others had shorty pajamas just visible beneath their robes. Propped on their bellies, the girls' hands worked away at their knitting. Like Madame Defarge, I thought, knitting and cheering on the executioner.[1] All we needed was a guillotine.

I sat next to an older woman with a hard face. A plastic shower cap covered her rollers. I watched her needles clickety-click. "What are you making?"

"A sweater for my baby."

"Are you keeping your baby?" I asked.

She looked at me and stopped knitting. "What are you, about twelve?"

No one else had commented on my age.

"Sixteen," I said.

"Jailbait."

Flinching and feeling my face grow warm, I leaned forward, looking down the corridor to the clinic.

"Your first?" she asked.

I nodded.

"I was once a good little Catholic girl like you."

"How did you know I was Catholic?"

"Half the girls in here are."

"Did you lose your faith?"

"Among other things." The corner of her mouth crimped. "Where are you from?"

"California."

"They have laws out there. Hell, one time I got arrested for soliciting, and I was just standing on the corner at a gas station."

"Soliciting what?" I asked.

"You know. Soliciting and gambling. Things that in Vegas are legal."

"Oh," I said.

"In most states a working girl can't hardly spit on the sidewalk, let alone stand there."

I looked at the yellow sweater unfurling from her needles. "Your sweater's pretty."

"You've got to do something while you wait. Otherwise, you go crazy."

A nurse in white stockings and a starched cap came out into the corridor. She carried a clipboard and looked down the row. "We still have about two dozen," she called back to someone in the clinic. Walking down the aisle, she looked at faces. "Paula, we'll take you now."

Paula wound up her yarn and tossed it in her knitting basket.

"See you around," I said, throwing my arm over the back of Paula's chair.

Buttoning her robe, Pam came from the clinic. "Mind if I sit?"

"No, please," I said, pulling my thighs in. I was inclined to spread out, and I hoped that didn't mean I was gaining too much weight, because I did feel sort of big, compared with my normal self. But of course I was big. The baby was making me bigger day by day. The only time I could almost forget this was happening was when I was dead asleep.

Pam leaned down and pulled her yarn and knitting needles from a raffia bag. "I gained a quarter pound."

"Is that good?"

"Yes, it's good. We're not supposed to gain more than a half pound a week."

"Why not?"

"It complicates the pregnancy. Plus, if we gain more than twenty pounds, we won't be able to fit back into our clothes. Oh, and before I went in, I ducked into Gloria's. She's awake, and the nurse came in and said Marianne had delivered."

"Good." Good because that was what Marianne must want: to have this over and get out of here.

Pam settled back into the rhythm of knitting. The stitches were small and regular, like knit garments from a store.

"I've never seen anyone knit as fast as you," I said.

"It's the European way."

"Mary?" The nurse smiled down.

"Marylee," I said.

"You're next."

I scuffed along, holding my robe tight and hoping I wouldn't have to take off my panties. In the clinic, the nurse asked me to step up on a scale.

"Should I keep my robe on?" I asked.

"Take off your robe, but keep on your slippers," the nurse said.

I took off my robe, feeling its weight and glad, as I laid it over the back of the chair, that it wouldn't add to the already heavy feeling of my body. As I stepped on the scale, one end tipped up like a teeter-totter.

"One forty-nine," the nurse said when she'd balanced the scale. "What is your normal weight?"

"One twenty-three," I said, plus or minus five. But one forty-nine! I was an elephant.

"Hop up on that table," she said, indicating an examining table near the door. "The doctor will be with you in a moment."

While the nurse was weighing me, they'd brought in another girl and had her go behind a folding screen, where they had another examining table. The doctor was over there, asking questions. The new girl's name was Barbara.

"She's not a prime ip," the doctor said. "Have you had other children?"

"Yes," Barbara said, in the gargling voice of a smoker lying on her back. "One other."

"Did you keep it?"

"No," Barbara said.

"Okay," the doctor said. "It looks like you're five or six months along. Have you had any prenatal care?"

"No," Barbara said. "I was hoping this wasn't happening."

"You can get dressed."

A young, square-jawed doctor who reminded me of my Physiology teacher, Mr. Parsons, came out from behind the screen. It made me blush to think of Mr. Parsons looking inside me, but then, he'd had no trouble slicing open a dead cat, so what was the difference? I was pretty much a cat on a dissecting table, two nurses walking back and forth, another girl coming in, and me sitting there in front of God and everybody.

"Lie down," the doctor said, and I did, unbuttoning my robe, as the nurse instructed. When the doctor raised my gown, I stiffened. His fingers, poking and prodding and pushing down into my abdomen, moved across my stomach. He reached into his pocket for a tape measure and planted his thumbs on my sternum and pubic hair.

"Can you feel the baby move?"

"Yes," I said.

"A lot?"

"Yes, a lot."

"Good." He pulled down my nightgown. "That's what we want to hear. It looks like you're six and a half or seven months along. When was your last period?"

"I'm not sure," I said, "but you should know I have to be back by second semester."

"When's that?"

"January twenty-eighth."

"I'm going to guesstimate January sixteenth as your due date, but as the time gets closer, we'll see if that's accurate."

"Okay," I said.

He held out an arm. "Here, sit up."

I sat, and while I turned my head, he felt the lymph nodes on my neck. So far, so good. This was a lot better than the doctor's visit that had confirmed my pregnancy.

"Now, about your weight," he said.

I looked over to the door. The girl, Barbara, who'd been behind the screen, was dressed now, and I saw that her skin was the color of dark chocolate. She had a narrow face, sharp nose, and hazel eyes, and she was wearing clothing designed to disguise a pregnancy: a loose, hip-length beige sweater with a cowl neck. The nurse, who had been straightening a pile of sheets, went over to Barbara's side. "I think they need to see you back in the office."

Barbara paused by the door and turned her inquisitive eyes on me.

I got off the table and assembled myself.

"I'm afraid we're going to have to put you on the diet table," one of the nurses said.

The diet table. The one thing I knew about diets was that they made the cravings worse. To lose weight, I would have to endure a hunger headache at a time when my only pleasure came from food. But at least I now had a date to put on the calendar, and the exam hadn't been as bad as the last one, where the doctor had gooped nasty-smelling jelly on that cold metal spoon thingy and spread me apart.

Half the girls were still waiting in the hall. This clinic routine took an entire morning.

When she saw me, Pam put away her knitting and stood. "Well?"

"You were right," I said as we headed back to our room. "They're putting me on the diet table."

"I'm sorry," Pam said, "but if you have a good weigh-in next week, you'll be eating normal food."

From the clinic came a shout: "Men on the hall!"

Pam pulled me into an empty room.

Two male ambulance attendants came from the direction of the clinic. Marianne lay on a gurney, a white flannel blanket up to her chin. Sweat had curled the hair around her face. She looked pale and spent but wide awake, and the bulge where her baby should have been was now just a small pooch.

With Pam just behind me, I leaned out the door. "Welcome home."

"Thanks," Marianne said, rolling past. "Come see me."

"All right. This afternoon." Marianne had just delivered. Maybe she could tell me what to expect.

CHAPTER 34

A VOICE FROM HOME

*G*irls who had gone to clinic early were lining up for lunch. The rumble of conversation reminded me of high school, except there, the metallic slam of lockers reached a crescendo right before the bell. Ahead of me, I saw the math-whiz Rhonda, one of the few girls in the home who rarely smiled, opening the door to the phone booth. She was the designated hitter giving Barbara, the new girl, the tour.

"No one on the phone for more than ten minutes," Rhonda said. "Outgoing calls only. No giving out the number."

Since when? Pam hadn't told me not to do that. Maybe the rules for Rhonda's wing were different. Or maybe Rhonda was a stickler for rules? Or was it because Barbara was black?

Eager to change out of my flimsy robe and put on a bra, I went into my room and knelt by my underwear drawer. Roonay, who had been in one of the visiting rooms with a social worker, stood facing her mirror and undoing the clasp of a pearl necklace.

"And what about visitors?" the new girl asked.

Roonay's head whipped around. "That voice. No, it can't be."

"What voice?" I said.

"That ratty-ass Barbara." Roonay's shoulders rose and fell, and her nostrils flared. "I don't remember her last name, but she know mine 'cause my daddy's a captain."

"You *know* her?" I asked.

"She from Fort Benning," Roonay said in a quiet voice. "You have to understand, I came here so my daddy wouldn't be embarrassed, and now who show up but the base's biggest slut. And she gossip. Lord, does that girl know how to tell tales. She the kind have to know everybody's business."

"Couldn't you turn the tables?"

"'Bout what?"

"Having a second child."

"This her *second* child?" A slow smile broke across Roonay's face. "You mean she done got herself knocked up twice?"

"Apparently, yes."

"Ha!" Roonay slammed a fist into her palm. "That changes everything."

Sitting on the edge of my bed, I put on my shoes. They felt tight. "Should we go get some lunch?"

"Sure," Roonay said. "I been puking my guts out for three months, but all of a sudden, I got me an appetite."

We joined the flow of girls, chattering about their weigh-ins and exams and homework and calls from boyfriends and due dates and letters, and Roonay and I stood together, not saying anything, because there was only one thing on our minds. Roonay anticipated meeting Barbara, and I anticipated seeing Barbara's reaction when she saw Roonay. I hoped Roonay could figure out how to make Barbara keep her mouth shut. Why were we here, if not to keep our pregnancies secret from anyone who might blab to the people back home?

The line advanced. Roonay took deep breaths, the way I did when I swam underwater laps. And then the line turned the corner and we entered the dining room. The cook, Ruby, raised the aluminum tambour. Her eyes went to the front of the line and the new girl, Barbara. Ruby passed her a plate and nodded in our direction. Barbara turned. Her plate sagged, and her mouth dropped open.

Roonay threw her arms out in a kind of cheerleader's V. "Barbara! You here, too! How you doin', girl?"

Barbara's tentative smile drained from her face. She put her plate on a table. "Roonay," she said flatly.

Roonay stepped out of line and a moment later held Barbara in a bone-crushing hug. "I'm fixin' to get my lunch. I'll be right back, and you can tell me all the gossip."

Barbara's eyes teared. "Please don't tell your daddy."

"No way, chile," Roonay said. "We got to stick together."

I started to take a plate for myself, but Ruby wagged a finger and pointed to the end of the counter where the diet plates sat. Two scoops of cottage cheese, two peach halves, a leaf of lettuce, and a slice of white bread. I picked up my plate and a carton of skim milk. Knowing I was going to leave the table hungry, I watched Roonay, with her smile and friendly manner, disarm whatever mischief Barbara might have made.

What an actress Roonay proved to be, offering Barbara a fake friendship until she could win Barbara over with her genuine and effusive personality. Barbara, I soon learned, was herself a member of the armed forces. She was older than Roonay by four or five years, and rather than go to college, she had worked her way up to staff sergeant. If anyone had known she was pregnant, she would have been bounced out of the army. Whether Roonay ever mentioned Barbara's previous pregnancy, I don't know, but from then on, they were inseparable.

CHAPTER 35

MARIANNE

*G*rimacing, Marianne held the bedrail and shifted her weight. Like a bowl of half-congealed Jell-O, her stomach flopped sideways. A round Band-Aid covered a bruise in the crook of her arm. I wanted to ask what had happened in the hospital, but Marianne was a grown-up. Still, she'd said come talk to her. Ask questions.

I raised my hand.

"Yes?" she said.

"Um, one thing I was wondering about is chores. Nobody gave me a job."

"They're probably just busy." Wincing, Marianne propped herself up and shifted her bottom. "It's hard to work in the kitchen. Anyhow, Ruby has favorites. You might see if early-morning hall sweeper is open."

"What does that involve?"

"Waking up at six and sweeping the halls. There's a push broom in the janitor's closet."

"I don't like getting up early."

"The good thing about that job is that you're free the rest of the day. The dishwashing detail is hard, especially once your stomach gets big, which yours definitely is."

I linked my fingers and rested them on my shelf. What did I, a girl of sixteen, have in common with a kindergarten teacher twice my age? Nothing whatsoever, but her eyes were kind. Maybe she could tell I was scared.

"Another thing. I was wondering . . ."

"Yes?"

"Um, did it hurt?"

"I won't lie. Yes, of course, but they give you a shot to dull the pain."

"Did you scream?"

She laughed. "If you want to know the truth, I cussed a blue streak."

Cursing God or the father of her child? The latter, I supposed.

"How am I going to know if I'm going into labor? Besides that 'show' thing."

"Well, your water could break, in which case you'll be standing in a puddle. But that might not happen right away. Sometimes the nurse breaks it—kind of like popping a balloon—but that's normally after labor starts. The first sign could be pain starting in your lower back. Then steel fingers reach around your belly. Your stomach turns rock hard. After a minute, the pain eases up and you have a couple of minutes to catch your breath."

"And then?"

"You're in the hospital and you push the baby out and the pain goes away."

"How did you survive it?" I asked. "I mean, you seem so cheerful all the time."

Marianne blew out a stream of air and patted her empty abdomen. "I try not to think."

"How am I supposed to do that?"

"Do you drive?"

"Yes," I said.

"Then put the car in neutral. Let the engine idle."

Let my brain idle? My thoughts were like an electrical current, humming in the background. The middle of me—my core—had always been a void, not just an informational void, but a physical void, like a deflated volleyball, and now, periodically, I felt the rounded shape of a head or back. I hadn't thought about the birth so much, but I couldn't stop thinking about John, wondering if he loved me, wondering if I would get a letter. But what Marianne meant, I supposed, was that I shouldn't think about the baby.

I had never questioned that the Virgin Mary's pregnancy had come about in some miraculous fashion. Now, I thought it ludicrous that she was held up as an icon. No way was Mary a virgin. Someone had knocked her up. Probably not Joseph. The story made him seem like her protector, an older man who'd taken pity on a young, unwed mother. Traveling on an ass at the end of her pregnancy, she must have felt mighty uncomfortable. And to give birth in a stable. Before, the story of the Nativity had been plaster figurines set out beneath the Christmas tree. Now, Mary could have been me.

A chubby nurse with white stockings and a starched cap poked her head in.

"Time for your *sitz* bath, Marianne." She gave the curtain a tug. "I'm sorry, but you'll have to leave."

"I have a stupid question," I said.

"There are no stupid questions," Marianne said.

Typical teacher comment.

"What's a *sitz* bath?"

"They bring a pan of warm water for you to sit in."

The nurse made a shooing motion. "It's for your episiotomy. Now, scoot."

Back in my room, I wrote down the word in my diary, except that I spelled it "appeaseotomy." Not until I'd given birth would I finally understand that the purpose of a *sitz* bath was to aid in healing the cut made to allow the baby's head to come out, except that in my case, the doctor didn't have time do an episiotomy. The birth ripped me open.

CHAPTER 36

AMBER

Sundays from two to four, we could sign ourselves out and leave in small groups[1] for a walk around the neighborhood, but any other time, the rules required a parent's signature. On Saturday, as we had arranged, my mom came into the waiting room to sign me out. I picked up my satchel of books. My absence from her daily life ought to have reduced the strain she was under—I hoped so, anyway—but as she bent over the clipboard, her hand trembled and she dropped the pen. Not good. I picked it up. The lower right side of her face twitched and grimaced as if she were chewing on a raw carrot, unable to decide when to swallow.

She looked over at two adjacent doors, each labeled VISITING ROOM. The mumble of voices came from inside.

"Besides the library," she said, "do you have any other errands?"

"I need shampoo," I said, "and if we could stop at a fabric store, I'd like to find a remnant."

"I have your allowance," she said, stopping just outside the door to open her purse and hand me a $5 bill, "but, unfortunately, I think we left your muumuu pattern back home."

"I'm sure they'll have patterns in the sewing room."

She looked at my stomach. "In your size?"

"Please don't stare," I said.

She flinched as if I'd slapped her.

My belly might be big, but at least I could bend over and pick up a pen. I held out my hand for the keys. "I'll drive."

She dropped her keys into my palm.

On the way to the library, looking down at her lap, she opened and closed the fingers of her right hand. Maybe this was a strengthening exercise. If so, good. Not once the entire summer had she gone in the pool or even taken a walk around the block. If she'd brought her sewing machine, that would have given her something to do during all those hours she spent alone.

"Are you going to wait in the car?" I asked, parking as close to the entrance as I could get.

"I'll come in," she said. "I want to check the supermarket sales."

"All right," I said.

"Could you take my elbow?" she asked.

"Which one?"

"The left."

I slid my arm through hers. With my body as ballast, she could walk.

At the library, I led my mother to the periodicals section, where newspapers, like wet laundry, hung from wooden poles. She picked up an *Arizona Republic* and settled into an easy chair across from a white-haired gentleman, his head rocked back, a gentle snore escaping now and then. Even though it was November, the man wore a Hawaiian shirt and leather *huaraches*, the casual sandals worn throughout Mexico. One of the snowbirds who would soon be filling up the other units in our motor court.

I hurried off to Adult Fiction and smiled at the unfettered conversation and the stream of patrons, each seeking information, ideas, and interpretations of experience that would help them in their daily lives. If my mom didn't tell me how to live, books would. Then I stood at the counter, waiting to check out.

The librarian inked her date stamp and looked from my stomach to my face. "Aren't you awfully young to be having a baby?"

"I'm nineteen," I said. "I look young for my age."

~

CARRYING my book bag and fabric remnant, my muumuu wet from defrosting my mother's refrigerator, I signed myself in. Now, I was safe. The outside world couldn't touch me.

In the sewing room, I found a box of patterns. A wan, thin girl, with skeins of yarn and knitting needles in the straw bag at her feet, sat at one machine. The other machine wasn't being used.

The girl looked up. The fluorescent light accentuated her sunken cheeks. "I'm Amber."

"What a beautiful name," I said.

"Thanks, but I hate it."

I'd never heard anyone but me say that.

"Who are *you?*" she asked.

I pronounced my name and spelled it.

Taking the remnant from the bag, I spread it out on a table and looked around for shears. There were none. "That's funny," I said. "I swear the last time I came down here I saw scissors on the table." I made a snipping motion with my hand.

"They're here," Amber said, taking pinking shears from a straw bag on the floor.

Pinking shears were expensive. If they were hers and she needed to leave, I didn't want to hold her up. "Are those your personal scissors?"

"No. I was just using them."

I spread the fabric on a table and pinned the pattern pieces. This wasn't going to take me any time at all, and, as Marianne had promised, just keeping busy made me feel better than if I'd done what I felt like doing: curling up in bed and pulling the covers over my head.

"So, when are you due?" I asked.

"March," Amber said.

"That's a long time."

"Forever."

"You're barely showing."

"Once you let yourself show, it's a lost cause."

"What do you mean, 'lost cause'?"

"People find out."

I hadn't *decided* to let myself show. My stomach had just popped out. Good luck to her if she thought she could hide it for long.

"What are you making?" I asked.

"A dress to wear to my grandma's ninetieth birthday," she said, not looking up. "I'm almost done." Amber stepped on the machine's foot pedal. The whir was like the buzzing in my head, what Marianne said I should stop.

"These old Singers remind me of junior high," I said.

"For straight-stitching they're okay," she said.

"Yeah, but they can't do zigzag."

Amber pushed back her chair and went to the ironing board. She spread the seams and pressed them flat, then folded them along her stitching line and pressed again. *French seams*, I thought. *Fancy.*

"If you're in here to hide from your family, how on earth are you going to show up for your grandma's party?"

"You'll see," she said. "In the dress I'm making, no one's going to know."

It didn't seem like she wanted to talk, but for some reason, I did. Maybe just because of all those months with my mother. I had a kind of pent-up feeling, a desire to let myself be myself. It was like the day I stopped wearing a girdle. Who cared if people knew?

THE MAILMAN HAD COME LATE, and Karla, the secretary, was taking her sweet time blacking out names. "Sit down, girls. I'll be done in a minute."

"That's okay," I said. "We'll just stand."

When we stood by the window, she would hurry up. Otherwise, if the phone rang or Mrs. South told her to type a letter, Pam and I would have to wait another twenty minutes.

"For Thanksgiving," Pam said, "Ruth says she's making a turkey, dressing, sweet potatoes, and pumpkin pie."

"That'll be a welcome change from meat loaf," I said.

The hall door opened.

"Holy cow," Pam said.

I turned.

Amber carried a turquoise train case and wore heels. I wouldn't have recognized her as the girl from the sewing room. The dress she'd been making had a form-fitting top with puffed sleeves. The skirt belled out over her hips. She had put up her hair in a chignon and wore makeup. Her cat's-eye glasses had rhinestones in the corners.

"You look like a million," Pam said. "How'd you ever get into that dress?"

"A girdle," Amber said, wheezing in a breath. She smoothed a hand down her front. "Am I showing?"

"Not at all," Pam said.

Amber picked up the clipboard and signed herself out. "My mom's supposed to pick me up."

"Does your family know?" I asked.

"My mom and dad do," Amber said, "but not my aunts and uncles or my grandparents. My parents would die if my sisters found out, so I have to sleep in the den, not my own bed."

"Where does your family think you're living?" I asked.

"In an apartment."

"I can't believe they're letting you go on an overnight," Pam said.

"I got special permission," Amber said.

"Is your boyfriend going to be there?" Pam asked.

"Not unless he's wearing a bulletproof vest."

Watching the screen swing shut, I said, "If she keeps her girdle laced up that tight, she won't have to worry about the weigh-in. She'll barf up anything she eats."

"She doesn't have the body type to gain weight," Pam said.

"What body type is she?"

"Amber's an endomorph." She sliced parallel lines through the air.

"What are we?"

Pam pointed at me. "You're an ectomorph, and I'm a mesomorph."

"And what's an ectomorph?" During an entire year of Human Physiology, I had never heard this term.

"You gain weight easily."

That was true. Especially when I had something to eat besides cottage cheese and Melba toast. I wondered what the diet table was going to get for Thanksgiving. I had a hunger headache.

CHAPTER 37

THANKSGIVING

The smell of bacon wafted down the hall. Gathering dust bunnies, I pushed the three-foot-wide mop. My stomach growled. Soon I would have breakfast. If I wanted, I could have a poached egg and a piece of dry toast. The alternative was cottage cheese and peaches and dry toast, and then I could begin listening to my stomach growl in anticipation of Thanksgiving dinner.

I had a Strathmore sketchpad I was supposed to be using for various drawing projects, but the assignments said things like, "Go sit on a park bench and try sketching the feet of the person next to you" or, "Set up a still life with a tablecloth, a vase, and pieces of fruit. Capture the reflections on the fruit." After breakfast, I sat on my bed and sketched Pam's foot. She had propped up her pillows and was reading *Too Late the Phalarope*. I asked what a phalarope was, and she said a kind of bird from South Africa. I asked if the bird was going extinct, and she said no. The bird was a metaphor for black-white relations, and she would loan me the book so I could read it myself. Okay, so she wanted me to shut up.

Because the library was closed for the holiday, my mom used the motor-court-manager's phone to call and wish me happy Thanksgiving. Rather than cook a turkey, she was going to take herself to a restaurant in Scottsdale. "Maybe you could go to a movie after that," I said, and she said yes, maybe she would.

At noon, I saw that everyone had put on nice clothes. The girls had seen me in the same five muumuus day after day. My new top wasn't formal, and the brown pants I'd picked off the clothes rack were slightly faded, but what the heck. At least the top was something different.

After changing, I returned to the line. We girls on the diet table got a large slice of breast meat, cranberry sauce but no dressing, and boiled potatoes instead of mashed. Our dessert was pumpkin pie with no crust.

"What about going for a walk?" Pam said.

"John said he'd call."

"All right. Then I'll go help Diane with the dishes."

"He's going to call at two. I should be done by two fifteen. We could go then."

"Sure," she said. "I want to stretch my legs."

I'd been sitting around too much, not doing my homework. Just staring into space.

I went back to my room and took the rug and my remaining rag ball from my closet. The rug had grown to five feet in diameter. Where could I get more dark clothing? Goodwill, maybe? Phoenix didn't look like a place where men wore dark wool pants, but maybe there were widows from cold climates who'd decided to clear out their husband's clothes.

The phone rang. I threw the rug on the bed and dashed across the hall, saying, "Hello, can I help you?" This was the way we were supposed to answer the phone in case of a wrong number.

"It's me," John said.

"Thank God." Heat rose to my cheeks, and my heart beat fast. I closed the door of the phone booth, sealing myself in.

"Did you eat already?" I said.

"No, we're about to sit down," he said. "I can't talk long."

"What have you been up to?"

"Watching the Army-Navy game."

I pictured John and his brothers in the TV room, all jostling for

228 | MARYLEE MACDONALD

space on two couches while his sisters helped their mother in the kitchen.

"You keeping out of trouble?" he asked.

"What kind of trouble could I possibly get in here?"

"I don't know."

"We're already grounded," I said. "No going out except on Sundays. Oh, and today. After I get off the phone, I'm going for a walk."

"Good. You can show me around."

Was he dreaming? "Show you around what?"

"Phoenix. What is there to do there?"

"John, how would I know? It's not like I'm a tourist."

"Then you can show me where you're living."

"I can't."

"Why not?"

"They don't let men inside. Even my mom can't come in."

"Great, just great."

"What's that supposed to mean?"

"I don't know. Forget it," he said. "Are you going over to your mom's for Thanksgiving?"

"I ate here."

"How was it?"

"They put me on the diet table."

"I hope you're not getting fat."

I rolled my eyes. "John, I'm pregnant."

"Yes, but pregnant's not the same as fat."

"How long are they going to make you be on this diet table?"

"Until Tuesday." I'd have my weigh-in at the clinic. The other girls said that to get off the diet table I'd have to lose weight or stay the same. At 149, I was already over the twenty pounds they let us gain. I knew my body, and with what they'd been feeding me, I was pretty sure the next weigh-in would be good.

Because I didn't have too much new to report, or really any way to describe what it was like in this place with all its new names and faces, I let John go on about Friday night's game. When he and I were together, I listened with the kind of rapt attention *Seventeen* magazine said girls should fake if they wanted boys to like them. Pretend to follow sports. Ask them about their interests. "I was 'that close' to intercepting a pass," John said, describing the details of his attempts to catch up to the receiver and reach out and grab the ball. After he finished talking about the game, he went on about quizzes and a test in Advanced Physics and the SATs, which he'd taken for the second time. His scores hadn't come back yet, but he felt pretty good about how he'd done in math, so he'd had the scores sent to his congressman. Each congressman got to pick five people for West Point, and he was hoping to be one of them.

"Are you sure you want to go into the military?" I said.

"No, but if I go to West Point, I can get a free education and get out from under my father's thumb."

John had recently taken the Academy's Physical Aptitude Examination, which meant he had to do a certain number of pull-ups, push-ups, standing long jumps, and sprints. His football coach had administered the test and written him a recommendation.

"What are your odds of getting in?" I asked.

"Pretty good," he said, then paused.

I waited for him to pick up the thread of conversation, to talk about some record he'd bought or maybe say he had to break off and go eat dinner, or maybe ask me how I was doing. If this place was getting me down.

"Uh, I was wondering," he said, "would you be upset if I asked Ginger Dawkins to the Christmas dance?"

Ginger, the cute redhead from Mercy High who had the hots for him? Instead of a phone booth, I was sitting in an elevator, dropping fast. The Christmas dance. Last year, I'd been his date. He would rent a tux and give Ginger a corsage. They would have their picture taken by a photographer. He would hold her in his arms and dance. His dick would get hard. She would feel it.

"Are you still there?" he asked.

"Yes, I'm still here."

"I haven't asked her yet."

"Good," I said. "Don't."

"I thought I should mention it before I did," he said.

"Are you going to Teen Club?"

"I can't sit home all the time."

My teeth, clacking, felt like Novocain was wearing off. "I need to free up the phone."

"See you, then," he said.

"I love you," I said, but it was more a reflex than the truth.

I WAS TOO upset to go for a walk.

"Here I am, having his baby," I told Pam, sitting on her bed and doing her nails, "and he has the nerve to ask me if he can take another girl on a date. Is he stupid or what?"

Pam screwed the top back on her polish. "At least he told you."

Oh, yeah, great. I should give him a gold star for honesty.

"Let's go down and see Gloria. It'll get your mind off him."

"I thought we loved each other," I said, standing.

"See what he says in his next letter."

God! Men! I needed to put my mind on something else.

Down in the infirmary, I stood on one side of Gloria's bed and Pam on the other. Pam, who had been Gloria's roommate for four months before I arrived, asked how she was doing.

"My blood pressure still hasn't come down, and I'm retaining water." Gloria held up a hand that looked like a water-filled rubber glove. A needle in the back of her hand connected to a bag of clear fluid hanging from a pole. A bruise spread from beneath the Band-Aid. "They're going to do a C-section."

"What's that?" I asked.

Gloria sliced across her abdomen. "They cut me open."

"When?" Pam asked.

"Tomorrow," Gloria said.

Pam picked up Gloria's puffy hand and pressed it to her cheek. "I'm sorry."

"That sounds horrible," I said.

"I have to be in the hospital for a week or two," she said.

"Will you come back here?" Pam asked.

"I don't know," Gloria said.

"What about school?" I asked.

"They won't let me back in," she said.

"Gloria goes to the Indian school," Pam said.

"But how would they even know you're pregnant?" I asked.

"The school arranged for me to come here," Gloria said. "My mother doesn't even know."

"Why not?" I asked.

"She lives on the streets up in Window Rock."

Pam looked over at me. "Gloria's mother's an alcoholic."

An alcoholic.

"What are you going to do?" I asked.

"Go back and live with my grandma on the rez, I guess."

Mute with sorrow, I stroked her fingers. I had driven through the Navajo reservation many times. Old women still wore long velvet skirts and lived in mud hogans. The hogans were far apart, the Navajo primarily shepherds and weavers. Would Gloria have to sit all day at one of those vertical rug looms?

"I can't imagine how you're going to get your life back," I said.

Gloria shrugged. "I want to get home. I miss my people."

The nurse looked in and said it was time for us to leave. We said our goodbyes. Very likely, this was the last time we would see Gloria. Pam wiped her eyes.

We were heading back to our room when I saw Joanie, the tall girl who helped Ruth in the kitchen, bounding toward us.

She flung open Mrs. South's door. "Amber hurt herself!"

"What's wrong?" I heard Mrs. South say.

"She's lying in a pool of blood in the bathroom."

"Which one?" Mrs. South asked.

"The back bathroom."

"Stay with her," Mrs. South said. "Karla's calling the ambulance."

"I don't understand," I said to Pam. "Amber went home yesterday."

"She came in late last night," Pam said. "I was awake and saw her tiptoe down the hall."

"But I thought she was supposed to stay over."

"Yeah. I don't know."

The ambulance screamed up to the gate. The door to the waiting room flew open. The attendants rushed in.

"Men on the hall," Pam called out.

Moments later, the paramedics returned with Amber—white as Dracula's sister—on a gurney. It all happened in a blur: The door slammed, the ambulance siren blared again, and I stood there with my heart racing, thinking that if not for my grandmother's having been carried out on a stretcher, John might have been just another one of the boys I dated.

Over a supper of cold cuts and American cheese, we spoke in subdued voices. Amber had attempted to abort her pregnancy with knitting needles. We speculated about what might have happened to make her that desperate. The thing was, in our hearts, we were all Amber. We were women who had what a Freudian analyst I saw years later called a "hysterical reaction," in which "hysteria" referred to the womb and all the yearnings of women that (it seemed) men did not understand.

Outwardly, we acted like normal people. We brushed our teeth. We did our homework. We helped in the kitchen and swept the halls. We did these things without ever talking about our feelings. We had none. We were like Stepford wives, women going through the motions and suspended between the past, where we had governed our own affairs, and the future, where we might yet govern them again.

The home and the months we spent waiting to deliver were a holding zone. A holding pen, if one were to make an analogy about cattle being driven to market. Part of the job of those who were in charge of the home and the social workers who came to broker adoptions was to deaden us to the day our babies would be taken. Then we could get out from under the cloud of shame.

CHAPTER 38

SIGNED OUT

I could well imagine that the party for her grandmother had pushed Amber over the edge. A scowl from a cousin. A neighbor's oblique remark. Any signal that people had guessed could have created an emotional tsunami and driven Amber to think, *I can't do this anymore*. It was our families, as much as ourselves, we were trying to save.

I was in nearly the same state, wanting *it* to be over and wanting my mother to love me again, but so far, she'd shown no sign that she was willing to take back what she'd said: "You're just like your mother." I had to make the first move.

It was Saturday at 1:00 p.m. on the dot when her '52 Chevy pulled up by the gate.

"Did the mail come yet?" I asked Karla.

"Not yet," she said. "But I'm sure it'll be here by the time you get back."

"I hope so." It had been five days since I'd received a letter from John, and I was still waiting for an explanation. Why would he even think it was okay to ask Ginger Dawkins out on a date, let alone to the fanciest formal of the year? She'd think he liked her. And what would that do to Ginger when I came back? Now, he was messing with two girls' lives.

My mother signed me out. I needed two arms for all my library books. She held the back door, and I threw them in.

"Should you be carrying all that?" she said.

"How else am I going to return them?"

"I thought there'd be someone to help you."

"Oh, sure," I said. As if the place had porters.

"After the library, what about a movie?"

"It's a nice day, and I'd rather be outdoors, but let me think about it."

After Marianne's heartfelt goodbye hug, Gloria's departure for the hospital and a C-section, and Amber's attempted abortion, pushing a mop down the home's dark corridors made me feel like Sisyphus pushing his rock uphill. At 6:00 a.m., when I'd woken up to do my job, everyone else was still asleep; only the breakfast cook was up, banging around in the kitchen. By afternoon, I wanted a nap, but here I was, getting into a car with my mother.

The car was the one place she could corner me. Once, she'd made me sit in the car in our driveway after I'd gone to the dentist. I'd bitten his hand, and he had tattled to her, and she had made me sit there, which I had, but saying over and over, "I didn't do it," hoping she'd believe me, until I had repeated myself so many times, I'd convinced myself that what I was saying was true.

"Have you been thinking about where you'd like to go?" she asked.

"No," I said.

"The paper's in the backseat. You could check the new features."

I turned. My books had landed on the movie section. Besides, I was big.

"I can't reach it."

"Don't the girls have any movie magazines?"

"They might, but we don't talk about movies."

"What do you talk about?"

Our boyfriends. How long until it's over. Our weigh-ins. Amber's abortion.

"Nothing," I said.

In the right-hand lane, going fifteen or twenty miles an hour, she drove in silence. It was like being back in the sweltering motor court with the swamp cooler.

She pulled into the library's parking lot. "While you get your books, I'll talk to a librarian and see if there's someplace she'd recommend."

That was my mother in a nutshell. Always having to ask someone in a position of authority. Never having her own opinions. Certainly, never sharing them with me.

"I won't be long," I said, and headed for the Z's. I'd done a book report on Émile Zola's *Germinal* my freshman year and thought it might be worth rereading. But wait! Here was a writer I'd never heard of: Sigrid Undset. I picked up three volumes of *Kristin Lavrans-datter* and kept searching for more women writers. Not finding any at the end of the alphabet, I walked down to the A's to see who might be there at the beginning. Austen, of course. But Pearl S. Buck had some tomes. *Imperial Woman.* I read the book flap. About a woman in China. I scooped up all the books by her and carried them to the circulation desk.

My mother was waiting. "Find something?" she asked.

The librarian who had told me I was too young to have a child averted her eyes and stamped my books. I gave her a hate glare.

Outside, I stared at the clouds, all bunched up like bedclothes. They were gray, and when I rolled down the window, the air smelled like rain. Far off, above South Mountain, sheet lightning crackled above the peaks.

Instead of heading back to the home, my mother turned east on McDowell.

"Where are you going?" I asked.

"The botanical garden," she said. "Then I thought we could stop for an early dinner."

"I have to be back by five o'clock," I said.

"If you just tell them you're out with me, I'm sure it'll be fine."

"It won't."

Her lip started twitching, and I could see the jerking on her right side begin. She pulled over to the curb. "Would you mind driving?"

"Just take me back," I said.

"No, the librarian said we had to go."

In 1961, the botanical garden was a dirt road that wound up and down the hills and gullies between Papago Peak and Hole-in-the-Rock's orange-red outcroppings. There were saguaros and ocotillo and barrel cactus and prickly pear, specimens I marvel at now. There was no place to get out of the car and sit, just sit and breathe the rain-laden air.

It was five fifteen by the time we returned to the home. I opened the back door and gathered my books.

"Would you like to come over for dinner tomorrow?" she asked.

"You can't really cook a dinner, can you?"

"I thought we could go out."

"Go *out?*"

"For a steak dinner. Maybe at one of those places in Scottsdale?"

"Mom, don't you realize I'm *in jail?*"

She frowned. "Is that how you see it?"

"See what?"

She nodded toward the door and the porch light that had just come on. "What this place is."

"You've never even asked me what it's like," I said. "Not over the phone. Not when you came to visit. And even not today, when all we did was drive around."

"I thought I was protecting you," she said.

"From what?" I said. "From *whom?*"

"Your father and John."

"You know something?" I said to the woman whose chin quivered and who sat with her shoulders hunched, trying with all her might to control the spasms. "You know what!" I said, more loudly.

"No. What?" she said, cowering behind the wheel.

"I hate you. I really hate you, and I wish I didn't."

PART V

DARK NIGHT OF THE SOUL

CHAPTER 39

CATHOLIC CHARITIES

I was turning into my father. When he couldn't stand listening *one more time* to my mother's stories, he'd slam a fist down on the table. "Goddamn it, Lorene! If I have to listen one more time . . ."

Waves of hot and cold prickled my skin. Still shaking with the enormity of what I'd done—I had *screamed*, not raised my hand, not said "ma'am"—I dropped coins into the phone and closed the phone booth's door. *Please, God, please. Let John be home.*

He picked up on the first ring, his deep "hello" so welcome that I sank down onto the phone's seat.

"John . . . John . . . I . . ." Jerk-sobbing, unable to form a coherent thought, I fed the last of my quarters into the phone. What was the matter with me? One minute enraged and shaking, the next inconsolable.

"You sound upset," he said. "Are you still mad?"

"Mad! What?"

"Because of Ginger Dawkins. I was being a butthead."

A butthead. "You were, but no, it's something else."

The operator came on the line: "To continue your call, deposit more coins." I fished in my pocket. Damn it! "John, I'm out of my money. Could you call me back?"

"Let me run upstairs."

I shouldn't take up space in the phone booth, but I couldn't let my roommates see me like this. Standing with my back to the door, I blew my nose on the hem of my muumuu and waited for the ring.

"Now, tell me what's wrong," he said when he had me on the line.

"I lost it," I said.

"What, the baby?"

The baby? Did he want me to lose the baby? But no. He couldn't.

"I meant my temper. I just totally lost it. I told my mother I hated her. I screamed."

The wheezing told me he was breathing through his mouth. His mom must not have dusted his room.

"Your mother only wants what's best for you," he said.

What's best for me. "She has no idea what's best for me."

"What did she say?"

"That she was protecting me."

"From who?"

"From my father and you."

"From me! Where does she get that?"

"I know."

A chair creaked. He'd propped his feet next to the stack of record albums. Bo Diddley. Little Richard. The Trashmen. Another long silence. The phone bill was going to be huge.

"Maybe she has a point," he said.

"About what?"

"About protecting you from me. I'm the one who got you into this mess."

"You're not the problem. At this point, I hate her so much, I never want to see her again."

"You probably won't like my suggestion, then."

"What?"

"Write her a letter. Apologize. The letter doesn't have to be long."

"What's the point?"

"It'll make you feel better."

"No way."

"Yes way. We all do stupid things."

"Yes, we do." Especially him.

One of his sisters was knocking on his door, saying she needed to use the phone.

"I've got to get off," he said.

"I love you," I said.

"I know," he said. "I love you, too. Hang in there."

"I will." But how? Blasting out anger at my mom wasn't like getting a C on a term paper. I couldn't revise what I'd said.

Sitting a moment longer in the phone booth, I stirred the pennies in my pocket. It would be dishonest of me to apologize. I had not an ounce of true contrition but putting words on the page might help me defuse the powder keg. The next time I saw her, maybe I could at least manage to be civil.

There was a bathroom next to the phone booth. I blew my nose and splashed cold water on my face. My nose was still stuffed up and my cheeks, pink and blotchy. A five-minute cry had turned me into a wreck, and it was all my mother's fault. Another surge of internal heat threatened to spill out. I had to get that letter written and retreat into the book I had just renewed: *Out of Africa*, by Isak Dinesen.

I opened the bathroom door and looked left and right. The dinner line had already begun to form, and those in the line had their backs turned. Amber's three roommates were talking about how Karla had bagged up Amber's things. No one had told us if Amber and her baby had lived or died. Girls just disappeared.

Our room was dark. I dashed across the hall, closed the door partway, and turned on my reading lamp. Stationery from the drawer. A pen. I plopped down on my bed and picked up the book, my writing surface. If I could get this letter written, then after dinner I could step into the flow of another life.

Dear Mom,

    I know you want what's best for me. You always have. What you said today made me angry. Hearing you lump John in with my father just lit a fuse. I said things I regret. I'm sorry. I didn't mean to hurt you.

XOXO,

    Marylee

    There. Enough said. I was violating one of my personal cardinal rules—*Never be a hypocrite*—but in the moment I had screamed at my mother, I had violated the First Commandment of being a good adoptee—*Always show gratitude for having been chosen.* It was worse to break that commandment than to be untrue to myself.

    I licked the envelope and sealed it.

CHAPTER 40

THERAPY

I don't remember how, exactly, my mother came up with the idea of going to a therapist. Possibly my letter, although she never responded to it directly, not even to acknowledge she'd received it. Possibly she realized that our relationship had been deteriorating for some time. On Wednesday, she called the office. I had to take the call on Karla's phone. Standing next to her desk, a finger in my ear to block out the key-taps of the IBM Selectric, I listened to my mother say she'd gone over to Catholic Social Service, the agency that would handle the adoption of my child, and asked if they had any counselors.

"You mean like a guidance counselor?" I said.

"No, a counselor where you can talk about your feelings. A therapist. I've already spoken to her. She has an appointment on Friday at four o'clock. I could swing by and get you at three thirty."

"Are you asking me or telling me?" I asked.

"I'm asking," she said.

"Let me think."

Karla stopped typing and gave me a questioning look.

Usually, my mother was like a limpet clinging to a rock and

getting pounded by the waves, but after my outburst, she had every right to think I was crazy. Hell, maybe I was.

"All right, I'll go." I handed the receiver back to Karla.

"Is your mom okay?" Karla asked. "She said it was an emergency."

"It wasn't an emergency." More like a siege with my heart walled up inside the castle of myself.

I hoped that saying yes would make me begin to come around, but when Friday came, I wished I'd said no. On the drive over, my mother drove like Mr. Magoo, leaning forward, going twenty miles per hour in thirty-five zones, and stalling at intersections. A couple of times, her foot slipped off the gas, and I was on the verge of screaming, *What are you trying to do? Get us killed?* But then I told myself the leg jerking wasn't as bad as it could sometimes be, more like a dog having a rabbit dream, and that maybe my going with her would help.

I should talk to her. I wanted to, but I couldn't think of a single thing to say. *How are you?* would sound banal. Besides, we'd never had a true conversation, not about who we were as people, what we loved, feared, were outraged by, and craved. Our common life, the life that constituted the sum total of our existence, was all about tasks and routines: what time we would eat, when we would go shopping, what day we would pull off the sheets and go to the Laundromat. I'd had years of that.

Catholic Social Service occupied a brown stucco house on a busy street. A secretary sat at a desk next to an unused brick fireplace and told us to take a seat. The counselor would be with us soon. If I sat, my mother would feel the heat waves of loathing. It was safer for me to linger by the bookcases on either side of the fireplace and see if there was a book I could dip into if she insisted we come back.

She took a seat and, bending over her purse, caved in on herself. *Poor woman,* I thought. *Protecting her heart.* Then her eyes lifted and she looked obliquely at my belly. Her eyes were devoid of compassion. I turned my back and pulled out a book. Words blurred. Why on earth had she dragged me here? This wasn't going to help.

Promptly on the hour, a trim woman with close-cropped black hair, a tennis player's haircut, short and practical, came to greet us. Her white blouse had a Peter Pan collar buttoned to the neck, and she wore a camel-hair skirt. She must be a native Phoenician. The heat of the summer didn't bother them in the least, but the instant the temperature dropped below eighty, they dug out winter clothes.

"Dolores Hudson," she said, smiling and offering a hand.

When had an adult ever shaken my hand? Teachers didn't. Priests didn't. I stared at the hand for a moment, then shook it.

"I'm Marylee," I said.

"Yes, I know. Your mother told me all about you."

Great. Just great. What could my mother possibly know? She was old.

When we were seated in her office, Mrs. Hudson behind her desk and my mother and I side by side, Mrs. Hudson said, "Your mother tells me your grandmother died recently."

If I had expected anything, it wasn't this. "Not recently. Over a year ago."

"I gather you became involved with your boyfriend the night your mother allowed him to pick you up at the hospital," she said.

"First of all, he didn't pick me up at the hospital," I said. "The hospital was in San Francisco. He picked me up at the Greyhound station in Redwood City, and it wasn't night. It was noon."

"But you were unchaperoned," Dolores said.

"God," I said, turning to my mother, "you are so dumb."

My mother flinched.

The night Grandma fell ill, I hadn't slept. John had dropped me off at home. Did she really think this was when we'd begun to have sex? Or that it was the only time? Back then, he was just some guy I'd been dancing with at Youth Club. He had a car, and he happened to be home when I called him. We barely knew each other.

"I told her that was the only time I could think of when he might have . . . taken advantage."

"You know nothing about me," I said.

"I'm only trying to help."

"Then *leave me alone!*"

"Why are you doing this to me?" she said, wiping a nose drip with one of the used tissues in her purse. "I only want what's best for you."

"And who defines what's best for me? You?"

"I'm your mother."

You're just like your mother. "No, you're not," I said.

Mrs. Hudson held up both hands. "Whoa! Whoa! Mrs. Benham, would you mind sitting out in the waiting room and letting me talk to Marylee alone?"

My mother gave her whipped-dog nod.

I sucked in a breath and closed my eyes. I had to get myself under control.

"Take as long as you want," Mrs. Hudson said.

If I took as long as I wanted, the hour, or however long this session was going to last, would be over.

"I'm all right," I said, opening my eyes.

Elbows on her desk, Mrs. Hudson leaned forward. "Why don't you tell me in your own words what's going on."

"I don't know," I said.

"Don't you have any idea?"

"No."

"She says you refuse to talk to her."

"I don't refuse. I just don't have anything to say. I told her I hated her, but I was angry."

"Yes, she told me you'd said something like that. We all say things in the heat of the moment." Mrs. Hudson opened a manila folder and consulted her notes.

Mrs. Hudson was undoubtedly right. Everyone loses their cool. Except I wasn't everyone. Grandma would have washed out my mouth with soap.

"Your mother says you're very intelligent," Mrs. Hudson said.

"I don't know about intelligent, but I love school."

"She says you work very hard."

"True."

"Would you agree that she wants what's best for you?"

God, not that again. "I'm sure she does." I folded my hands over my belly. "But I'm not a little kid."

"How would you describe the problems you're having?"

"I'm not having any problems."

"You're having a baby," she said.

"A baby wouldn't be a problem if our parents would let John and me get married."

"Does he want to marry you?" she asked.

"His father won't let him."

"Why not?"

"He's a cheap bastard. Plus, he doesn't want John to get trapped."

Mrs. Hudson smiled. "Well, I may not be able to help with John's father, but I'd at least like to help you and your mother get on speaking terms."

I blew out a stream of air. "I try to be civil."

"That's not what she wants," Mrs. Hudson said.

"I know what she wants," I said. "She wants me to talk to her, but honestly, we never had anything to say to each other before I got pregnant, and we have even less now. Like I told her, she doesn't even know me, apart from what she can see on the surface. My grades. Whether I keep my room picked up and do my chores." I pointed at my chest. "She doesn't know *me*, and *not once since she found out I was pregnant has she ever asked how I was feeling*. She says she cares about me, but there's only one thing she really cares about!"

Mrs. Hudson drew back. "And what's that?"

"What the neighbors think."

"Pardon me? I don't quite get that."

"She grew up in a small town in Colorado," I said, "and everybody knows everybody else's business."

"But you live in the Bay Area," Mrs. Hudson said.

"Yes, but she still has that small-town mentality. She doesn't want people gossiping, and she's constantly worried about her reputation."

"Can you give me an example?"

"When my father was on the front page of the *Redwood City*

Tribune, a photo showed him with his hands wrapped around the bars of his jail cell. It was the lead photo of the day. He was in jail for refusing to pay one dollar in alimony. 'Blood money' he called it. My mom took a sick day from school and kept me home. She spent the day locked in her room. I didn't think it was such a big deal, but she did."

"What was your father trying to accomplish, do you think?"

"He wanted to embarrass her and make her feel like she couldn't hold her head up."

Mrs. Hudson made some notes. "Did you love your father?"

"He was my father," I said. Impulsive and volatile, yes, but also passionate about politics. My birth mother, the person I was "just like," was a hazy figure. My birth father sounded just like my father, a guy with a blue-collar job, so why swap the shadowy father for the one I knew? "He was a better father when I was young."

"When was the last time you saw him?" Mrs. Hudson asked.

I tried to think. "A year ago, maybe? He came by shortly before my grandmother's death."

"You didn't let him inside, did you?"

Did she think I was stupid? "What are you getting at?" I asked.

"There's no chance that he touched you inappropriately, is there?"

"No!" Of course not. I wouldn't . . . but what about Vera Cruz? Blind drunk, he'd sat on the bed and let his towel drop open. My first glimpse of a penis. And then he'd stood. If I hadn't punched him . . .

My face was on fire. "Where are you getting this?"

"Your mother thought he might have," Dolores said.

"My father was a scary person," I said. "What did she say, anyway?"

"That he's suing for custody."

Suddenly breathless, I gripped the chair's armrests. "Of who?"

"You, of course."

"He doesn't want custody."

"If he found out you were pregnant, he could claim your mother's not a fit parent."

"On what grounds?"

"That she let you run around."

Like squirrels on a tree?

"I wasn't running around."

"Her lawyer's in court right now, trying to get your father to pay back child support, and he countersued, saying he wants custody. Apparently, there was a hearing last week."

A swiftly dropping elevator jolted to a stop. "This is the first I've heard of any of this."

"*Is* it," Mrs. Hudson said.

"Yes, it is," I said. "My mother is a private—a very self-conscious and self-pitying—person."

"Do you think she would describe herself that way?"

"She would say 'shy.'"

"And how would she characterize you?"

"Outgoing. Popular, probably. But I'm not that outgoing, and I'm not all that popular. In fact, my mother doesn't know me. She doesn't know what I think or feel. Being pregnant at my age is really hard on me."

Mrs. Hudson checked her watch. "I'm sorry, but our time's up. We'll talk again."

"All right," I said, relieved that the hour was over. What I longed for most, apart from getting back to high school and my normal life, was to get away from grown-ups.

CHAPTER 41

CHANGING OF THE GUARD

*W*hen I returned from the therapy appointment, I signed myself in and Karla handed me a letter. I tore it open. John had bought a plane ticket. He'd see me in three weeks. Thank God.

"And there's something else," Karla said. "Tonight is Director South's last day. She'll join you girls for dinner and introduce her replacement, our new social worker."

I looked past Karla's desk to the director's office. The door was closed. If Marianne had been here, she would have given us a heads-up, but she was gone, and now Mrs. South would be gone, too.

The dining room was the largest room in the home, and we had not yet carried our dinner plates over to the kitchen counter. Mrs. South waited by the door while we finished dessert. Beside her stood a tall, thin, thirtyish woman in a black, kick-pleated skirt, its waistband buttoned and not even tight.

After we'd bused our dishes and reseated ourselves, Mrs. South read from a piece of paper. "What a pleasure it has been to know you individually. Each of you has such potential, and beyond this period in your lives will come other periods with far less stress. I wish you well on your journeys, and I am proud that the Florence Crittenton Home has provided you safe haven. That has always been our mission—to protect women in their time of trouble."

"Are you getting canned because of Amber?" Paula, the hooker, called out.

Mrs. South blanched. "Thank you for your concern, but no, I'm not getting fired. We're simply adding a new person to our staff." She looked down at the paper. "I'd like to introduce our new social worker, Ernestine Fennel. She comes to us after having served as a probation officer here in Phoenix and before that in the armed forces—"

"What branch?" Barbara, the sergeant from Ft. Benning, called out.

"Women's Army Corps," Mrs. South said.

"Where'd you train?" Barbara interrupted again.

"Fort McClellan," Miss Fennel said.

With hair clipped army short, Miss Fennel looked us over the way a spectator at a zoo might look at a flock of ducks and not notice any one duck in particular. Instead, she would be thinking, *What a noisy, gaggling, silly flock! How superior they make me feel!*

Roonay elbowed me. "What you have to do to get that bitch to crack a smile?"

Miss Ernestine Fennel stood with her arms crossed, swaying a little. "Miss South is going to be a hard act to follow. I know you all must have great affection for her. I'll do my best not to change things too fast and to respect the solid foundation she's laid down. Now, let's hear a round of applause for Miss South. Job well done." Miss Fennel saluted.

Miss South. It was *Mrs.* South. Women thumped the table with the flats of their hands. We liked frumpy Mrs. South, with her flowered jersey dresses and flyaway hair. She stayed in her office and left us alone.

After clearing our plates, we ran the gauntlet between the two women. Miss Fennel didn't know us from Adam, or, rather, Eve, and her hand, cold and limp, made me shudder. But maybe I was wrong. Cold hands, warm heart. I wanted to give Miss Fennel the benefit of the doubt and assumed she'd be like a vice principal, a person whose office you didn't visit unless you'd done something wrong.

CHAPTER 42

DEVELOPMENTAL TASKS

*E*ven by 2018, when I had gone through my diaries, read my mother's old letters, looked at the forms I'd filled out, and gotten down the basic outline of this memoir, I still did not fully understand whether my sense memory—the emotions I recalled and that occasionally welled up from the deep—matched the objective facts, what would be observable and quantifiable to anyone standing outside the picture. Having seen my own kids grow up, and now watching my grandchildren, I knew that hormonally overwrought teens do not have a complete grasp of how the world works—what my mother liked to call "adult responsibilities."

When I was pregnant, my emotions were all over the place, but now, looking back, I understand that I was stuck in a situational crisis that led to a situational depression. My boyfriend wouldn't marry me. Our parents had come up with a plan that would allow me to stay in school but that would ultimately take my baby away. I wasn't allowed to tell even my best friends where I'd gone. My coursework was boring and stupid, more like eighth-grade home-work than the rigorous classes at my high school.

But it wasn't just the unplanned pregnancy that threatened my mental health. My parents had divorced. My grandmother had died. My father had disappeared, but now he was back in court. As anxious as my mother must have been about her physical and financial health, she'd found the chutzpah to stand up to him. As many people had tried to tell me, she had my best interests at heart. That might have been easier to acknowledge if I had not been a teenager.

Like all teenagers, I saw the world through the lens of my own developmental tasks: pushing away from my mother, dealing with attraction and rejection from friends and the opposite sex, establishing independence, and trying out versions of the self that I would be when I grew up. In 1961, I would have been about halfway through my formative years.

In her paper about identity formation, psychologist Elizabeth Crocetti[1] writes that adolescents enter their teen years with a preliminary sense of their identity, based on what they've understood about themselves from their families and the mirroring that takes place when relatives make offhand remarks about a child looking like a parent or having aptitudes that run in the family. Under ordinary circumstances, teens make a preliminary commitment—they plant a flag in the sand—and then test and reconsider that commitment, based on their experiences. *Yes, I am like my artistic mother. No, I don't want to work in my father's hardware store.*

Crocetti writes that the formation of identity is a dynamic one. If teens are testing parental boundaries all the time, then they are also testing themselves against markers from the outside world. Some teens, Crocetti writes, are also acutely aware of their inner landscapes, meaning their moods. That was me in a nutshell. Always gazing at my navel. Self-absorbed. Trying my best to stay afloat. However, moody though I was, I still needed adult help in discerning the path ahead.

"Although commitment and in-depth exploration imply attempts to develop and maintain a sense of self, reconsideration represents questioning and rethinking this sense of self (identity confusion)," Crocetti asserts. Over the long term, asking the deep questions about who you are and what your life is all about "is important for finding more satisfying commitments," she believes;

however, the loss of familiar routines and certainties "can lead to a temporary crisis."[2]

Miss Fennel's arrival altered our routines and signaled a change in tone. From then on, we were under surveillance. We lowered our voices when she approached, and her scrutiny pushed me closer to the precipice of despair.

I HAD SLEPT LATER than I normally did and so had not finished my chore until eight thirty. I stood at the open janitor's closet, putting away my mop.

"When you're done with that, could you come see me in my office?" Miss Fennel said.

"Sure," I said, my heart beating fast.

"No rush," she said.

Was she going to dish out a demerit? Make me stand in the corner with a dunce cap? A few minutes later, I knocked on her door.

"Come in," she said, her voice a high and low syllable, like a doorbell's chime.

"You wanted to see me?"

"Come in, come in." She rushed toward me and took my elbow, guiding me to a seat, and then she went back behind her desk and, like a nesting heron, folded down into her chair.

The former director, frumpy and plump, too many trips to the cookie jar, had somehow belonged here, but Miss Fennel did not. Mrs. South had opened her eyes and looked us square in the face. Miss Fennel squinted, as if staring at a bright light. *She's going to trap me*, I thought.

"Well," she said, rocking back and making a tent of her fingers, "I thought we should get better acquainted."

"Okay." Grown-ups liked it when you sounded cooperative.

"So!" Her mouth turned from a flat, nothing expression to a fake smile. "Your file says you are able to establish paternity."

I had no idea what she meant. "Okay," I said.

"Okay what?" she said. "Are you, or aren't you?"

"Aren't I what?"

"Do you know the father of your child?"

"Of course," I said.

"How many times did you have relations with him?"

"Sex, you mean?"

"Yes," she said.

I had her number. This was like one of my father's trick questions.

"Once," I said.

"Once." She wrote something on my file. Then she looked across the desk and her eyelids lowered until her irises all but disappeared. "Are you sure it was only once?"

"Yes, I'm sure," I said. "We were unlucky and got caught."

"Are you telling me the truth?"

I looked at the bookcase. It was completely empty—no books, no pictures of family. There was a pen stand and a Rolodex on her desk. Who exactly was I talking to? What did she want to know?

"I'm telling you the truth," I said. "We're Catholics, and Catholics aren't supposed to have sex before marriage."

A smirk played at the corner of her mouth. "Plenty of Catholics do."

"You're not Catholic, I gather."

"No, I'm not."

"Sex outside of marriage is a mortal sin."

"Does the Catholic Church believe birth control is a sin, too?"

"You mean condoms?"

"In part, but there are other ways to prevent pregnancy."

The rhythm method. "I know."

"You do understand how you got pregnant, don't you?"

I made a circle with my thumb and stuck my index finger through it.

"When did your parents tell you the facts of life?"

"Sixth grade," I said.

"And which one told you?"

"My mother," I said. "We were canning peaches." Even the

thought of that made me want to throw up, the idea that my mother and father had actually "had relations" and the cringing, clinical explanation of what a man did and what a woman had to put up with because of the man.

Sex with John was nothing like that. Sex with him was in a whole other category. He made me feel alive.

"Why do you even care how many times we had sex?" I said. "It's really none of your business."

"Oh, but it *is* my business," she said. "We want all of our girls to leave here better people than when they came in."

I was a fine person when I came in. "Can I go now?"

"We'll have another chat next week," Miss Fennel said. "By the way, Miss South left me a note that you were taking correspondence courses. How are you coming with them?"

"Fine," I said.

She looked down at her notes. "Do you think I should call your mother?"

"She doesn't have a phone."

"Then how do you reach her?"

"She calls me from a pay phone."

"The next time you talk to her, please ask her to stop by the office."

"Sure, but why?"

"Because of your age," she said. "I gather you were fifteen when you got pregnant."

"Yes, but I'm sixteen now and quite mature for my age," I said. "At least, that's what people say."

Her eyes flicked up. "Close the door when you leave."

CHAPTER 43

BANANA SPLIT

*I*t was Sunday, the day Pam and I had started walking a mile and a half to a donut shop.

She picked up a book from the nightstand. "I want to finish my novel and take a nap."

"Okay. I'll see if someone else is going out."

I sat in the waiting room, thumbing a magazine, until Joanie, the tall girl who helped Ruby in the kitchen, and Karen, the acne-scarred, heavyset girl from the diet table, came out. "Could I tag along with you guys?" I asked.

They looked at each other. "Sure," Karen said, in that real slow way that made me realize it wasn't okay, but they weren't going to tell me no.

We signed the clipboard and wrote down our departure times, and then we were on the sidewalk. Instead of turning left, which was the direction of the donut shop, we turned right, walking two by two. The odd one out, I brought up the rear. I wasn't sure why they didn't want me with them, except that they didn't, because they whispered among themselves and Karen kept looking over her shoulder to see if I was still there.

She crossed the road and turned down a side street, where I saw a small market. At the market, she opened the screen and held it while Joanie and I filed in. The market was dim and had three double-sided shelves with canned goods, crackers, and pet food. On one wall was a cooler with bottles of Coke. Then I saw a soda counter with five stools. A bald man so short I could barely see his face stood behind the counter. Karen and Joanie sat down on the stools.

"What'll it be, ladies?" the man asked.

"Chocolate-banana shake," Karen said.

"Hot fudge sundae," Joanie said, smirking in my direction and patting a stool.

I hesitated, then made up my mind. "Banana split."

"Cherries?"

"Sure."

A banana split was my favorite dessert. Throughout sixth grade, I'd been on a dentist-enforced no-sweets diet, but, after a successful checkup, the dentist lifted the ban. Soon after, my father took us on a driving trip through thirty-six states, and once a day, I ate a banana split. When I saw the two slices of banana, three kinds of ice cream, and caramel, chocolate, and pineapple sauce, topped with whipped cream and peanuts, my mouth watered. I couldn't believe this place was here, a mere three blocks from the home, and that Pam and I hadn't discovered it. Maybe Pam didn't know, or maybe it was just concern about her weight that kept her away. She cared a lot more about her appearance than I did. And obviously Karen didn't care at all, because she was huge.

I spooned up the ice cream slowly, savoring each bite. This was different than the ice cream cups with the paper tops that Ruby served us on special occasions. There was a half a cup of ice cream in each container, and we had to dig it out with a wooden spoon. This was three scoops of ice cream, plus the banana, plus the sauces, and most of all the heaping mounds of whipped cream. The flavors mingled on my tongue and reminded me of my childhood. One day I would be happy again. Not that I was unhappy. I tried not to be. But trying not to be was different than actual happiness.

When we were done, Karen held me by the shoulders for

inspection. She wiped a smidge of chocolate from my lips. "Be careful about dripping on your dress," she said, dipping a napkin in my glass of water and scrubbing at the sticky caramel. Luckily, I had worn my paisley muumuu and the drips blended in with the design. Also, luckily, I had phone coins in my pocket, or I would have had to borrow.

"Now, don't rat on us," Karen said. "Pam's sort of a goody two-shoes, and she might feel compelled to say something to Miss Fennel."

I stuck out my tongue. "Miss Fennel. Ugh!"

"Don't you like her?" Joanie asked.

They looked at each other.

"That *dyke?*" Karen said.

"What's a dyke?" I asked.

"Dykes, otherwise known as lesbians, are women who have sex with other women," Joanie said.

I frowned and looked from one to another. They looked at me, expecting agreement. They weren't trying to pull my leg.

"But how is that even possible?" I asked.

Karen smirked and rolled her eyes. "You'd have to ask Fennel."

"But are you sure?" I asked. "I mean, how can you tell?"

"She gives off a certain vibe," Joanie said.

"A vibe," I said.

"Yeah, a vibe," Karen said. "We knew the moment we saw her."

"Oh, yeah," I said. "Roonay and I picked up on it, too. We just didn't know it was *that.*"

I had thought it was just that there are some people you don't take a cotton to, without ever having a reason. Unlike Mrs. Hudson, the lady my mom had hired to try to talk me out of my silence, Fennel seemed more interested in interrogation. She made me feel like a witness on *Perry Mason.*

CHAPTER 44

THE RUG

On Monday, I was still pondering what Joanie and Karen had said, when I heard Miss Fennel's heels clicking along the hall. She made the rounds four or five times a day and would brace herself against the door jamb, smile momentarily, and, unless she found something amiss, be on her way. Pam, doing her nails, sat on her bed. I had just decided to take a nap.

Miss Fennel looked in. "No shoes on the bedspread."

I kicked them off.

"Don't leave your things lying around," she said.

I leaned over for my shoes and shoved them beneath the bed.

"That's not where they belong," she said.

Sighing, I fished my shoes out and opened my locker. The hooked rug, which now had the diameter of a wading pool and which I'd rolled up and crammed next to my muumuus, fell out onto my bed.

"What on earth is that?" Miss Fennel asked, entering the room.

"It's a rag rug," I said. All the balls of rag I'd brought had gone into it, and I'd been thinking of taking some of the clothes down in the clothes room and cutting them up.

Miss Fennel took three strides and reached my locker. She slid open my drawers one by one and saw the collection of shredded underwear, including my old training bra, pantyhose, hair clips, scarves, and mismatched socks. In the drawer below, I had crammed my pajamas and robe, which made the drawer hard to close. And in the very bottom drawer, I kept my art supplies: watercolors, sketch pads, lead pencils, gum erasers, and brushes.

Miss Fennel straightened up and put her hands on her bony hips. "Put your things in order," she said. Then, looking at the rug that lay like a dead body across my bed, she said, "That thing belongs in the luggage room."

Pam blew on her nails. "It's her hobby."

"I'll be back to inspect in half an hour," Fennel said.

"That's not much time," I said.

"I know," she said. "Get busy."

She crossed to her office and slammed the door. I don't know why my messy drawers annoyed her. My closet at home was a lot messier, but my mother said it was okay to confine my mess. If my bed was made, she didn't care.

I began straightening my art supplies.

"I can help you," Pam said. "I'm good at organizing."

I passed her the drawer.

"Faber pencils." She held one up.

I passed her my Strathmore sketchpad. She opened it and fanned through the pages. "Who's this?" she asked, turning the sketchpad around.

"My mom," I said.

"She has an interesting face."

I stuck out my tongue. "She's ugly as a toad."

"She reminds me of my grandmother," Pam said. "A wrinkled-up, old apple doll."

"She's old enough to be my grandmother," I said.

"My parents are old, too."

"Not as old as her, I bet. I was adopted when she was forty-four." The elastic in my nylon undies was so shot, they weren't worth keeping. I threw them in the "toss" pile.

"Are you done yet?" Miss Fennel stood behind me.

"Almost," I said.

Miss Fennel pointed to the collection of lipstick, nail polish, and tweezers on the shelf below my mirror. In his last letter, John had sent me a picture, and I'd stuck it in the mirror's frame.

"We can't have that there," she said. "You're not allowed to leave any personal items within view of the other residents."

"I don't care if people see my boyfriend's picture."

Hands behind her back, she leaned in and scowled. "Hmm! He's got a big nose."

Stork! Crane!

She straightened up, then checked the drawers I had put back. "Much better."

"Okay," I said.

"Keep it picked up," she said, "and make sure you put that rug away."

"I'll give it to my mother when she comes," I said.

"In the meantime, don't keep it in here. You girls don't have much room."

"That's the truth." Pam's eyebrow shot up, and she looked at Miss Fennel, who'd said what she'd come to say and was leaving to go back to her office.

As if feeling Pam's eyes on her back, Miss Fennel spun around and pointed at me. "I'll see you in my office tomorrow."

"What did I do?" *Now*, I could have added.

"Nothing," Miss Fennel said. "I just want to get to know you."

Women who make love to other women. I really didn't want to go into her office again.

When Miss Fennel had left, Pam handed me back my art drawer. "The only reason she's interested in you is because you're the youngest."

"What does that have to do with anything?"

"I think she's trying to save you."

"From what?" I asked.

"Getting pregnant again."

Good grief, Charlie Brown. Just let me focus on one thing at a time and have the first baby before anyone worries about a second one.

I carried the rug down to the luggage room. I was completely not in a mood to draw.

"I've been thinking about getting a bridge group going," Pam said. "Joanie plays, and so does Rhonda. Do you?"

My father had been a big poker player. I associated cards with a crawly feeling in the pit of my stomach. "The only card games I know are Fish and War," I said. "I think I'll write a letter."

"Okay, then," Pam said. "We won't include you."

I turned on the bedside lamp and fluffed my pillow. *Ka-ching, ka-ching, ka-ching.* Across the hall, someone was dropping nickels into the phone.

December 14, 1961

Dear John,

How did you do on midterms? Have you filled out your other college applications yet? Are you still thinking about applying to Dartmouth? I know they have a good engineering school, but there aren't any really good women's colleges nearby, and it would be good if we don't wind up too far apart.

I've still got my sights set on Pembroke. I think it'd be easier to get into than Radcliffe, and I definitely don't want to go to a single-sex school like Smith, even though my History teacher said she'd write me a letter of recommendation and that Smith would be a good place for me. Because of my mom's illness and my dad moving out, she thinks I wouldn't have too much trouble getting a scholarship.

Have your parents filled out the FAF? Maybe if you got a scholarship and I did, too, we could both go to the same school. Wouldn't that be cool? We could take the same classes and have a lot to talk about when we see each other.

My roommate Diane, who showed me the path around the building, said her boyfriend is thinking about becoming a mechanic, and she's thinking about taking a secretarial course. They're one year older than me—seniors—and when Diane leaves, she'll have one more semester before she graduates. She's going to try to keep her baby.

When you come down here, maybe we can figure out what to do. It's hard in a letter.

Love,
   Marylee

PS: I can't wait to see you.

I had one envelope left, and I was out of stamps. Karla had some I could buy. Crossing the hall to the waiting room, I saw Pam in the phone booth, her elbow on the chrome shelf where we laid out our change. So much for getting Joanie and Rhonda to play cards. What Pam was really doing was calling Dougie.

CHAPTER 45

CHRIS-TOWN MALL

*C*alling from the library, my mother told me that she'd made another appointment with the counselor, Mrs. Hudson, but that it would be just the two of them this time.

"Are you going to talk about what a bad daughter I am?" I asked.

"Not necessarily," she said. "But I need some emotional support. Your father's giving me a hard time."

My father. Who had stormed out after calling me a whore.

"If my lawyer can get him to pay what he owes in child support," my mother said, "it will help."

"Maybe you should let it go," I said.

"No, I have to try."

She explained that their counseling session would take place at the Catholic Social Service office. However, since I had no way of getting over there, she suggested that Mrs. Hudson come by the home and meet me in one of the two visiting rooms: windowless, white-walled spaces, each with a small, rectangular table and six chairs. "Is that okay?" she asked.

"I don't mind," I said.

Mrs. Hudson met with me two more times. Rather than grill me about my behavior, she asked open-ended questions. How was I doing? Was anything going on that I wanted to talk about? How was the baby? How was I spending my free time?

I told Mrs. Hudson how easy the extension classes were, which was odd because the curriculum came from UC Berkeley. I told her how torn I was by what had happened. I had put the boy I loved in a bind and brought shame on both our families. Now, I couldn't even get forgiven for my sins because my mother wouldn't let me go anywhere near a Catholic church. Mass was the one place my father, if he happened to find out we were down here, might come looking. (Little did any of us know that her vigilance turned out to be prescient: Rex remarried and moved to Phoenix around 1962 and passed away four years later. A private first class in World War I, he was buried in Phoenix's Greenwood Memorial Park cemetery.)

"Are you able to get to Mass?" Mrs. Hudson asked.

"Not now, but I will when this is all over."

I didn't tell Mrs. Hudson why I hadn't been going to Mass. A priest from the local parish regularly came by the home to hand out Communion wafers, but John and I had had sex in the garage, and since then, I hadn't gone to confession.

"I miss going to Mass," I said. "It's important to check in with your conscience on a regular basis."

"Don't beat yourself up," Mrs. Hudson said, smiling. "God's not going to punish you any more than you're already being punished."

I felt a slight shift inside. Mrs. Hudson had put into words what I'd been feeling—that pregnancy was a kind of punishment for my having had sex outside of marriage. "I can't wait to put this all behind me," I said. "It's killing my mother to see me pregnant. I don't think she'll get better until this is all over."

"Meaning?" she said.

"Until I'm no longer pregnant."

"Sounds like you're worried about her."

"If she's in this bad shape when we go home, I don't see how she can go back to the classroom."

"Would it be fair to say you care?"

I looked inside. The dirty clay of disgust was still there.

I shook my head. "Deep down, I suppose I must care. After all, she is my mother, and I owe her, but . . ."

"Leave the 'buts' for the moment. Let's stick with the positive. That's a big win."

Mrs. Hudson proposed that she, my mother, and I go someplace "neutral"—the new Chris-Town mall at North Nineteenth Avenue and West Bethany Home Road. Normally, I couldn't leave on a weekday, but Mrs. Hudson got special permission. After she picked me up, we swung by to get my mother.

Outside every little dwelling in the motor court, a car was parked. Illinois. Idaho. Saskatchewan. I thought of that old license plate game we used to play on the long driving trips with my father. I wished I could go back to being the kind of daughter I'd been at nine and ten.

My mother locked the door. Hunched over as if carrying a safe, she climbed in the back. I turned and said, "Hi, Mom," and Mrs. Hudson added, "How are you today?"

"Not good," my mother said.

"What's the matter?" Mrs. Hudson asked, pulling out of the motor court and looking at my mother in the rearview mirror.

"Just the usual."

"The usual" meant the jerking had gotten bad again. Sometimes it was her face and arm. That was bad enough. It made her self-conscious.

"Are you having trouble walking?" I asked.

"I always have trouble walking," she said. "It's a matter of degree."

Mrs. Hudson raised her eyebrows and looked at me. "Don't worry. We'll take it easy."

At the mall, Mrs. Hudson and I walked as if we were slow walking in a swimming pool, but even then, my mother could not keep up. What I knew to be true about myself, I told the counselor, was that I was hardwired to have a smile on my face and to think that affection and love and connectedness were what mattered. I kept reaching for that will-o'-the-wisp, that connection to my mother, but I could not find it. Where my mother and her parents came from—the small towns of Missouri and of the Colorado plains—people did not share their feelings. They did not gush or enthuse. They talked of who they visited and how long they stayed and from whom they'd had a letter. Because my mother shared so little about herself—her own hopes, dreams, loves, or yearnings— she was not someone I could confide in.

When my mother caught up, the talking stopped. I could not explain to this kindly social worker what was wrong. My mother was a good mother. She tried hard. With a shy, homely, introverted girl —someone with thick glasses and an overbite, someone who'd been teased and shunned—my mother could have drawn on her decades of teaching experience and found a way into that child's heart. My mother and I were mismatched. I was the wrong daughter for her.

CHAPTER 46

FROM MONDAY

*M*iss Fennel pointed to her office chair and I sat. "Thank you for asking your mother to drop in," she said. "We can't meet all the parents, because some live so far away, but we like to meet the locals."

"She's not a local," I said. "We're from the Bay Area."

"You know very well what I mean."

She made a tent with her fingers. Behind them, I could see her smirk.

"I'm curious," I said, "just why you *did* want her to come over."

"It helps us triangulate."

"On what?" I said.

"Your home situation."

My home situation. My home situation was a wreck, and I had ruined my mother's life. I knew it. She knew it.

"Your father wasn't an easy man to live with, I gather," Miss Fennel said.

He hadn't been easy to live with, but now my mother was rid of him.

"When I was talking to your mother, I discovered an odd coincidence," she said.

"What?"

"We both have ties to Missouri," she said. "I come from Moberly."

"I've been to Moberly," I said.

Moberly was the large town next to the small town when my grandma, grandpa, and I went to stay in the summers. We'd driven through Moberly, but always on the way to the farm. The farm was in Yates, Missouri, and it was where Grandma had lived when she fled the sod house in North Dakota where my mother had spent two years of her early life.

"What else did my mother tell you?" I asked.

"Some details about your biological family."

Like a slowly filling glass, a line of heat rose from my neck.

"Did you hear me?" Miss Fennel asked.

"I heard you," I said.

"You're looking out the window."

Was I? Yes, I was looking at the little spaces between the slats. I forced myself to look at her again. Miss Fennel's hair had grown out a little. Now she had a curl in the middle of her forehead. *When she was good, she was very, very good, and when she was bad, she was horrid.* Grandma used to say that.

I imitated Fennel's bit with hands, an isosceles triangle.

Miss Fennel tapped her pencil and sucked in her lower lip. "We like to know what our girls plan to do when they leave us."

"I'm going to college," I said.

"What will you study?"

"Biochemistry or Spanish," I said. "I'm also somewhat interested in anthropology because of Margaret Mead. Have you read *Coming of Age in Samoa* or *Blackberry Winter*?"

"Never heard of them. Or her. What are they about?"

"Adolescence and maturation. One is the story of her childhood. The other is the story of her fieldwork in Samoa."

"And why is this of interest to you?"

"Because Margaret Mead writes that women in Samoa are mothers at sixteen. She says America forces teens to live in a period of prolonged adolescence. That runs counter to our biological imperatives."

Miss Fennel's mouth gaped open. "Is that right."

"Yes, and she's quite convincing."

Miss Fennel was making some notes to herself. While she wrote, I looked at the books that had begun to populate her shelves, but they weren't books, exactly. Just pastel-colored volumes with titles like *Journal of Health and Social Behavior* and *Journal of Abnormal Psychology*. I hoped to God she'd had enough of this getting-to-know-you stuff and would let me leave the room.

"Let's talk about your adoption."

This again. "There's nothing to say."

"When did you learn you were adopted?"

"I've always known."

"I see," Miss Fennel said.

The seat cushion began to slide out from under me, and I straightened up, gripping the arms of the chair.

"Your mother told me she's fairly sure you and the father of your child had relations more than once."

"We didn't."

"Did he force it on you?"

My eyebrows pinched. "Force what on me?"

"Did he force you to have sex."

"No."

"Did you tell him to stop?"

Why didn't she just shut up?

"If he did, then I wouldn't be in love with him, would I?"

Miss Fennel checked her watch. "All right, but if you don't open up, we can't help you. We need you to work with us."

"Work with you how?"

"To discover the causes of what brought you here."

I knew what brought me here. I liked sex.

CHAPTER 47

MOVIE NIGHT

One day at lunch, Miss Fennel made an announcement. After dinner, we would watch a movie.

"If we've already seen it, do we have to?" someone asked.

"Yes," Miss Fennel said. "I would like everyone to see it. The nurse will be here if you have any questions."

A movie would be neat, I thought. Maybe *Ben-Hur* or *Gone with the Wind*. Anticipating an epic, I went back to my room and took a nap.

After dinner, the nurse set up the kind of portable screen people once used to show their vacation slides. There was a sixteen-millimeter projector. The nurse slid a dinner knife under the film can's lid, popped it off, and loaded the reel.

Karen, Joanie, and I ate our dinner, bused our dishes, and returned to the diet table. Joanie had joined our elite ranks, and, probably because of our trips to the soda fountain, Karen's acne had flared up.

"I hope this isn't some kind of World War II movie," I said.

Joanie and Karen looked at each other and gave me a "how dumb can you be" look.

"It's about childbirth," Karen said.

"And we've both seen it," Joanie said.

The movie was a black-and-white movie with scratchy sound and the kind of alternately dramatic and sappy music that played behind the voice of an announcer. I wondered if this production was by the same people who'd made the movie I'd seen in sixth grade. It repeated some of the same information. There was the sperm swimming upstream. There were the fallopian tubes. There was the embryo implanting itself in the wall of the uterus and the baby beginning to grow.

But this movie went far beyond where that movie stopped. Drawings showed the baby getting larger. The baby looked like a Martian: all head. Then the drawings had the baby turn upside down, its bald white head wedging into the birth canal.

Pam sat at the table behind me. She leaned back and patted her stomach. "Two more weeks."

My due date wasn't for another three and a half. We were midway through the second week of December, and John wouldn't arrive until the twenty-sixth.

The movie shifted to an operating room. A woman was lying on a bed. Her knees were up and covered by a sheet. Leather straps held her wrists. The announcer said that when the woman went into labor, she would have to push. The screen went black. Then a doctor pulled a baby from beneath the sheet. A cord spiraled from the baby's navel. The doctor held the baby upside down and slapped its butt. The baby's mouth opened, but we could not hear a cry. The doctor cut the umbilical cord and handed the baby to a nurse. The nurse took the baby away.

I think my attention kind of flagged at that moment. This was a real baby, with jerky motions, its squashed head turning in a startled way. It looked wet. I put my hand on my stomach. My poor baby! When it came out, it would get a slap on the butt. It would breathe on its own but would no longer be inside me, squirming about, taking naps. It would begin its sovereign life.

The movie then showed the mother back at the home. It showed a room with cribs. Half of the cribs had babies. The mother, in a robe, walked into the room and picked up her baby. She felt the baby's diaper and put on a clean one. Then she wrapped the baby tightly in a blanket, carried it to a rocking chair, sat down, and began to feed it from a glass bottle of formula.

Another woman came into the room. This one wore a dark skirt and a blouse with a ruffled collar. She went to a crib and picked up a baby. The camera followed her as she went to a second rocking chair. She lifted her blouse, and the baby began to suckle. I felt a stinging sensation in my breasts. Then there was happy music, like a toothpaste jingle, and the words "the end."

The nurse, who had been leaning against the wall, turned on the lights. She walked back to the projector and put it on rewind. The whir of sprockets filled the silence. The end of the reel whipped.

No one smiled. We just looked at one another as if we'd been horsing around while the teacher was out of the room.

When the rewind finished, the nurse came to the front of the room. "Any questions about the birth process?"

There were no questions.

Finally, Pam raised her hand. "When I'm loading the dish-washer, I get pains around my back. Is that normal?"

"What's your due date?" the nurse asked.

"The fourth of January," Pam said.

The nurse frowned. "I'll talk to the office. We can reassign you."

I wasn't having any pains. I raised my hand. "She can do my job, and I can do hers."

"Thank you for volunteering. I'll tell them tomorrow. What's your name?"

"Marylee," I said, then spelled it out. "And she's Pam."

"I know who Pam is."

The nurse looked around. "One more time. Does anyone have any questions about childbirth?"

No one did.

I wanted to ask about the babies. Why were there cribs in the movie but no cribs here? Why did the movie show mothers taking care of babies? As far as I knew, unless our boyfriends decided to marry us, the social workers took our babies away.

"I'll show you what to do in the kitchen tomorrow," Pam said.

"Okay," I said. "I'll show you the hall."

"I know what to do," she said. "That was my first job when I moved in."

When I went to bed, I kept seeing that room with the cribs. The two women in the movie had Dorothy Lamour hairstyles: curly bangs and hair swept back at the sides. The room did not look like any room in the home. The building had high ceilings and dark woodwork. What year had this movie been made? Seemed like the era of Jeanette MacDonald and Nelson Eddy, the musicals they'd shown at the Fox Theater's Sunday matinees. Even the lilting background music sounded similar. I could not get it out of my head.

CHAPTER 48

THE KITCHEN

The dishwashing area was in the back of the kitchen. Two deep sinks had a sprayer. It was the older woman, Paula's, job to rinse food off the plates. She dumped out the drinking glasses and checked the rims for lipstick. If she missed something, Pam grabbed the dish rag and cleaned off the pink. Paula had soap and was supposed to hand over plates that looked clean. The dishwasher wasn't a dishwasher, really. It was a sterilizer and had big gray trays that had to be loaded a certain way and then slid along the stainless-steel counter and lifted in. Pam showed me how all the dishes had to face front. If I didn't load the plates right, the sterilizer would have to run twice.

"Believe me," she said, "when you're done with this, you'll be ready to hit the sack."

I was amazed at how efficiently she worked. Her hands flew as she took the rinsed dishes, checked them for particles, and slid them in the tray, each slot filled. The glasses went in one tray and the cups in another.

Paula wiped her hands on a kitchen towel and pulled off her hairnet. "I'm finished. See you lovely ladies tomorrow."

"You'll see me," I said. "I'm taking over Pam's job."

"Yeah, I heard you," Paula said, "but one thing I've learned is, never volunteer. Keep your head down if you don't want to get it chopped off." She pulled the apron over her head and hung it on one of the hooks next to the sink.

"I guess I should wear an apron," I said, going to get one.

"And a hairnet," Pam said.

"Where are they?"

"In the bottom drawer." She pointed to a wheeled metal cabinet.

While I leaned against the counter, tucking my hair up into the net and feeling the steam come from the running water, I said, "Do you like working in the kitchen?"

Pam, whose hands were down in the deep sink, scrubbing the burnt chili from the bottom of an aluminum pot, looked over her shoulder. "It was okay till about a week ago."

"What happened then?"

She lowered her voice. "The baby turned."

"How do you know?"

"The feet are up under my ribs. My pelvic bones ache. It feels like he's about to drop out."

"He?" I said.

"Marianne said if you're carrying low, it's a boy."

My baby had dropped. I felt like I had a bowling ball between my legs, but it wasn't a bowling ball. It was a baby.

ON TUESDAY, I'd had my weigh-in. Not good. Pulling off her hairnet and throwing it on the nightstand, Diane, fresh from doing the lunch dishes, said, "I hear you're still on the diet table."

"Yes," I said. "What a drag."

"How much did you gain?"

"Another pound."

"I don't understand why you're not losing weight. They're only giving you twelve hundred calories a day."

"I must gain weight easily," I said, trying to remember what Pam had said. Ectomorph, mesomorph, or something else.

I had gone over to the soda fountain once. At home, one banana split a week wouldn't have put on the pounds. I would have been biking to the library—five miles, there and back. An hour-long walk to school. Here, I waddled around the building once or twice and called it quits.

As usual, Diane went out for her forced march, and when she returned, she climbed up on the bed and did her trampoline act. Pam and I and Roonay, with her big mound of a stomach, lay on our beds, wishing Diane would stop jumping so we could take a nap. *Creak, creak* went the bedsprings.

But Diane's jumping paid off. She woke up with pains in the early morning and delivered four hours later. When I went to visit her in the clinic, the nurse was wrapping a wide ACE bandage around Diane's breasts.

A girl who lived down near the exit to the clothesline occupied the other bed. A Southern girl from Atlanta with the dark beauty of Elizabeth Taylor, she could have won the Miss America pageant. She'd delivered the previous morning.

"They gave me a shot to dry up my milk," Diane said, "but guess what?"

"What?" I asked.

"They're bringing my baby over this afternoon."

"Here to the clinic?"

"To the visiting room."

"My baby's coming over, too," the girl from Atlanta said.

"How is that possible?" I asked.

"Normally they don't bring babies over," Diane said, "but my boyfriend wants to see him before they take him to foster care."

My heart beat fast. Nobody had told me about any of this, about foster care or boyfriends' visits.

"Are they going to let your boyfriend come back here to the infirmary?"

"He'll meet us in the visiting room. Could you bring my hair spray down? I've got to get myself together."

"Is your boyfriend coming over, too?" I asked the girl from Atlanta.

"No, he's back home, trying to find employment. My mom is."

"I thought you signed surrender papers," Diane said.

"Yeah, honey, I signed in the hospital," the other girl said, "but my mom was able to get that reversed. She's taking me and the baby to a motel so we can bond." She squeezed her breasts. "It better happen soon. My breasts are full to bursting."

"What made your boyfriend change his mind?" I asked.

"I had a boy," the girl said, smiling. "For the first time, he could imagine himself as a father. Throwing a ball around. Doing guy stuff."

"And if you'd had a girl?" Diane asked.

"Ya'll know without me having to say."

A nurse with an armload of linens swooped in and brusquely pulled curtains around the bed. She wanted to get the girls cleaned up.

I brought Diane's hair spray from our room and then retreated to the hall and sank down in a clinic chair. The girl from Atlanta, in flats and a skirt, and Diane, in her robe, hobbled down to the visiting rooms. Soon enough, the tiny visitors arrived, brought in through the waiting room to spare the rest of us the parents' happy chatter. *How cute! How adorable!* Sounds dimmed. A young man's voice joined women's voices. The babies' mewling cries were muffled by the door, which was kept closed. And it was as if that door stood between me and the rest of the world. All the experiences I might have wanted—to see my baby, to hold it, to keep it— took place out of sight, on the other side of the wall, and I didn't have the strength to stand, much less walk into the waiting room and demand to know how I could make one of these other options happen. Diane and the girl from Atlanta said goodbye, and I got up to go take a nap.

CHAPTER 49

THE IQ TEST

The thought of those babies never left my mind. I had never placed my demands on the table and said, *John, you've got to marry me. I can't bear this another minute.* And then there were my binders of unfinished lessons. God knows I spent enough hours sitting at the card table. I should have had them done by now.

I folded a sheet of binder paper in thirds, and my thumbnail pressed two lengthwise creases. The legs of the card table shook as my pen moved down the page. On the left, I recorded Spanish words. On the right-hand panel, I wrote their meanings. *Embarazada*: pregnant; *parto*: childbirth; *cordón umbilical*: umbilical cord. *Placenta* was the same. Every day I set up a card table between my bed and Roonay's, but this morning I saw Roonay's slippers, two pink kittens, peeking out from under her bed.

I stood and, holding the small of my back, kicked the slippers into the shadows of the spread, then sat back down on the folding chair I'd dragged in from the laundry room and had to return there once I'd finished my homework. The light was off and the room, dim. I slipped my feet out of my sandals. The floor felt cold.

Explosions of canned laughter came from the TV room, where

Paula, the older woman from Las Vegas, and Barbara, the sergeant, hung out, watching *Days of Our Lives*. The noise made it hard to concentrate. The Cal curriculum wanted me to translate a paragraph and then fill in blank spaces with the appropriate verbs, but this was so easy, it was like being back in seventh grade. With no one to talk to, no one making my brain switch gears, I felt my language skills slipping into the deep freeze. My Spanish teacher, Mr. Macias, would go apoplectic.

Click, click, click. Miss Fennel on patrol again. Thank goodness I'd pushed those slippers under the bed. A hand opened the door. After ducking under the lintel, Miss Fennel flipped on the light.

"Why are you working in the dark?"

"It's light enough."

Miss Fennel came around and stood over my shoulder. "Here," she said, covering my homework with a stapled booklet she'd brought in. There was also a single-sided answer sheet, questions with numbered ovals.

"What's this?" I asked.

"An IQ test," she said. "The notes in your file claim you're smart. I want to verify that."

Claim I was smart? I felt like a balloon with a pinhole leak. "I'll do it after I finish my homework."

"It's timed," she said. "I'll be back to collect it in twenty minutes."

I had taken standardized tests my whole life. I was good at them —well, not uniformly good, because if I let myself remember the test I'd taken in seventh grade, a test I didn't know till later was an IQ test that separated the smartest kids and put them on a fast track that included algebra, I hadn't done well enough on math. I'd been put in the second-smartest class, which divided me from my friends, who had started learning about factorials and quadratic equations in eighth grade, while I had to wait until freshman year and Algebra I.

As I filled in the little ovals, I barely read the questions.

I completed the last oval and pushed the answer sheet aside. In preparation for my return to high school, I needed to review the familiar plural conjugations of irregular verbs.

"Done?" Miss Fennel asked, appearing at the door.

"I'm done," I said.

Miss Fennel took the workbook and answer sheet. "I'll grade it."

I returned to my verb list. First, I went down the Spanish side—*vosotros querais; vosotros estáis; vosotros ponéis*—and repeated the verb and its subject three times. The familiar plural was the one verb form that gave me trouble. I wouldn't have dared speak familiarly to Mr. Macias, with his handlebar mustache and tufts of hair in his ears. I pictured him pacing around the cafeteria, hands behind his back, turning red like a cartoon thermometer when he saw students throw food in the trash. If he could see me now, struggling to keep an active vocabulary when I had no one to talk to, no way to practice, when I could barely thaw out my brain . . .

The door slammed back against Roonay's closet, and I looked up to see Fennel holding the answer sheet. "I graded it," she said, "and it looks like they made a mistake."

From the nape of my neck to the small of my back, I felt a zap of cold. "What kind of mistake?"

Miss Fennel looked at the answer sheet. "According to your intake file, you're supposed to have a high IQ, but according to this, your IQ is only 126."

"Is that bad?" I asked.

"It's not brilliant. You're a high average."

I looked down at the table. "I need to finish my homework."

"Do you have any questions?" Miss Fennel asked.

"No," I said.

"I can see you're concentrating," Miss Fennel said. "We can talk in my office another time."

Every conversation I'd ever had with Miss Fennel ran through my head. With the IQ test and her verdict that I was not as smart as I thought I was, she had pretty much kicked the props out from under me. If I wasn't smart, then what was I? Who was I? A phony? A liar? A slut?

I looked up from my list. *Comer*, eat—*vosotros coméis*—was the most regular verb in the language. I didn't need to practice the conjugation. From the kitchen came a smell that reminded me of hot roast beef sandwiches. Tomorrow was weigh-in day, and I should probably not eat a big meal, though I felt like it. I felt like stuffing myself. Even if they kept me on the diet table, at the next opportunity I would sneak out with Karen for a banana split. Rules be damned.

CHAPTER 50

DWARVES

*A*t lunch, Miss Fennel came into the lunchroom and rapped on the nearest table. "Attention, ladies!"

Heads turned. Eventually, the room fell silent.

"I gather that every year the Ladies Auxiliary puts on a Christmas party," Miss Fennel said.

"Do-gooders," Pam murmured.

"The ladies will bring over a Christmas tree, but they need some helpers. Can I see a show of hands?"

Joanie and Rhonda raised theirs.

Fennel looked at me.

Paula frowned at me and shook her finger. I kept my hand down.

"The Ladies Auxiliary will also be bringing over presents. The presents will be individually wrapped, and you can choose whichever you'd like. But in the meantime, we'll have them stacked beneath the tree."

"Where's the tree supposed to go?" Joanie asked.

"The dining room's the only room large enough for a party."

"Party?" someone said.

"We'll have a party on Christmas Eve," Miss Fennel said.

Pam groaned.

"Will we open presents then?" someone asked. Fennel said we would.

Pam whispered, "I have an idea."

"What?"

"We're going to make dwarves."

"Circus dwarves?"

Pam covered her mouth to stifle a laugh and talked behind her hand. "Snow White, silly. At home, I made dwarves to put out on our lawn."

"Not wise men or a manger?"

"We're atheists, so no."

A genuine atheist! How cool! "But why not Santa's elves?"

"Because I can draw dwarves from memory. They're fun and cute." She put a finger to her lips and looked up at the ceiling. "First, we need cardboard."

"Won't cardboard bend?"

"Gesso will stiffen it. Do you think your mom could take you to an art store?"

"Sure," I said. "She's planning to come over Saturday, same as usual."

I had always made presents for my family: one year, I'd used hot wax and indigo to make scarves. Another time, I'd made copper plaques pounded out in a technique called repoussé. An art project would lift my mood.

I was ready when my mom came to sign me out. I gave her a peck on the cheek, and her eyes bugged out.

"Almost Merry Christmas," I said. "Instead of the library, could we go back to that mall we went to with Mrs. Hudson?"

"If that's what you want," she said.

"It is. My roommate and I have an art project."

At Chris-Town, the parking lot was jammed. Christmas shoppers loaded down with bargains bumped into my mom. Hooking my arm through hers was the only way to keep her safe.

"Is this okay?" I asked.

"Yes, thank you."

"Everybody's in a rush."

"I don't want to fall and break a bone."

"You won't," I said. "You're steadier on your feet."

"Tomorrow, it could be worse. I can never tell until I get up."

I still hadn't made up my mind what to do about Christmas— tell her a lie and say I wasn't allowed out or let her take me back to her place for an excruciating nonholiday. But maybe I should do that. The bed would need clean sheets.

At the art store, I found a chair for my mother and made her sit. Pam had given me money for supplies: poster paint, gesso, kindergarten brushes, sticks of charcoal, an X-Acto knife, and Elmer's glue.

After the mall, my mom insisted we go to a matinee at the Camelview, a building that reminded me of Tomorrowland, where my parents had taken me the year Disneyland opened. We sat in darkness, or, rather, I sat, and she tried to. She could not keep still. Her leg twitched. She elbowed me. She sniffed and blew her nose. She asked if I wanted to go out to dinner, and I said I couldn't because I had to be back to wash dishes.

"All right," she said.

One day in her presence was enough.

Before she dropped me off, I told her John would arrive the day after tomorrow. She agreed to pick him up.

"Would it be okay if he drives your car while he's here?" I said.

"I would have to put him on my insurance."

"Could you do that?"

"I'd need his license number."

I should have thought of that.

"Then does that mean you're going to drive us around?" I asked.

"No, you have your permit."

"But Mom! Girls don't drive."

"This time you'll have to."

We'll see about that, I thought.

Back at the home, I got out of the car. "Thanks so much for the movie," I said.

"Did you like it?"

"Yes. Very much."

"What about Christmas Day?" she asked.

"I've already thought about that," I said. "I think I'm allowed to leave at ten. If you come sign me out, I could come over to your place. I could put fresh sheets on the bed. I'm sure it's hard for you to clean the bathroom, so I'll do that."

"I don't want you straining yourself," she said.

"I'll be fine," I said. Compared with washing the dinner dishes, it wasn't any strain at all.

"Maybe we could go out to lunch."

"Sure," I said. "How about IHOP?"

"That sounds fine."

"Good, then." I leaned in and brushed my lips against her cheek. "It'll be a fun day."

Excited that I'd actually felt a modicum of genuine kindness, I signed myself in. We had Sunday to make the dwarves.

Pam used my sketchpad to do the drawings. Dopey, with his toothless grin and trailing nightshirt, turned out perfect. She had a harder time with Doc because she couldn't remember if he had regular glasses or those half glasses, like the ones Miss Fennel used when she was looking at our records. Grumpy, with his sneer and uplifted eyebrow, looked truly mean. With a ruler, she made a grid to scale up the drawings, and while she lay resting on the bed, turned on her side and looking down at the space between our beds, I knelt on the cardboard and made a grid, scaled up the dwarves' outlines with charcoal, and cut them with an X-Acto knife.

Pam sent me to find empty tomato juice cans in the kitchen garbage, and then she mixed up poster paints. I painted the clothes

—red, blue, and green—and she painted the flesh-colored faces and white beards.

"How are we going to stand them up?" I asked.

"We'll use the scrap cardboard to make triangular props."

"Do you want to do that now?"

"No. That's the last step, and if we prop them up, we can't hide them under the bed."

"Do you think we're going to get in trouble for this?"

"We'd better not," Pam said. "It's Christmas. Besides, we're not going to be here that much longer."

CHAPTER 51

FESTIVITIES

*A*fter lunch on Christmas Eve, Miss Fennel appeared at the door of our room and told me to fold up the card table and bring it to the dining room. I didn't mind. All morning I'd been staring into space. Hopelessly behind and fearing that I might flunk my classes, I stacked the course binders on the floor of my closet and slammed it shut. Until *it* (the pregnancy) was over, the stupid classes wouldn't get another minute of my time.

A short while later, Karla opened the office door and shouted, "Man in the hall." The husband of one of the Ladies Auxiliary members was carrying in a five-foot tree. We scurried like mice to our holes. After he'd gone, we ventured into the dining room and found the card table jammed in a corner and covered with a green flannel sheet. On it sat the tree.

In spite of Paula's warning to me not to volunteer, that afternoon I joined the decorating crew: tall Joanie, who climbed the kitchen stepstool and put the star on top; Rhonda, the girl who liked math and who was due any day; and Pam, still gliding through the day despite her size. We were all short-timers, due in the next week or two. The strings of lights were still in their boxes, the cords not tangled, and I popped the bulbs loose and handed them to Pam.

The tree looked like the ones in banks. White lights. Red ornaments. At home, our tree would have had decorations made from brass Mason jar lids. Every year, I pasted cutouts from the previous year's Christmas cards on the circles and glued small red bows at the top. Back home, we hung the ornaments with paper clips. And at home we had tinsel. That was the last thing we put on the tree and the first thing we took off on New Year's Day, always while watching the Rose Parade.

"What about tinsel?" I asked the lady from the auxiliary.

"No tinsel," she said. "Fire department regulations."

Rules, rules, rules. Making the dwarves had been fun, but now, with that project done and the tree decorated, I gave in to the urge to take a nap.

On Christmas Eve, Ruth cooked a turkey dinner, pretty much the same as Thanksgiving, except that this time, thanks to my trip to the art store, I had skipped the banana split and, hence, had managed to get off the diet table. After eating a slice of the Yule log—a spiral of thin chocolate cake and vanilla ice cream frosted with brown icing—I did the dishes.

Two more ladies from the auxiliary showed up, each carrying in shopping bags of small wrapped presents. The women piled the presents around the tree. Fennel plugged in a portable stereo and put on *The Perry Como Christmas Album*. Then she left the room.

"Now's our chance!" I said to Pam.

We dashed to our room, brought back the dwarves, and set them up next to the tree.

"How adorable!" the lady from the auxiliary said. "You girls are so clever, but in all the excitement, I would hate for the little fellows to get knocked over."

Pam and I looked at each other. Her tongue made the ticking sound she always made when she was thinking. Unfortunately, the lady was right. The room was small, and the dwarves would be in the way.

"What if we just set them up in our room?" I said.

"And we could bring them back tomorrow."

I took Grumpy and Doc, and she took Dopey. The hall was dark.

"Who's that?" Pam asked.

Two figures—string beans—were coming down the stairs from the schoolroom. Both had DA's—duck's ass haircuts—and both wore heels and kick-pleated skirts. The tall one walked like one of those drinking birds they sold in Chinatown, the bob of her head matching her strides. Her companion held the leash of a miniature white poodle. Its toenails clickety-clacked on the linoleum. Fennel's hypocrisy floored me. All this time, even on the day of our admittance, none of our family members had been allowed to see our rooms. And yet here was Miss Fennel, strolling about with her gal pal.

"Quick! Hide!" I said.

"Why?" Pam said.

"I don't want her knowing our business." I pushed the dwarves behind the door.

Miss Fennel looked in. "Come on, girls. Don't miss the festivities."

Festivities! "Yeah, sure," I said.

Hands on the small of her back, trying to counterbalance the weight of her belly, Pam said, "We're coming."

Then, when they had passed, Pam said, "Does she think any of us want to be here?"

"'Not I,' said the cat."

Pam laughed. "'Not I,' said the pig."

Thinking of *The Little Red Hen*, I followed the two women down the hall. The poodle looked back. Fennel and her friend, intent on their conversation, paused at the dining room door and went in.

Fennel introduced three women from the Ladies Auxiliary. Then she rested her hand lightly on her companion's shoulder. "This is my friend Marge Wilkins. She and I trained together at Ft. McClellan."

People clapped halfheartedly. Barbara and Roonay looked at

each other. Roonay, unsmiling, shook her head. Barbara, lips pursed, looked down at the floor. I expected one of them to say something about the army. After all, these two women with their adolescent-boy haircuts had look-alike uniforms: skinny skirts, white blouses, and shined shoes. They looked like women soldiers in civilian dress. But Roonay and Barbara had melted back into the crowd, as if they wanted to stay as far away as possible. The military was a small world.

Karen edged past the tree and sidled over to me. "See what I mean?" she asked.

"Yeah," I said. Women with women. "Go figure."

"Figure what?" Pam asked.

"Nothing," Karen said.

The women from the Ladies Auxiliary handed out presents. "Who wants this red box with the pretty silver bow?" One held a present to her ear and shook it. "I hear jingling!" One by one, we opened our gifts. The box and wrapping paper were worth more than whatever was in them. Mine was a ceramic ballerina, an ugly, worthless piece of shit.

Back in the room, the new girl, Betty, a fifteen-year-old who still wore braids, had already gone to bed. Betty was barely showing, and since her arrival two days before, she'd gone to bed with her back turned, shivering or silently weeping. A girl that young—with buds instead of breasts—made me feel as old as Marianne. Of course, all of us wanted to console Betty, but there wasn't a thing we could do until she told us her story. How she got pregnant. Who her boyfriend was. Why her parents wouldn't let them marry, or why her boyfriend had skipped town or enlisted in the service.

Roonay, Pam, and I had dangled the hypotheticals in front of her. "Say, Betty," Roonay tried, "a girl in my high school got knocked up, and her boyfriend lit out for the navy." Then Pam, normally one to live and let live, gave it a try. "This girl in my college dorm, she was really shy, and no one could imagine she even had a boyfriend, let alone that she was sleeping with him." I added that there'd been a junior in high school, a cheerleader, who'd dropped out of school, seemingly for no reason. Just before I left, I'd seen her pushing a baby in a shopping cart at Lucky's and figured out what happened.

So far, Betty had not taken the bait. Whatever her story was, she kept it well hidden. During the party, she was the one girl whose eyes lit up when she unwrapped her present, a music box, and I wondered how we could draw her out.

The party wrapped up an hour after our normal lights-out. Betty, the music box hugged to her chest, crawled into bed with her clothes on. Roonay changed into her nightgown and wrapped a do-rag around her hair. Pam and I didn't bother with rollers, because tomorrow, actual Christmas, Pam was staying in and I was only going to see my mother.

I turned out the light. Padding around in my slippers, I took the dwarves from behind the door.

"What you got there?" Roonay asked, sitting up.

"Three dwarves," Pam said.

"But in the real story, there's seven," Betty said, her voice tremulous.

Pam and I looked at each other.

"You're right, of course," Pam said, "but we only had enough cardboard for three."

"I like Snow White," Betty said, turning over. "The dwarves are good. They watch over her when she's asleep. Nothing bad happens."

What bad could happen when you were asleep?

I set the dwarves up between the ends of Betty's bed and Pam's. I put Doc closest to Betty. He looked the most cheerful, and Betty needed cheering up. Grumpy went in the middle. If we'd been brave enough to show our true colors, his crossed arms and scowling face would have been the face we might have shown to the world. As for Dopey, with his dragging hem and guileless innocence, he was us, too.

"They're our guardian angels," I said, returning to my bed and pulling up the covers. "Now I lay me down to sleep . . ."

"I pray the Lord my soul to keep," Betty said.

"If I should die before I wake," Roonay said, "I pray Lord God my soul to take."

"'Course, you all know prayin' don't do no good," Betty said.

"Chile, you got to have faith," Roonay said.

"My daddy's a preacher," Betty said.

Someone went into the bathroom across the hall. A toilet flushed, and whoever it was walked back toward the dorm wing.

"Your daddy the one who got you in a family way?" Roonay asked.

A gasp came from Betty's bed. Then she was crying again.

"Go ahead and cry, honey," Roonay said. "We all got plenty a reason to cry."

"We do," I said, just in case Betty thought we didn't.

"Good night, ladies," Pam said.

Good night, we said.

When we woke up, it would be Christmas.

CHAPTER 52

CHRISTMAS

*A*s so often happens, I wasn't aware of my anger until Christmas morning. Partly, I was angry at Betty's preacher daddy, and partly I was angry at the auxiliary ladies who had cleared their shelves of bric-a-brac and pretended these were newly purchased presents. But more than the odd items we were supposed to be grateful for, I found myself enraged at being the object of anyone's pity. We didn't pity ourselves. We just had to get through *it*. Even the party, with the need to put on false faces and knee-jerk smiles, was almost more than any of us could bear. I was almost glad to be escaping the breakfast table's gloom.

My mom showed up exactly at ten a.m. When I unlocked the door of her little motor court abode, the cold made me take a step back.

"What gives?" I said. "It's like an icebox in here."

She dropped her purse on the couch and sank down. Apparently, the drive to and from the home had worn her out.

"Turn up the heat if you're uncomfortable," she said, elevating her feet on the coffee table.

I went straight to the thermostat. Fifty! What was she thinking? I heard a *whoosh* and turned to see a live flame leap from a gray wall furnace.

"You should tell the manager to fix this."

"I have, but they're busy."

"Why do you keep it turned down so low? Are you worried about the cost of heat?"

"I'm worried about asphyxiation. I'm waking up with headaches."

"Move into the bedroom, then."

"I moved the minute you left."

"But how can you sleep when it's so cold?"

"I'm fine once the bed warms up, and the rest of the time, I wear my winter coat."

I saw that indeed she had not removed her coat. It was a navy-blue wool coat with sand dollar-size buttons. A few years back, my mother and I had taken the train to the city. After buying winter coats, we'd ridden the cable car to Fisherman's Wharf and met my father at Alioto's. I'd ordered abalone.

By the looks of the place, she was spending all day in bed or shivering on the couch. She hadn't vacuumed the shag carpet, and dishes were piled in the sink. If we were going for lunch at IHOP, I had to get busy.

"Do you have clean sheets for the hide-a-bed?" I asked.

"The old ones are still on it."

"You knew John was coming. Why didn't you wash them?"

She took off her glasses and massaged her temples. Set off by the deep blue of her coat, the lenses glinted. Her face looked sallow. Gosh, maybe she did have carbon monoxide poisoning. Headaches and lethargy. Those were signs.

"Should I go down and borrow the vacuum cleaner from the manager?" I asked.

"Don't disturb her. It's Christmas."

"Okay, but, Mom, what's going on? This place is a mess."

"I've given up on housework," she said, lifting her head and putting her glasses back on.

"What? Why?"

"Because I'm a professional woman, not a maid."

"Can you move, please?" I said. "I need to pull the sheets off the hide-a-bed and get them in the wash." It would cost a quarter to use the dryer, but I wouldn't have time to hang them.

She moved to a chair. Thinking about my grandmother and how she had always done the housework, enlisting me as her helper, I wondered if my mother had always seen herself this way. Not as a housewife. No, as a "professional woman," whatever that meant.

I unfolded the hide-a-bed. The frame was heavy and clunky. I should have let her take the bedroom from the start. God, she'd been down here all these months, supposedly for her health, and she looked pale and utterly spent. Low oxygenation could do that. Carbon dioxide bonded with red blood cells. The cells lost their carrying capacity. Her body would need time to make new ones, and in the interim, she'd have to jump into a classroom where a long-term substitute had established her own routines. Why had I not thought of this before?

In the two months I'd been in the home, I'd seen my mother seven times: twice with Mrs. Hudson, once when she took me to the art store, and the rest when she took me to the library. I went into the bedroom and stripped the bed. I gathered towels. With the laundry in a bundle over my shoulder, I closed the door behind me. My mother should bring a chair outside. Soak up the sun and breathe the fresh air. It was a fine day: birds chirping, traffic on nearby Indian School a whisper. Passing the pool, I saw my bug friends still floating near the intake filter. Some things never changed.

I stuffed the washing machines. Fifty-five minutes for a wash, another forty for the dryer, and then I'd have to make the beds. By the time we arrived at IHOP, the brunch crowd would be gone.

Back in the apartment, I grabbed a broom and swept the carpet. I pulled out the stopper in the tub and cleared it of hair. Luckily, there was a bit of Comet left.

"Do you have Clorox, by any chance?" I called.

My mother hadn't moved from the chair.

"What do you need it for?"

"The tile grout's super moldy."

"The bathroom fan's broken. I asked them to fix it, but no one came."

I got up from my hands and knees and flipped the switch. Sure enough, the fan was on the fritz. Oh well. Nothing I could do about it. Hot and sweaty, I washed my hands. I'd better dash over and throw the sheets in the dryer. My pelvic bones felt like a wishbone slowly being pried apart, and the kitchen still needed attention.

Back from transferring the clothes, I opened the refrigerator. Three inches of ice coated the freezer compartment. The ice had locked in the half gallon of butter brickle I'd bought two months before. I dug out the box with a knife and managed to cram in a saucepan of boiling water. While the ice thawed, I moved refrigerator items to the kitchen table: limp carrots, sliced ham, cream cheese, a jar of Velveeta, a bunch of brown celery, and Wonder Bread. I sniffed a carton of milk. Sour! Even I, inclined to drop clothes on the floor, would never have lived like this. What would it take to cheer her up?

She hadn't bought a tree or done any decorating. No surprise, but it did feel odd, sitting on the couch and handing across a single present. I hadn't wanted to show up empty-handed, so I had boxed up the ceramic ballerina.

She thanked me and gave me a turquoise ring that had belonged to my grandfather. Gloria had worn a similar ring, until her fingers had grown so swollen that she had to take it off. Like the stone in Gloria's ring, the turquoise in my grandfather's ring had turned green.

"Thank you," I said, curling my fingers around it. "I will treasure this."

"He would have wanted you to have it," she said.

Sighing, I heaved myself off the couch and went to gather the sheets. Maybe the time apart had been good for us. She had told me two things I never would have guessed: She didn't like housework, and she saw herself as a professional woman. What I could have told her was that I loved putting a house in order. Ironing. Laying out bread for lunches. Sewing. Even running the sterilizer. My two months in the home had made me appreciate order.

CHAPTER 53

JOHN'S VISIT

*M*y mom was never late. If she said she would be there at ten, then the car would pull up at ten on the dot. John's flight was supposed to land at nine. It was 10:47.

Karla, a sprig of holly pinned to her hair, slid the window open. "You know what they say about a watched pot."

I turned. "My mom should be here any second."

"Oh?" she said.

"To sign me out."

She clipped a fresh sheet to the sign-out page. "Sign yourself out."

"Is that okay?"

"Just forge her signature. Don't make her walk all the way in."

"Thanks."

My mom's penmanship wasn't at all like mine. She began her name with a big looping "L" for Lorene, and her letters had a definite slant, like Sisyphus pushing his rock. I did the best I could and handed the clipboard through the window.

"Miss Fennel won't be in today," Karla said. "If you want to stand out by the gate, you can."

"Thanks," I said. "But first I have to pee. Can you watch my stuff?"

"Sure," she said, already back at her typewriter.

I left my purse and long wool coat on a chair. Lately, I'd been having to pee once an hour. The baby was sitting on my bladder, or maybe squeezing it the way boys in sixth grade used to squeeze water balloons before lobbing them in my direction. If I waited too long, the pressure turned into a low-grade ache and a feeling of mounting desperation. In the home, I was safe. Plenty of stalls. The walk to the ice cream counter took ten minutes, so I could leave with Joanie and Karen, eat my banana split, and be back in under an hour. But at IHOP there had been only one stall and six people ahead of me. I'd almost peed my pants.

I knocked on the sliding window. "Thanks, Karla."

She looked up and smiled. "I'll keep an eye out for letters."

"No need," I said. "My boyfriend's coming in person."

She stopped typing and turned. "Really?"

"Yes," I said. "For one day. He's staying with my mom."

"Then have an extra-good time," she said.

"I'll try," I said.

By now, I was so huge that my coat wouldn't button around me. It was a chilly day, but I folded it over my arm. Hide my stomach and lessen the shock.

I opened the door and stepped outside.

John came striding up the walk. Man on a mission.

"Hey, you made it!" I said.

His head jerked up, and he halted. He stood with his legs apart, a triangle torso, and the patchy beard of a boy who, not so long ago, had bought his first razor. Ants crawled on my skin, the months since we'd seen each other an uncrossable moat. Mouth-breathing, he let his eyes run up and down my body. The same look people in Chris-Town gave me. The same look I got at the library. His eyes welled with tears. He took out a handkerchief and wiped them.

"Here, let me help you with your coat," he said, reaching for it.

In the movies I would have rushed into his arms, but this wasn't Hollywood. I turned my back and felt for the sleeves.

He watched me button the top button, and his eyes fell on my stomach again.

My finger stabbed his chest. I made a V and pointed from his eyes to mine. "*I'm* up here."

"Yeah," he said, his eyes drifting down. "It's just kind of a shock."

"Let's get out of here," I said.

"Your mom says I'm not allowed to drive."

"She told me."

"But can you drive?" he said. "Like that?"

"Like what?"

"Like the Goodyear blimp." He pooched out his cheeks and encircled an imaginary belly with his hands.

Should I kill him now and get it over with? I laughed instead.

"If I move the seat back."

"How are you?" he asked.

"I'm fine."

"Are you fine?" he said.

When a person asked that question, they didn't really want to know. *Are you fine?* really meant *You look like I should worry about you, so please tell me I don't need to.*

How was I supposed to greet him, anyway? We couldn't really kiss right here on the front walk of a home for unwed mothers, and the last time we'd kissed, he'd turned me around and come at me from behind.

John opened the gate and let me pass. He climbed in the backseat, and I went around to the driver's side. My mom started to get out, but a corner of her mouth twitched worse than it had in months. Her arm was jerking, too, and I told her to just scoot over.

Her shoulders rounded, and she clutched her purse.

"The traffic at the airport was horrible," she said.

John leaned forward. "Sorry, Mrs. Benham. There was fog at SFO."

"I'm glad you made it," I said, turning the ignition and hoping my feelings would start to engage.

"Me, too," he said, resting a hand on my shoulder.

The weight of his hand was a heavy quilt, comforting, but a burden.

He sat back. "This is my first time in Phoenix."

"Pretend you're on the Rocket to the Moon."

"What's that?" he asked.

"A ride at Disneyland."

"Oh," he said. "I've never been."

My mom, in her teacherly voice, pointed out Camelback Mountain. We were driving down Indian School.

"Now, *there's* an attraction," I said, pointing off to the left. "The Indian school one of the girls in the home was going to when she got pregnant."

In the rearview mirror, I saw John shade his eyes. The massive brick complex sat far back, well beyond the athletic fields.

"Is it like the one in Pennsylvania where Jim Thorpe went?" he asked.

"I don't know," I said.

"He was a football player," my mother said.

"I know who he was," I said.

What a bitch I was being. I turned on the radio. "Love Potion No. 9" was playing. Stupid teenage songs.

My mother pointed to the motor court's entrance. "Turn here."

"You don't have to tell me," I said. "I was here yesterday, or did you forget?"

My mother turned to John. "She's been a little on edge since we came down."

"On edge?" I said. "You're damn right. I'm pregnant!"

"Hey, hey," John said, leaning forward. "Your mom's only trying to help."

"Don't try to placate me, either of you."

John sat back. He was cracking his knuckles. Poor guy. He'd flown all the way down here for this and forgotten his shining armor.

I steered around the swimming pool and wondered about the water temperature. A nice, warm dip would be the perfect thing. It would relax me. Well, no point. I couldn't fit in a suit, and I'd forgotten to tell John to bring his.

I parked by our unit—the green door with a peephole; the swamp cooler covered with tinfoil; the array of garbage cans next to the alley. Home sweet home.

"This isn't how I pictured it," he said, taking his suitcase from the trunk.

"Pictured what?" I asked.

With a sweep of his hand, he said, "Any of it."

"I told you about the pool."

"Yes, but you didn't say it was tiny."

"I told you about the motor court."

"Only how hot it was. Say, did you hear the Pope issued a papal bull? He's convening a second Vatican Council."

Why did he want to talk about the damned Pope? "John, I haven't gone to Mass in months."

"You aren't turning atheist, are you?"

"No!"

"I thought you might."

"Why?"

"Your roommate. She's not brainwashing you, is she?"

"Just shut up," I said.

My mom unlocked the door and went inside.

"You want to take your suitcase in?" I asked.

"Yes," he said, taking it from the trunk. "Then let's blow this clip joint. I'm starving."

"IHOP's close."

"Fine. It's cheap. After that, let's find somewhere we can park."

IN THE DESERT BOTANICAL GARDEN, single-lane gravel roads wound through the saguaros, growing where they had grown for a thousand years.

During the time we'd spent in the restaurant, talking about our classes and he filling me in on Greek and Latin and jazz band and the activities of his brothers and sisters, the bright morning had turned dark and cold. John, driving, had on his Bellarmine letter sweater and tan twill pants with a copper button. He found a place to pull over.

We sat on opposite ends of the bench seat. He scooted closer and told me to feel his neck.

Humor him, I thought, poking around and making appreciative *hmms*. "Your neck feels like a tree trunk."

"I have this weight belt I strap around my forehead."

He flexed an arm and had me feel his bicep, an apple inside his skin.

"Is that from pull-ups?" I asked.

"Yeah. I put a bar across my bedroom door."

"Impressive." Football had certainly bulked him up, not that I cared at all about football or his damn muscles.

He took out his billfold. "I brought my check and one from my dad."

"That'll be appreciated," I said, "but give them to my mom."

"Yeah, pound of flesh."

"She's not trying to punish you."

"I know, I know. I wasn't referring to her."

He told me about working at his father's shop and how much he hated his dad. John got the dirtiest and most boring jobs. Threading pipe. Sweeping the floor. Crawling in boilers and scraping out asbestos.

"He's always poor-mouthing," John said.

"What do you mean?"

"Oh, saying how much he's shelling out for uniforms and tuition. All the while, he's got an apartment up in Burlingame. He and his bookkeeper, who's still married, are shacking up."

"Does your mom know?"

"I don't have the heart to ask. Oh, and by the way, she says hello."

"Tell her hello back," I said.

Then he put his hand on my stomach and lifted my blouse, one I had taken from the stash of free clothes because my muumuus no longer fit. The pink striations on my stomach looked like snakes. His fingers were short. He spread them and moved them over my scarified skin.

"What do you want, a boy or a girl?" I asked.

"The oldest should be a boy." He put an ear down and listened. He felt a foot push against my skin. "How much longer? Did they say?"

"Officially, January sixteenth," I said, counting on the fact that he had listened to the baby and felt it move to make it real, to make him *want* to get married. Stroking his hair, I explained what Diane and her boyfriend had done, how she planned to work and put Brian through school, how she came from a big Catholic family just like his.

He lifted his head from my stomach, straightened up, and slid the seat back.

"I thought you wanted to go to college," he said.

"I do, but I could go to Foothill or De Anza."[1]

"Not if I'm at West Point," he said. "We'd be too far apart."

"No, John, I meant I could go to junior college and you could go to San Jose State. We could get married. You'll be eighteen soon."

"I want to go to West Point."

I'd watched *West Point Story* on television. I knew the academy's motto: "No wife. No horse. No mustache."

"Do you still want to marry me?" I asked.

"Yes, of course," he said. "After I graduate."

"Why not sooner?"

"Because until I graduate, I don't have any way to support a family."

Then he was telling me that he missed me, that he thought of me every day, that he loved me more than he ever thought it was possible to love another human being, that we would get through this and be stronger as a couple. He moved closer and wrapped me in his arms. End of discussion. Contortionists that we were, we dodged the steering column and made love on the bench seat of a '52 Chevy, steaming the windows and filling the car with our panted breaths. I had never felt so desolate and alone.

CHAPTER 54

BIRTH

*I*t was like a contagion, all my friends leaving one after the other. Roonay's parents, who had driven over to be with her for Christmas, had decided her father's military career wasn't that important. Roonay packed her suitcase, and they drove her back to Fort Benning. Their plan was to let her return to college while they raised the baby as their own. Paula had delivered and signed her surrender papers. Rhonda and Joanie had delivered and smushed themselves into girdles and put on makeup. They left with our good wishes. Pam had delivered a week ago, and by this time, I figured, she'd be back at the University of Minnesota.

I began walking on the path that Diane had walked and that Pam had walked, right up until the day of her delivery. Of the girls I'd been close to, only Karen and I, the diet table regulars, were left. And young Betty, of course, poor girl.

On Saturday night, I waddled down to the infirmary. The weekend nurse, whom I remember as a rotund woman with dimples like Shirley Temple's, had a couple of tricks up her sleeve. She could start labor by giving us an enema, breaking our water, or sticking her finger inside and scrambling the soft tissue of the cervix. For me, she did all three. Apart from the movie, I had had no childbirth or

Lamaze classes, and I was as ignorant about the birth process as I once had been about sex itself. I knew only one thing. John was not going to marry me anytime soon, so I had to focus on getting *it* over with and protecting my mother's precarious health.

My labor started at two in the morning. I went back to the infirmary and climbed up on the metal table. The nurse shaved my pubic hair into a kidney-shaped bowl. Then she called the ambulance to take me to the hospital.

In the labor room, I was alone in a narrow bed. Occasionally a nurse checked me. I held the guardrails and cried. As my pains grew worse, I screamed for help. A nurse gave me a shot of Demerol. As if I were plastered against the wall of a Tilt-A-Whirl, the room began to spin. Steel fingers wrapped around my abdomen and squeezed and squeezed, driving the baby out. I called for help again. Nurses surrounded the bed. One took a quick look. "The baby's crowning."

They pushed me into the glare of an operating room. I slid onto the table. The nurse strapped my ankles and wrists. Dizzy, I felt like a child myself, held by an arm and a leg and flung around and around in circles. The baby was coming out.

"She's so young," a nurse said to a colleague. Her fingers curled around mine as I let out a scream and pushed.

"Don't push!" the doctor said. "You'll tear."

What was he talking about? My baby had to come. The head slid from me. Then the shoulders. The doctor held a bloody, waxy mess by its ankles. For a long second, the baby didn't breathe. I lifted my head. The doctor put his finger inside the baby's mouth and slapped its butt. The baby squalled.

"It's a boy," he said.

A nurse held out a flannel blanket to accept the baby from the doctor's hands. "Do you want to see him?"

"Yes," I said.

She held the blanket open. Eyes squeezed shut, face red, he wailed. I saw his kicking legs, the little fists I had felt inside, a fringe of dark hair. The nurse folded the blanket around him and took him away.

"This is going to hurt just a little." The doctor thrust his hand deep into me, scraping the inside of my abdomen as if he were cleaning a pumpkin.

"Ahhh! Stop!" I screamed.

"He has to get the rest of the placenta," the nurse said. "Go ahead and cry—I know it hurts."

Instantly, I didn't have any more tears. I don't know where they went.

The doctor held a hypodermic needle to the light. I felt a stick in my crotch, then the tug of stitches.

While he worked, the nurse pushed on my abdomen as though it were a deflated pillow. Beneath the puffiness, she found the edges of my uterus and seized it, kneading it like a tennis ball. Apparently, my uterus was flaccid, and for days, big clots of blood plopped into the toilet bowl.

It was almost over.

CHAPTER 55

SURRENDER

I had hoped to see Mrs. Hudson once more, if only to thank her and say goodbye. Even on Catholic Social Service's sliding scale, the one-hour therapy sessions cost my mother money, and my mother did not think a final appointment necessary. Perhaps she was already calculating how much money she'd need for our drive back to California, or possibly she figured that our relationship had gotten better. All these years later, I have come to understand that Mrs. Hudson was a paid-by-the-hour sort of friend, someone, like my Evanston counselor, Jim, whose ability to listen empathetically provided help and perspective during an otherwise dark time.

Karla, the secretary, was another such person, paid, but going out of her way to help. Ordinarily, she stayed in the office to answer the phone, but the day I gave birth, she saw that I'd received a letter from John and brought it down to the infirmary.

"From your guy?" she said, dangling the letter in front of me.

I grabbed it and tore it open. "Wear something hot," he wrote.

God, what a one-track mind.

"He certainly has been a faithful correspondent," Karla said. "You and Pam won the lottery in the boyfriend department."

"Did we?" I said, reaching for the rail on the hospital bed and shifting my bottom. The middle of me—my core—had always been a void, not just an informational void, but a physical void, like a deflated volleyball, and now, without the baby's feet pushing up against my ribs or his little bottom just under my hand, I felt untethered and adrift. I remembered Marianne, the kindergarten teacher, blowing out a stream of air, patting her empty abdomen, and telling me not to think. About the baby, she meant.

"Your mother and a social worker from Catholic Social Service are coming over tomorrow," Karla said. "Are you well enough to walk down to the visiting room?"

"What are my choices?" I asked. "They can't come back here."

"They could wait a day."

"No, I'm sure I'll feel better tomorrow."

DURING THE BIRTH, I had lost a pint of blood. The nurse had wanted me to stay in bed until the bleeding stopped. The pain nearly made me pass out, but by afternoon, the bleeding had slowed. The nurse said if I had another gush of blood, I should call her, and she'd bring a wheelchair.

My ears rang and I felt short of breath, but at least I wasn't dripping on the floor. Holding my robe over the Jell-O of my stomach, I shuffled down to the visiting rooms, where Diane and the girl from Atlanta had come to see their babies. My mother, one corner of her mouth twitching ever so slightly, held out a grocery sack with my skirt and boat-neck blouse.

"Here are your clothes," she said.

I took the sack. "Thanks a lot."

"You look a little peaked."

"I think I'll sit down." I tossed a pillow on the chair and sat.

My mother pulled out a chair in the middle of the table.

Mrs. Mildred Freesh, stocky and with a practical demeanor, an adoption caseworker for Catholic Social Service, joined us. Sitting opposite me and next to my mother, she took paperwork from her briefcase. The ball was about to get rolling: the legal transfer of a baby from one family to another.[1] At the time of my son's adoption, and, indeed, mine, some sixteen years earlier, agencies attempted to find a suitable match based on hair and eye color, religion, and social class.

From the distance of sixty years, I can catch a glimpse—one akin to a faded Polaroid—of my own young self and of John. So young. So young.

- My hobbies: art, music, knitting, sports.
- Putative father's hobbies: hunting, football, outdoor sports.
- My personality: enjoys people; likes to have moments alone; even-tempered.
- John's personality: enjoys people; capable leader.
- My future plans: give baby up for relinquishment; return to school; complete education in Redwood City.
- John's future plans: may enter West Point.
- My parents: father, 57; mother, 58, graduate degree, health good, Redwood City schoolteacher.
- Parents of putative father: father, 44, Stanford grad, building contractor and electrical engineer, big build; mother: 44, Stanford grad, good health, algebra teacher, 5′7″, slim.

The information Mrs. Freesh took down, plus whatever Miss Fennel had to say about me regarding my intelligence or lack thereof, went into my son's case file. This snapshot would not have been shown to my son's adoptive parents, nor could they have asked for specifics. They would have been told our ages, the broadest outlines of our ethnicities, and that we had not been married.

What's glaringly obvious is the lack of even a rudimentary health history, apart from terms like "slim" and "big build." Ironically, my mother, sitting right there, her mouth twitching and her leg jerking, asserted that her health was good.

∼

ALTHOUGH I HAD HAD a shot to dry up my milk, my breasts were hot, heavy, and engorged. The weekend nurse in the infirmary showed me how to squeeze the areolae and expel as much milk as I could. To keep the milk from leaking through my blouse, I packed my bra with gauze pads.

Signing the official surrender papers was almost the last thing we did before leaving town, and for that, we went to the offices of Catholic Social Service of Arizona, Inc., 1515 East Osborn Road, Phoenix. Mrs. Sherron, the woman who later asked me to make a tape for prospective adoptive parents, passed papers to me and handed me a pen.

"By signing," she said, "you agree to relinquish your child forever."

I read the text.

Know all men by these presents: That I, MARYLEE BENHAM, the undersigned, being the mother of BABY BOY MACDONALD, a minor child born in the State of Arizona on the 13th day of January, 1962, being unable to adequately provide or care for said minor, hereby surrender/s the custody of said minor to Catholic Social Service, a child welfare agency duly licensed under the laws of the State of Arizona to care for, maintain or place children in family homes for care or adoption; and I (we) also hereby relinquish to said agency all rights of every kind or nature which I (we) may have to the custody, services, earnings, or control whatsoever, over said minor child and hereby consent to the adoption of said child by any person or persons deemed by said child welfare agency to be fit and proper as adoptive parents. To the best of my (our) knowledge, said minor child WAS born out of wedlock.

Signed: Marylee Benham
    Witnesses:
    Ruth P. Johnson

Catherine M. Donnellan
January 23, '62
Ramona K. Sherron
Representative of child welfare agency

Seeing me hesitate, Mrs. Sherron said, "You know, this is a self-less act."

I stared at her concerned gray eyes and lined face. A grown-up. She didn't have any doubts.

"I know," I said. "It's just that …"

"You're giving a childless couple the greatest gift possible," she said, "and you should feel good that your son will be raised in a loving Catholic family."

I sat there, wanting to feel a saintly glow. What was wrong with me? My son would have two parents. Catholics. They would give him all the advantages.

I picked up the pen and signed.

Mrs. Sherron called in two witnesses and affixed her signature. "Now you can go on with your own life. Put this experience behind you."

Over the years, I have wondered if she, or any of the social workers who facilitated adoptions, truly understood what those words meant.

PART VI

SO CALLED "NORMAL LIFE"

CHAPTER 56

DRIVING HOME

*E*leven days after I had given birth, *it* was irrevocably over. My mom and I were heading back to Redwood City. At the wheel of the car once again, I was sitting on a pillow. My son's birth had torn me open, and the rip had not healed.

By the time daybreak burned away the blue-black night, we were halfway to Wickenburg. From the vast wilderness of the Sonoran Desert sprang basalt cones of ancient volcanoes, and the earth, stripped bare, yielded up its inventory of geologic time.

My mom unfolded the AAA map. The map had routed us up through Kingman, a diagonal, and the quickest, way back to the Bay Area. I kept looking in the rearview mirror at the cars heading for Phoenix, and at the saguaro, their spiny arms uplifted to the sky. I was thinking—with a kind of dental numbness to the brain— about going home, back to my "real life," whatever that might entail.

At the state line, an inspector in a khaki uniform waved us forward. Leaning in, he said, "You don't look old enough to be driving, young lady."

"She's been driving for almost a year," my mother said.

The inspector saw the rug in the backseat. "Got a wetback in there?"

I hadn't heard anyone say "wetback" since my father had left.

"No," I said.

"Any citrus, ladies?"

"No fruit of any kind."

He waved us through.

Welcome to California.

Kingman, Barstow, San Bernardino. The highway took us past an old Burma-Shave sign, faded from red to pink. BABY YOUR SKIN.

A mile down the road, another sign said KEEP IT FITTER. Who knew what that meant?

"Let's stop for lunch," my mother said. "Give you a break."

"I'm not tired." Wide awake, glassy-eyed, even, I knew another part of me wanted to curl up in the backseat and suck my thumb, and an even less acknowledged part wanted to lie down on the road and let the traffic finish me off. Not that I was suicidal. Just bone weary.

The two-lane highway washboarded under the Chevy's tires, and then the car bumped back onto a smooth slab. Somehow, staring out at the landscape, I'd let the speed climb to seventy-five and had to slam on the brakes. My mother reached for the strap above the door. At fifty-five, the car stopped its shimmy. My mother looked out the window and saw another sign. With Burma-Shave, the trick was to remember all the words, to guess the final rhyme. Silently, she mouthed, OR BABY.

A few miles down the road came the rest of the rhyme.

WILL GET ANOTHER SITTER.

My mother repeated the lines.

> *Baby yourself*
> *Keep it fitter*
> *Or baby*
> *Will get another sitter.*

"I guess that makes sense," she said.

"It's pure doggerel," I said.

She was silent for a moment.

"I never thought I'd see the day," she said, "when I'd agree to let a grandchild of mine be put up for adoption."

I wanted to look at her—the receding chin, the turkey wattle, the thin lips—to see if I was going crazy or if she was as ugly as I sometimes made her out to be. Because then I could hate her. It would be easy. But I had never known my mother to intentionally wound. Provoke, yes. Goad other people into behaving like monsters, yes. Utter a stupefying remark that exposed a listener's greatest vulnerability, yes, that she could do, too. Had done.

"But, Mom," I said, "I did this for you."

"And I did it to protect your reputation." She opened her purse and took out a tissue.

I had to stop, or I'd bleed through my skirt. At a dilapidated Esso station with hubcaps nailed over the holes in the vertical boards and the dried skeleton of a horned bull above the door, I took my purse and went out back to find the restroom. A trickle of water came from the cold-water tap and dripped into the rusty sink. I closed the door.

The lady at the agency said that once I signed the papers, I had to forget. I wanted to believe her.

The granular pink powder that came from the soap dispenser, its strawberry smell, reminded me of the restrooms on the docks in San Francisco, and I wondered what made a person stop wanting what they'd wanted before. How I, or anyone, was supposed to forget. First, there had been the *it* I was so eager to have over, the birth itself. However, I was beginning to see that *it* was only the beginning. Now a new *it*—the years of my child's absence—loomed ahead.

I washed my face and yanked the towel roller. I didn't even have a word for what this *it* encompassed. *It* felt so large that I couldn't wrap my arms around it.

CHAPTER 57

SKYLINE

I hadn't been certain my mother would let me see John again, or that his father would let him use the car. My mom set a ten o'clock curfew. If I didn't get an adequate amount of sleep, she believed I would get run down. She attributed my constant exhaustion to anemia. In any event, there John and I were, driving up Old La Honda Road in his dad's white Fairlane, just as if nothing had happened—no shame, no secrecy, no alteration of the life plan. But on the inside, everything had changed. I was a ninety-year-old woman going on a date with a teenager.

"Where are we going?" I asked.

"To this new place I found," he said.

It was pitch black out, black made blacker by the redwoods. At an overlook near Sky Londa, I looked down at the bay and the twinkling lights and thought of the stupid presents all the Ladies Auxiliary members had put under the Christmas tree. Pam had gone back to Minnesota. I wondered how she and Doug were doing. If, after her thirty-six-hour labor, she still loved him. Or, for that matter, if I still loved John. Love—the idea of love, the enchantment of it, the belief that he and I were a modern-day Romeo and Juliet, love's *necessity*—had begun collapsing the moment our families got together to come up with the goddamn plan.

John looked the same as he had at Christmas—the same white gunk at the corners of his mouth, the same tan jeans with the zipper he'd strike matches on when he lit his farts. He'd always said he wanted the oldest to be a boy, and now he had a boy. A boy who was somewhere, with someone else. He must feel as sad I did.

On my own, I had no right to go back to the agency and see if we could get him back, but if John and I went as a couple, we might stand a chance.

The lights down below grew blurry in the fog, and a gray mist enshrouded the car.

"Nice place," I said.

"It's okay." He crossed his arms on the steering wheel and looked out toward the bay.

"We have to talk," I said.

I had worn a purple sweater and a black wool skirt. A safety pin held the waistband together. The pin felt like it might spring open and jab me in the side.

"I'm growing horns," John said.

"Did you bring a condom?"

"Tillie gave me one."

John didn't look happy. During my pregnancy, I had gained forty pounds. I had lost only sixteen since the birth. My belly looked like a striated marshmallow. Not sure I could bear having sex so soon after giving birth, not sure how I would say no if John insisted, I huddled against the passenger door.[1]

He sighed and leaned back against the seat. His mouth crimped, and he swiped the corners of his lips. "I've got a confession to make."

He'd been a coward, I expected him to say.

"What kind of confession?"

"I parked up here with Ginger."

"When, back in November?"

"After Christmas."

"Wait a sec! While I was down in Phoenix, having our baby, you came up here and made out?"

He shrugged and rolled his eyes.

I pulled up my sweater and undid my bra. A gauze pad fell out. I grabbed it before it grossed him out. "Is this what you want? You want to suck a girl's tits? Well, suck mine. Milk's coming out."

Then I threw my head in my hands and surrendered to great, heaving sobs. I had no body left, only my face, wet and covered in snot, and screams that rose from my very soul. When Michelangelo painted the Sistine Chapel, he painted a self-portrait of an empty skin, freshly flayed by a sculptor's knife, and that is how I felt.

John turned toward me and threw an arm over the back of the seat. "Don't get hysterical. It's not like we went all the way."

My throat hurt. Too empty to go on, I sat up.

As if weighing a cantaloupe, John cupped my breast. "Get dressed."

I guessed we weren't going to do it after all.

He leaned down and turned on the ignition. By the time the heater started, I had fastened my bra and stuffed in my boobs. He backed the car and turned it to face the road. Headlights came toward us, and a truck passed.

I put a hand on his arm. "It's not too late," I said.

He reared back, and his eyebrows shot up. With his foot on the brake, he shifted into neutral. The engine idled.

"We're not getting married," he said. "And anyway, you signed the papers."

A red-hot pressure built up behind my eyes. Great, gulping sobs swamped me again, and I pitched forward.

John pushed me aside and opened the glove box. "I brought some Kleenex. Help yourself."

I took out the box and blew my nose.

Guilt was the only weapon I had in this fight, and if it meant I had to make him feel like a coward and a shit, then I would.

"I want my baby back," I said.

"I'm waiting to hear if I get into West Point," he said.

"And then what?"

"If I don't, then maybe we could think about it."

"John, the baby will be adopted by then. It might already be too late. At least now we'd have a chance."

"My dad won't let me."

"If we went together to our parents and insisted, if you insisted, he'd change his mind. We could drive to Reno or West Virginia or somewhere it's legal for people our age to marry."

"If I get in, I'll spend the summer at Camp Buckner," he said.

"What's that supposed to mean?"

"There's a chance I won't like the army. I could drop out then."

"You're missing the point. We have a baby. Your—our—oldest son. Every day we delay makes it less likely we could get him back."

"I don't want to do anything I'd regret."

"*You'd* regret! What about me?" I said something about all the feelings I didn't know what to do with.

"What did they tell you there at the home?" he asked.

"They told me to forget," I said.

"Then that's what you should do."

"I can't forget."

"You can if you try. I don't ever want you to bring this up again."

For all the years of our too-short marriage, it was this moment that hung between us, not just the fact of the surrender, but that he would never allow me to speak of our son. I hated him for that. I hated him and I married him anyway and had four more kids. Because, despite the ways in which we were not a perfect fit, there was that magic between us, that ability to read each other's bodies the way blind people read Braille.

CHAPTER 58

THE DREAM OF WEST POINT

*W*hen my mother and I had arrived back in Redwood City, we couldn't move back into our house. The tenants wanted to rent it for another year. My mother had found an inexpensive two-bedroom apartment on busy Woodside Road. She arranged furniture delivery for two Danish modern couches and a matching dinette, and I made multiple trips over to our real house to get our kitchen supplies and her sewing machine. Over the course of my pregnancy, I had gone from a size 12 to a size 16, and I had to make myself a new wardrobe.

My mother resumed her teaching and said I needed to find an after-school job.

"I'm stopping your allowance," she said.

"What for?" I asked. "To punish me?"

"Because you need to learn financial responsibility, and you'll need spending money for college."

The following week, I took a job at a steak house called the Char-Pit. I worked from five thirty to ten thirty, four nights a week, and from eleven a.m. to closing on Saturdays and Sundays. My job was to dress up as a hostess and take orders or to work behind the counter as a waitress, and I earned minimum wage. I was entitled to a hamburger or fish sandwich and a trip to the salad bar as part of the job. The weight fell off.

At home, conversations centered on chores and tasks: when we would go to the grocery store, what day we would go to the Laundromat, whether it would be better to go to the Department of Motor Vehicles early or late. A month after I returned home, I finally got my driver's license and my mother made a new friend, a fellow teacher. Years later, this woman told me, "Never doubt that your mother loved you. She always said you were the one good thing that had happened in her life." *Really?* I thought. *How sad.* After our return from Phoenix, my mother kept a roof over our heads; however, we had said things to each other that could not be unsaid.

Because I was busy, John and I saw little of each other. We talked on the phone, yes, and I told myself I was in love with him. Of course, I was. We had had a child together, and in God's eyes we were as good as married. But I was also scared of him. The striated scars on my abdomen were a vivid reminder of what could happen if we had sex, and then there had been that awful reunion up on Skyline when he'd told me never to mention *it* again.

Rather than going out on dates, I used the excuse that I was behind at school and needed to catch up. It wasn't a lie. I had a ton of homework: all the content from first semester that I had missed (I was trying to speed-read the textbooks), plus the incompletes from my correspondence courses.

Although his family still included me in brunches and birthday celebrations, on Sunday morning John no longer picked me up for Mass. Because of my schedule, I went to the 8:00 a.m. service at St. Pius. As for friends, prior to my departure for Phoenix, John had occupied every spare moment. I knew it would be good for me to make new friends, but how could I have friends when *it* had happened, and I had been told not to share *it* with anyone? Besides, I was working thirty or more hours per week.

Then John got into West Point. On April 25, 1962, three

months after I had signed papers surrendering our son, a photograph in the *Redwood City Tribune showed* John receiving his appointment letter to the Academy.

> Congressman J. Arthur Younger said that MacDonald was the highest scorer among four finalists in a test given in March at Stanford University. Eighty-four boys took the preliminary examination given in Redwood City last November. He was selected by the commandant of the academy and his name was put in nomination by Congressman Younger.
>
> In addition to his scholastic honors covering a college preparatory course in mathematics, language, and other difficult subjects, MacDonald last year was given the award as outstanding lineman for the "Bells" varsity football squad on which he played guard and tackle.
>
> He is a member of the student council, vice-president of his class, a staff member of "The Cardinal" school newspaper, member of the Block B society, and president of the Bellarmine school band, playing saxophone. . . . Younger said that MacDonald has accepted the nomination and will report to the Academy on July 2.

John is pictured at San Francisco Airport the day he flew back to West Point.

John, the big man on campus. The local hero.

CHAPTER 59

MY SENIOR YEAR

Fall semester of my senior year, I scored 690 on the verbal half of the SAT. I managed to get my math score up to 620, which was a miracle, considering I hadn't had a math course in two years.

My History teacher, a Smith grad, told me I should apply to the Seven Sisters colleges on the East Coast and wrote letters on my behalf. My employer gave me Christmas week off so that my mother and I could fly East for college interviews, and on that trip, we stopped at West Point, where John and I went to the Christmas formal.

Marylee and John attended the Christmas formal at West Point. This photo was taken when the author was on a trip to visit colleges during her senior year. John was a freshman (plebe) at West Point.

Standing apart from myself, in the same way I had done on the drive back from Vera Cruz, I hovered above the girl who'd believed herself a modern-day Juliet. Who was I kidding? I was no different than any other love-struck teen. And if I got into a decent college, I didn't want to blow a chance to live life on my own terms. Maybe I could become an archeologist like the father of the twins I'd met down in Mexico, or maybe I could study anthropology and live among primitive cultures like Margaret Mead. My Spanish was pretty good. In either of those fields, the whole of Central and South America would be open to me.

Second semester of senior year, what had felt like an unbreakable connection began to fray. In late February, John wrote:

> I can tell that you've changed since we've been apart. You have some strange ideas about having a career. Once we have children, I don't want you working outside the home. My mother didn't, and she has had a happy life. I think you should date other people to make sure you're ready to settle down, and I will do the same.

He'd already had two blind dates and gone to a party in Newburgh, just outside West Point's gates.

"All right," I wrote back. "That's probably a good idea. We are a little young, and people change."

I didn't have a lot of extra time, but a couple of guys had been asking me out. I went to senior prom with a boy I'd had a crush on freshman year. Nothing serious. Nothing that ignited sparks.

In March, I learned that I had been admitted to Pembroke (now part of Brown University), the University of Massachusetts (my safety school), and Vassar. The money for tuition and room and board would come from a trust fund set up at the time of my grandfather's death beneath the wheels of the Southern Pacific train. My grandmother had also left me a third of her portion of the settlement. Had the times been different, or had I been one or two years older, this money could have been redirected to help me support myself and a child. In the end, I chose Vassar because of its academic rigor and because of its proximity to West Point. John and I agreed that if our relationship were to survive, he and I needed to see each other.

I packed two metal footlockers and shipped them off to Poughkeepsie. The week before I left for college, my mother's *hemichorea* kicked in full force. I could only conclude that my pregnancy was not the only source of her anxiety: She was anxious about the prospect of my being so far away. I thought about not going, but I couldn't face starting the application process all over again.

When I arrived on campus, I found that they'd assigned me to Jewett, the dorm where Mary McCarthy, author of *The Group*, had lived. I shoved a big oak desk beneath the window and took pictures of my grandmother's crazy quilt. Oddly, although I was three thousand miles away, in a long letter to my mother, I poured out details about the week devoted to orientation.

The first night, we had gathered in the chapel to hear the president of the college give us a pep talk about how all of us were smart and how, now that we were here, we should feel free to be genuinely excited about learning for the sake of learning.

The following night, we went to a lecture hall for a talk by Dr. Mary Calderone, daughter of the photographer Edward Steichen and niece of Carl Sandburg. A Vassar grad herself, she was brought to campus to address the incoming class about the importance of birth control, which still wasn't available to women.[1] By this time, I certainly knew how girls like me got pregnant, but not a single medical person at the home had talked to me about how I could avoid getting pregnant again, nor did Dr. Calderone's talk go beyond a general warning that sexually active women should consider the consequences.[2] I knew the consequences and didn't intend to have sex with John or anyone else.

Classes started. Three of my four professors were women. My History professor, Miss Rappaport, taught us to make note cards for our research in "primary sources," meaning original texts written by the likes of Herodotus and Thucydides. My English professor had us do a mix of creative writing and expository prose. Raised in India and the child of a British army officer, she had four children, two novels in progress, and a PhD on Thomas More. My Spanish teacher spoke with the soft Castilian of Spain but made it his mission to teach us about the vast reaches of the Spanish empire. For the first time, I was reading literature from the diaspora, such as Rómulo Gallegos's classic novel, *Doña Bárbara*. And then there was Chemistry and my struggle to understand covalent bonds.

Apart from Chemistry, Vassar did not grade freshmen. Professors gave feedback on assignments, and I soon learned that problem sets, labs, language quizzes, essays, and primary source readings would occupy my every waking moment. The library was full of musty old volumes I couldn't wait to explore. To take advantage of this wealth of knowledge, I would have to take myself seriously as a scholar: buckle down and study as I had never studied before. Finally, I had vanquished Miss Fennel and her damn IQ test. I had arrived at a place I truly belonged.

I wrote to John and asked him to call. He wrote back and proposed a time, saying he couldn't wait to see me in person. I rolled my eyes. I didn't look forward to the conversation I was about to have.

When he called, I was sitting at my desk, looking out on Vassar's spreading lawns and majestic trees. A rubber-banded stack of note-cards sat by a copy of Huizinga's *The Waning of the Middle Ages*. I had homework to do, and I wanted to get this over with.

"Sorry I'm late," he said. "There was a line for the phone."

"That's all right," I said.

"How are you? How are your classes?"

"Good, but hard," I said. "You know I told you I had a Chem lab on Wednesday afternoons? Well, my instructor was standing at the end of my lab bench and collapsed."

"What happened to him?"

"*Her*," I said. "My instructor was a woman. My lab mate ran over to Student Health, but by the time the doctor arrived, the instructor was dead."

"That must have shaken you up."

"It did. Very much." Our time on Earth was finite. I wanted to make the most of it.

"What did you want to talk to me about?"

"Listen, John, I don't know how to say this, except directly. I don't want to be a housewife, or least not *just* a housewife. I want a career."

"I've heard there's a bunch of lesbians at Vassar."

"Not that I've seen."

"A guy on my hall has a girlfriend at Vassar, and that's what she says."

It was stupid to argue. Who cared what people did in their

private lives? Next, he'd say there were communists under every bed. "Listen, John, what we had was not love. It was infatuation. I've outgrown this relationship, and I don't want to be tied down."

The other end of the phone went quiet. Outside, it was dusk and there were halos around the streetlamps. My eyes, reflected in the window glass, looked sad.

"Come down," he said. "Let's talk about this in person."

"I don't know. I think it would just be better to part friends."

"It sounds like you're giving me the old brush-off."

"Maybe I am." And it was long overdue.

"Please," he said. "I have to see you."

The following weekend, there I was, at the end of a long taxi ride, annoyed at myself for squandering my hard-earned savings on a relationship I had outgrown. Girls visiting West Point for the weekend waited in Taylor Hall.

John, in his trim gray uniform, strode toward me. His blue eyes, full of longing and affection, bore down on me. He could not touch me because the academy forbade public displays of affection. We could not hold hands or kiss. But the instant I saw him, I knew I had deluded myself. There was no one for me but him. Two long years earlier, I had planted my flag in the sand of loving this man and bearing his children.

We walked side by side along the parade ground and stopped to look inside one of the cannons.

"Want to go to Flirtation Walk?" he asked.

"Sure," I said, following him toward the woods.

And we began again, sinking down into the fall leaves and believing that, against all odds, what we shared was simple. We could be happy with no one else.

CHAPTER 60

BRUCE AND ME

*B*y late 2018, I had gathered most of the material for this memoir. The last pieces of the puzzle were dropping into place. Even though I had moved to Phoenix with my second husband, Bruce, and, for the most part, had managed to wear my "supportive spouse and good sport" beanie, he still did not understand, on a visceral level, why I had freaked out in our therapist's office back in 2005.

Bruce was a scientist. If I forced him to, he could check in with his feelings, but most of the time he spent his life examining "data." I needed him to validate my hypothesis—that being in a home for unwed mothers was a second adoption-related trauma. The "crying baby" had turned into a sullen, hurting teenager. Being in the home had been life-changing and something I might well never recover from emotionally. To that end, I'd been digging around in the newspaper archives and wanted to show him some of my "research findings." I proposed meeting at Thai Basil, a restaurant across from his lab.

When the waitress had cleared our plates, I turned my iPad so he could read an article from an old copy of the *Arizona Republic*.

Pressed always by requests for service which cannot be met because of space limitations and staff size, the focal point of all planning has been to help, guide and aid the girls who are admitted to Crittenton, states Mrs. James Henderson, president of the board of directors.

For them, the open door of the Crittenton Home tries to be also an open door to understanding and to social adjustment.[1]

"Really?" Bruce cleaned his glasses with a handkerchief and reread the article. "This kind of reminds me of *Alice's Restaurant* when the guy in the army uniform leans over and looks at the misfits and felons sitting on the Group W bench and says, 'Kid, have you rehabilitated yourself?'"

"Exactly," I said. Nothing that happened in the home would have rehabilitated me, short of a lobotomy. I went back into the world and felt myself free the same way a prisoner stepping outside the gates of a penitentiary feels free. Some part of me had been permanently imprinted by my confinement. And no one had done more to destroy my tentative sense of self than Miss Fennel.

"And there she is," I told Bruce, pointing to the picture. "My nemesis."

He stared at the picture for a long time. "She's exactly the way you describe her. A stork."

"Read the rest of the article," I said.

Part-time parent. That's how each staff member at Florence Crittenton Home of Phoenix regards herself. So says Miss Jeanne Fennell, staff social worker.

Understanding, support, love, acceptance, patience, judgment, wisdom—these are only some of the attributes staff members contribute to the life of the unmarried mothers for whom this nationwide network of services has been established.

Whether she be a cook, a housemother, a nurse, a teacher, an executive director, each staff member realizes her responsibility is making a particular period in the life of an unwed mother a new beginning rather than an interval of bitterness without meaning.

"An interval of bitterness," Bruce said. "Was it an interval of bitterness for you?"

"Actually," I said, "my time in the home was not an interval of bitterness. The interval of bitterness began after I left, when it dawned on me that I would have years of not knowing if my child was alive or dead. The inability to mourn my absent child, or, on an equally profound level, to mourn the death of my young self, made it impossible to put the surrender behind me."

Bruce placed his hand on mine and then leaned across the table and kissed my cheek. "Condescending sons of bitches."

"Not all of them," I said. "The first director, Mrs. South, was kind, and the weekend nurse was on our side—never judgmental. Willing to help a girl go into labor if she was near her time."

"How did she do that?"

I told him.

He grimaced. "And Miss Fennel? This article makes it sound like she cared."

"Oh, I think she cared. She was getting paid to care, and I do think she was trying to get me to be honest with myself."

"What about the lesbian thing?" he said. "Wasn't there something prurient about her line of questioning?"

"No, even at the time, I never thought that. She wasn't sexually attracted to me, except as a possible target for her good intentions."

"I don't understand."

A waitress came to clear our plates. I closed my iPad and reached across the table for his hand. "Growing up with my father, I was hyper alert to a certain type of personality."

"And that was?"

"One that didn't respect boundaries."

"What kind of boundaries?"

"Power boundaries. If my dad thought I'd gone against him, he'd give me an Indian burn or twist my arm up behind my back. If my mom went against him, he'd haul her into court or get his picture plastered across the newspaper. It was a power play."

"And with Fennel?"

The enigma of Miss Fennel. I could only speculate about her

intentions. "Let's just say Fennel saw it as her mission to fix whatever had landed me in the home."

"Did you resist?"

"She had all the power."

"And?"

"She tried to break me."

"Did she?"

"For a time, yes."

When I went back to high school, I was determined to prove her wrong. No matter what her stupid IQ test said, I was smart enough to get into a good school.

In 2018 Bruce Rittmann was awarded the Stockholm Water Prize, often called the "Nobel Prize for Water." His work ethic played a role in the four children we raised together getting PhDs. Pictured left to right are Marylee MacDonald, Dr. Jacqueline MacDonald-Gibson, Dr. John Michael MacDonald, Dr. Bruce Rittmann, Dr. Ted MacDonald, and Dr. Robert MacDonald. Because of work commitments, my oldest son was not able to attend the ceremony.

CHAPTER 61

THANKSGIVING

I had gotten into a good school—Vassar—but it was close to West Point. By Thanksgiving weekend, I had missed a period, and by the following weekend, I'd gone to a gynecologist and had my pregnancy confirmed. I called John and broke the news. "What are we going to do?" I asked.

"I don't know," he said. "I'll get back to you."

West Point's Catholic chaplain advised John not to drop out. John was one of their top ten students, a "star man" with gold stars on his collar. The chaplain promised that the academy's lawyers would fight any potential paternity suit.

"John," I said, "I can't go through this again."

"It's a pretty big deal to drop out."

"Getting married is *not* the end of the world!"

"Maybe not for you," he said.

Morning sickness had already started, except that I was fine in the morning and nauseated in the afternoons. Just like last time. Distraught and overwhelmed, I called the Catholic chaplain at Vassar. He suggested we drive down to West Point.

"I don't have a car," I said.

"No problem," he said. "I do."

Father Donovan, in his twenties, not much taller than me and with a puckish grin, was the only priest I'd ever talked to outside the confessional. I hadn't been at Vassar all that long and didn't know him well. After eleven o'clock Mass, he drove to campus and fetched me. On the drive down, as I bent over, hiccup-crying and blowing my nose, he talked about the weather and the cost of gas and the services he had planned for Advent. He was an avid Ping-Pong player, and next weekend he had a big tournament in New York City, so it was a good thing we were going down to West Point this weekend. Next weekend he wouldn't have been available, and he supposed, given my pregnancy, that I would want to have this resolved. When I finally got control of myself, he asked how long I'd known John.

"Since my sophomore year of high school," I said. "I got pregnant and had to give up our oldest son for adoption."

"What do you want to do now?"

"Get married," I said. "I wanted to do that then, but our families wouldn't let us."

Almost there. Highland Falls, a town of shuttered storefronts, taverns, and faded signs, lay just outside the academy's entrance. I had a feeling of dread. John wouldn't want to drop out of West Point. Getting married wasn't in his life plan. At least, not in the short term.

Father Donovan signaled to the guard at the gatehouse, and he waved us through.

"How old is your cadet?" the priest asked.

My cadet! I didn't own him.

"Nineteen," I said.

"And you?"

"Eighteen."

"Then you don't need your parents' consent."

Good thing, too. John's dad was not going to like this one bit.

Father Donovan craned sideways and looked up at the fortress-like Hotel Thayer. The previous December, when my mother and I had come back for John's Christmas dance and my college visits, she and I had shared a room. John and I hadn't been sleeping together then.

Farther on, outside Taylor Hall, John stood clapping his arms against his winter greatcoat and blowing on his fingers. After getting in the backseat, he leaned forward. "So, what's the plan?"

"Are you allowed to leave campus?" Father Donovan asked.

"Yes," he said.

"Good, because I used to be at Sacred Heart, and I asked the priest to leave the sanctuary open. It will give us a private place to talk."

"We can't get married today," John said, sitting back.

"Of course not," the priest said. "There's the matter of the banns."

"What about the banns?" I asked.

"They have to be read or published on three successive Sundays before a wedding can take place."

"I didn't know that," I said, fearing that a wedding wouldn't take place at all. John thought it was the man's job to support a family. To do that, he needed to finish college. Otherwise, he'd be stuck in some dead-end job.

In Sacred Heart's freezing-cold sanctuary, John and I slid into a pew and sat holding hands and looking up at a crucifix above the altar. Father Donovan genuflected, crossed himself, and, after taking a seat in the pew in front of us, swiveled around and looked us in the eye.

"You know, our Lord created the sacrament of marriage to honor the commitment of a man and a woman. Do you understand that?"

John rolled his eyes. "Yes, of course. I went to a Jesuit high school."

"Do you love Marylee?"

"Very much," John said, without hesitation and folding my arm into his.

"And do you love John?" he asked me.

"Yes."

"Then you should get married. Trust in God. These things have a way of working out."

John laughed. "You make it sound simple."

"It is," the priest said. "There will be hurdles, but take them one at a time. Now, what's the first hurdle?"

I looked at John. Not a trace of a smile. Was he going to marry me or balk?

Finally, he said, "Telling our parents."

The priest stood. "All right, then. Where's the nearest phone?"

"There's one at a deli down the street," John said. "It's not very private. Just a phone hanging on the wall."

"You don't need to have a long conversation," the priest said. "Just tell them what you're going to do, and don't be ashamed."

"All right," John said. "I'll try."

At a pay phone in the deli, as the owner looked at us over a glass display case of mortadella, pastrami, and potato salad, John called his mother. "Not again!" she said, and John had to say, "Yes, again."

When I called my mom, she said, "Is he going to marry you?"

"We're with a priest right now," I said.

"Good," she said.

Using the excuse that my mother's ill health required my presence at home, I dropped out of Vassar. Vassar's dean of students arranged for a Stanford professor to proctor my exams. John came home for Christmas, we planned our wedding, and he returned to West Point for finals. No point losing a semester's worth of credit, not when he'd be racing to finish his degree.

In late January, the priest from Teen Club, now a monsignor, married us. While waiting to see if Stanford would let John in and whether it would give him financial aid, we lived in a small apartment in San Mateo and John worked for his dad. Two months later, Stanford awarded John an Atomic Energy Commission fellowship. He didn't want to work on nuclear energy, but he took the money, and we moved to married-student housing.

I spent a semester at De Anza Junior College and then transferred, graduating from Stanford with honors in English and a senior thesis on Kierkegaard and Saul Bellow. Because of John's liberal-arts credits from West Point, he was inducted into both Phi Beta Kappa and Tau Beta Pi, the engineering honor society , and while I babysat, repaired washers and dryers, built and sold planter boxes, and tutored undergrads, he continued on for a PhD.

After graduation and shortly after my mother's death, we packed up the family and moved to Germany where John had a postdoctoral fellowship at the Max Planck Institute for Plasma Physics, a research lab north of Munich. He was a wonderful father, never too tired to give our children a bath or carry the little ones on his shoulders. We were raising three kids and expecting another when a semi-truck barreled into his car and killed him. It was December 2, 1971, and he was twenty-seven.

CHAPTER 62

SEATTLE

*I*n late 2019, I visited my oldest son John in Seattle. He was fifty-seven, and I was seventy-four. Since our rendezvous in Phoenix in 2013, my son has had heart surgery to correct an irregular heartbeat, and he's fine now. His cardiac surgeon told him he's a "good healer."

I suppose that's true for both of us and for our relationship as a whole. At this point, I have known him two and a half times as long as I have not known him, and when we were sitting at his neighborhood's Starbucks, catching each other up on our lives, I heard the echo of his father's voice and saw in his posture—elbows on the table, leaning forward, intent on what I had to say—that my son cares about me and values my opinion.

In one of our conversations, he said, "I'm so glad you chose to have me."

"It wasn't a choice, exactly," I said.

I know that it's hard for anyone in my kids' and grandkids' generation to fathom what life was like back then: that there was no birth control, apart from diaphragms and condoms, and for teens, those were hard or impossible to come by. That abortions were illegal and done in back alleys.[1] That oral contraception did not exist, nor did the idea of reproductive freedom.

From the end of World War II until the start of the 1970s, four million parents had children placed for adoption. Two million of those adoptions took place in the 1960s. For white, middle-class girls

The author and her son in Seattle.

like me, a child born out of wedlock would have so shamed our parents that they could not have walked around with their heads held high. Even though I had doubts about my own adoption, I had bought into the myth of the chosen child. And because I thought that being a chosen child was a good thing, I allowed myself to believe that my firstborn child would benefit from having two parents who would choose him, rather than two parents who were his biological kin. What it came down to was this: To save my mother, I surrendered my son.

Some people have no stomach for looking back and excavating the layers of the past, but I have always been part archaeologist. As we age, do not all men and women seek to bend the brittle branch of age and touch the green, pliant twig of youth? Perhaps our attempts to come to terms with how we wind up where we are, to sort out the trail of accident and circumstance, hidden drives, and unintentional blindness, will prove futile. My "crying baby" will never go away, nor will the anguished teenage mom struggling to understand where she stood on the nature-versus-nurture divide.

It is these cast-off selves that build the layers of who we become in our maturity. Only with hindsight can we understand where this journey was leading all along. I do not regret any of it because it made me who I am.

Left to right are Bob and Ted MacDonald, John Lauer, Jackie MacDonald Gibson, and John Michael MacDonald.

NOTES

CHAPTER 3

1. Nancy Newton Verrier, *The Primal Wound* (London: The British Academy for Adoption and Fostering, 2009).
2. Jack Hinman, "Adoption, Trauma and Attachment Disorder in Teens," a blog post by a therapist working with teens who struggle with behavioral problems associated with adoption trauma.
3. Judith S. Gediman and Linda P. Brown, *Birthbond* (Liberty Corner NJ: New Horizon Press, 1991), 4.
4. Although this quote has been variously attributed to author Rita Mae Brown, Einstein, and even Mark Twain, a more recent investigation by blogger Garson O'Toole from the website Quote Investigator found earlier instances of its use.

CHAPTER 5

1. Bruce had never officially adopted the kids. The youngest was seven by the time Bruce joined the family, and it was simpler to leave well enough alone.

CHAPTER 6

1. It had taken me seven years to find my birth parents. I maintained contact with my birth mother, but not with my birth father, with whom I'd been in touch by phone. My mother maintained that I was the product of a sexual assault.
2. Peter Claes et al., "Genome-wide mapping of global-to-local genetic effects on human facial shape," *Nature Genetics* 50, vol. 3 (2018): 414–23.
3. Joyce Wadler and Johnny Greene, "Anne Rice's Imagination May Roam Among Vampires and Erotica, but Her Heart Is Right at 'Home,'" *People*, December 5, 1988.

CHAPTER 9

1. Historian Jens Jorgensen found historical records that suggest Andersen was indeed an "ugly duckling"—the illegitimate son of Denmark's crown prince, Christian Frederick, and a Danish aristocrat, Elise Ahlefeldt Laurvig. Their child was born on April 2, 1805, in the castle of Broholm, and, according to oral tradition, "given away to good people." It's possible Andersen learned the truth of his birth shortly before he began work on "The Ugly Duckling," a story that took him a year to write and that he called his "autobiography."

2. The first chapter of Walter Isaacson's book *Steve Jobs: A Biography* begins with the story of Jobs's birth and subsequent adoption. By placing this information in the first chapter, the biographer invites the reader to contemplate the ripple effect that adoption played throughout Jobs's life.
3. Christa Hoffman-Riem, *The Adopted Child: Family Life with Double Parenthood* (New Brunswick, NJ: Transaction Publishers, 2016), 113.
4. Ibid.
5. For a poignant reminder that even well-intended social-work interventions can have devastating personal consequences, see Victoria Golden and William Walters's memoir, *A Last Survivor of the Orphan Trains* (Orphan Books, 2017).

CHAPTER 10

1. According to Wikipedia, "The School Mathematics Study Group (SMSG) was an American academic think tank focused on the subject of reform in mathematics education. Directed by Edward G. Begle and financed by the National Science Foundation, the group was created in the wake of the Sputnik crisis in 1958 and tasked with creating and implementing mathematics curricula for primary and secondary education, which it did until its termination in 1977.

"The efforts of the SMSG yielded a reform in mathematics education known as New Math, which was promulgated in a series of reports, culminating in a series published by Random House called the New Mathematical Library (Vol. 1 is Ivan Niven's *Numbers: Rational and Irrational*). In the early years, SMSG also produced a set of draft textbooks in typewritten paperback format for elementary, middle, and high school students."

CHAPTER 11

1. The union is now called the International Longshore and Warehouse Union.

CHAPTER 12

1. An excerpt from *The Primal Wound* can be downloaded from the Gap Academy's website. The download link is listed in Works Cited.
2. Clifford R. Adams was the author of widely read advice books: *How to Pick a Mate*; *Sexual Behavior and Personality Characteristics*; and *Preparing for Marriage*. For more about Adams and the mindset about women's roles, see Martin Halliwell's *Therapeutic Revolutions: Medicine, Psychiatry, and American Culture, 1945-1970* (New Brunswick, NJ: Rutgers University Press, 2013), 141.
3. Divorce Statistics Analysis: United States—1962.

CHAPTER 13

1. Table 75: "Estimated average annual salary of teachers in public elementary and secondary schools: selected years 1959-60 through 2005-06" (Washington, D.C.: National Center for Education Statistics, 2007).

2. "Women's Wages—1950s" (Columbia, MO: Government Documents Dept., University of Missouri, 2020).
3. According to the National Domestic Violence Hotline, risk factors include isolation, denying and blaming, being physically abusive, and using threats and coercion.

CHAPTER 18

1. Nancy Newton Verrier, author of *The Primal Wound*, writes that adoptive parents report that their children often act out on their birthdays.
2. Morris Kaplan, "City Expanding Birth Control Clinics," *New York Times*, March 28, 1965, 66.
3. Rickie Solinger, *Wake Up Little Susie* (New York: Routledge, 1992), 211.

CHAPTER 19

1. Verrier, *The Primal Wound*.

CHAPTER 22

1. Mary Bloch Jones, *Birthmothers: Women Who've Relinquished Babies for Adoption Tell Their Stories* (Chicago: Chicago Review Press, 1993), 15.

CHAPTER 25

1. A swamp cooler, also called a "desert cooler," cools the air by means of evaporative cooling. This was the only means of lowering indoor temperatures prior to the invention of air-conditioning.
2. *Santa Cruz Sentinel*, October 7, 1960, 8.
3. Verrier, *The Primal Wound*.
4. During the five-week interval between birth and adoption, I was cared for in a foster home. My son was also placed in an interim foster home.

CHAPTER 27

1. *Arizona Star*, November 16, 1954, 10.

CHAPTER 28

1. Arthur D. Sorosky, Annette Baran, and Reuben Pannor, "The Reunion of Adoptees and Birth Relatives," *Journal of Youth and Adolescence* 3, no. 3 (1974): 195–206.

CHAPTER 31

1. Verrier, *The Primal Wound*.

CHAPTER 32

1. Solinger, *Wake Up Little Susie*, 68.

CHAPTER 33

1. Madame Defarge was one of the villains in Charles Dickens's *A Tale of Two Cities*, a novel about the French Revolution. The book was especially meaningful to me because it was one of my grandfather's favorites.

CHAPTER 36

1. In the 1960s, the Florence Crittenton Home did not allow women to leave the premises one at a time.

CHAPTER 42

1. Elisabetta Crocetti, "Identity Formation in Adolescence: The Dynamic of Forming and Consolidating Identity Commitments," *Child Development Perspectives* 11, no. 2 (2017): 145–50.
2. Ibid.

CHAPTER 53

1. Foothill and De Anza are junior colleges in Santa Clara County, California.

CHAPTER 55

1. When my son visited me in Phoenix and asked about his birth story, I told him I had hired a "confidential intermediary." In Arizona—indeed, in most states—neither an adult adoptee nor a birth mother is entitled to look at the records of a child's birth. When adoptions are legally finalized, birth certificates are amended; the time of birth remains the same, but the names of the parents are replaced. Birth certificates are locked. The original is sealed and held in the Department of Vital Statistics, and only a court order can unseal it.

CHAPTER 57

1. In 1961, the Florence Crittenden Home offered no sex counseling, and even at the clinic, the doctors spent no time directly counseling patients about their sexuality.

CHAPTER 59

1. Calderone served as president and cofounder of the Sexuality Information and Education Council of the United States (SIECUS) from 1954 to 1982. She was also the medical director for Planned Parenthood. She wrote many publications advocating open dialogue and access to information at all ages. Her extensive work with popularizing sexuality education has often been compared to Margaret Sanger's campaign for birth control.
2. According to a *New York Times* obituary written by Jane Ellen Brody, Mary Calderone's most notable feat was overturning the American Medical Association's policy against the dissemination of birth control information to patients.

CHAPTER 60

1. "Mrs. Charles Pickrell Is Chairman of Event," *Arizona Republic*, April 21, 1961, 71.

CHAPTER 62

1. The Supreme Court would not issue its verdict on *Roe v. Wade* until 1973, a full eleven years after my son's birth. *Roe v. Wade*, 410 US 113, 1973.

ACKNOWLEDGMENTS

Authors depend on reader feedback. We need to know our books are worth the time we spend at our desks. If you enjoyed this book, please take a moment to leave a comment in your favorite online bookstore. Even a line or two makes all the difference. And, please stop by my website and say hello.

www.maryleemacdonald.com

This book could not have been written without the support of my editor, Annie Tucker, whose faith in the possibilities for this story kept me going during the many times I felt like giving up. Over the years my writing groups in both Chicago and Phoenix have seen pieces of this manuscript, and I thank them for encouraging me to believe that the work in its entirety might one day become a book.

I owe a special debt of gratitude to Mary Clark, Polly Baughman, Chandra Graham Garcia, Deborah Bauer, Debra Borchert, my sister Kathryn, and my son Ted MacDonald, who read the almost-finished draft and helped me see that the text could be even better if I removed a few remaining stumbling blocks.

Thank you also to my many friends whose lives have been

touched by adoption. Special thanks to my amazing and patient husband, Bruce Rittmann, for reading the manuscript on his vacation and for believing that a painful personal experience could be transformed into a work of literature.

One of the most gratifying aspects of having put this story down on paper is that it has opened a dialogue with my grandchildren. I especially appreciate Jonathan, Erika, Alisa, Carolyn, Kelly, and Jenny for the frank discussions we've had about "then and now."

Most of all, thank you to my son John.

You are a blessing in our lives.

ABOUT THE AUTHOR

Marylee MacDonald is the author of *Bonds of Love and Blood, Body Language, Montpelier Tomorrow, The Rug Bazaar,* and *The Big Book of Small Presses and Independent Publishers.* Her fiction has won the Barry Hannah Prize, the Jeanne M. Leiby Chapbook Award, the Ron Rash Award, and the *American Literary Review* Fiction Prize, among others.

WORKS CITED

Arizona Republic. "Mrs. Charles Pickrell Is Chairman for Event." April 21, 1961, 71. Accessed May 19, 2019. www.newspapers.com/clip/31591673/jeanne-fennel-and-florence-crittenton/.

Arthur, Max. "Historian Says Author Was Son of Swedish King: Hans Christian Andersen: Royal Child?" *Los Angeles Times.* August 9, 1989. Accessed April 14, 2017. www.latimes.com/archives/la-xpm-1987-08-09-mn-254-story.html.

Biography Online. "Steve Jobs Biography." March 19, 2019. Accessed June 2, 2019. www.biographyonline.net/business/steve-jobs.html.

Brody, Jane Ellen. "Mary S. Calderone, Advocate of Sexual Education, Dies at 94." *New York Times*, October 25, 1998.

Burnham, Bo. "Director Bo Burnham On Growing Up With Anxiety—and an Audience." *NPR*, December 27, 2018. Accessed March 28, 2019. www.npr.org/2018/12/27/680356663/director-bo-burnham-on-growing-up-with-anxiety-and-an-audience.

Claes, Peter, et al. "Genome-Wide Mapping of Global-to-Local Genetic Effects on Human Facial Shape." *Nature Genetics* 50, no. 2 (2018): 414–23. www.nature.com/articles/s41588-018-0057-4.

Cohen, Stanley. *States of Denial: Knowing About Atrocities and Suffering.* Malden, MA: Polity Press, 2012.

Crocetti, Elisabetta. "Identity Formation in Adolescence: The Dynamic of Forming and Consolidating Identity Commitments." *Child Development Perspectives* 11, no. 2 (2017): 145–50. www.srcd.onlinelibrary.wiley.com/doi/10.1111/cdep.12226.

Fox, Robin. *Kinship and Marriage: An Anthropological Perspective.* Cambridge, UK: Cambridge University Press, 1983.

Ganz, Sheila. *Unlocking the Heart of Adoption.* DVD. 1999. www.unlockingtheheart.com/essays.

Gediman, Judith S., and Linda P. Brown. *Birthbond.* Far Hills, NJ: New Horizon Press, 1991.

Golden, Victoria, and William Walters. *A Last Survivor of the Orphan Trains.* California: Orphan Books, 2017.

Government Documents Department. *Prices and Wages by Decade: 1950-1959.* May 24, 2020. Accessed December 7, 2018. www.libraryguides.missouri.edu/pricesandwages/1950-1959.

Halliwell, Martin. *Therapeutic Revolutions: Medicine, Psychiatry, and American Culture, 1945-1970.* New Brunswick, NJ: Rutgers University Press, 2013.

Herman, Ellen. "The Adoption History Project." University of Oregon, February 24, 2012. Accessed October 17, 2014. www.darkwing.uoregon.edu/~adoption/topics/adoptionstatistics.htm.

Hinman, Jack. "Adoption, Trauma and Attachment Disorder in Teens." Sunrise Residential Treatment Center. Accessed June 15, 2018. www.sunrisertc.com/adoption-trauma-and-attachment-disorder-in-teens/.

Hoffman-Riem, Christa. *The Adopted Child: Family Life with Double Parenthood.* New Brunswick, NJ: Transaction Publishers, 2016.

Isaacson, Walter. *Steve Jobs: A Biography.* New York: Simon & Schuster, 2015.

Jones, Mary Bloch. *Birthmothers: Women Who've Relinquished Their Babies for Adoption Tell Their Stories.* Chicago: Chicago Review Press, 1993.

Kaplan, Morris. "City Expanding Birth Control Clinics." *New York Times*, March 28, 1965.

National Domestic Abuse Hotline. "What Is Domestic Violence?" 2017. Accessed December 12, 2018. www.thehotline.org/identify-abuse/power-and-control/.

O'Toole, Garson. *Quote Investigator*, March 23, 2017. Accessed July 9, 2018. www.quoteinvestigator.com/2017/03/23/same/ [URL inactive]

Solinger, Rickie. *Wake Up Little Susie.* New York: Routledge, 1992.

Sorosky, Arthur D., Annette Baran, and Reuben Pannor. "The Reunion of Adoptees and Birth Relatives." *Journal of Youth and Adolescence* 3, no. 9 (1974): 195–206. www.link.springer.com/article/10.1007/BF02214749.

Steenbarger, Brett. "The Mirror Principle: Shaping Your Experience, Shaping Your Self." *Forbes*, June 30, 2015. Accessed July 22, 2018. www.forbes.com/sites/brettsteenbarger/2015/06/30/the-mirror-principle-shaping-your-experience-shaping-your-self/? sh=46297bd03ec0.

US Department of Education. *Estimated Average Annual Salary of Teachers in Public Elementary and Secondary Schools: Selected Years 1959-60 Through 2005-06.* 1959-2006. Accessed December 4, 2017. www.nces.ed.gov/programs/digest/d07/tables/dt07_075.asp.

US Department of Health, Education, and Welfare. *Divorce Statistics Analysis: United States, 1962. Vital and Health Statistics* 21, no. 7 (1965). Washington, DC: US Department of Health, Education, and Welfare. www.cdc.gov/nchs/data/series/sr_21/sr21_013acc.pdf.

US Supreme Court. *Roe v. Wade.* 410 US 113, January 22, 1973. www.supreme.justia.com/cases/federal/us/410/113/.

Verrier, Nancy Newton. "The Gap Academy: An Alternate Approach to Educating Teens." *Gap Academy,* 2009. Accessed July 14, 2017. www.gapacademy.ca/files/The_Primal_Wound_by_Verrier.pdf

———. *The Primal Wound.* London: British Association for Adoption and Fostering, 2009.

Wadler, Joyce, and Johnny Greene. "Anne Rice's Imagination May Roam Among Vampires and Erotica, but Her Heart Is Right at Home." *People,* December 5, 1988. Accessed September 22, 2017. www.people.com/archive/anne-rices-imagination-may-roam-among-vampires-and-erotica-but-her-heart-is-right-at-home-vol-30-no-23/

BOOK CLUB QUESTIONS

$\mathcal{H}$ ere are questions to help book groups discuss the issues raised in the memoir.

1. What did you already know about adoption before you read this book?

2. Why do you think the author chose to tell this story?

3. What else have you read on this topic, and would you recommend these books to others?

4. Have you seen any movies or TV shows that deal with the subject of identity, genetic heritage, or adoption?

5. How honest do you think the author was being?

6. Think about the other people in the book besides the author. Was the author "fair" in her portrayal?

7. What aspects of the author's story could you most relate to?

8. What new things did you learn?

9. Do you think nature or nurture played a bigger role in the author's young life?

10. What aspects of the author's personality seemed most related to her biological heritage?

11. If you had a chance to ask the author one question, what would it be?

Printed in Great Britain
by Amazon